CBSE Term II
2022

Accountancy

Class XI

CBSE Term II 2022

Accountancy

Class XI

- Complete Theory Covering NCERT
- Case Based Questions
- Short/Long Answer Type Questions
- 3 Practice Papers with Explanations

Author
Areesha Naaz

ARIHANT PRAKASHAN (School Division Series)

ARIHANT PRAKASHAN (School Division Series)

卐 **Administrative & Production Offices**

Regd. Office
'Ramchhaya' 4577/15, Agarwal Road, Darya Ganj, New Delhi -110002
Tele: 011- 47630600, 43518550

卐 **Head Office**
Kalindi, TP Nagar, Meerut (UP) - 250002, Tel: 0121-7156203, 7156204

卐 **Sales & Support Offices**
Agra, Ahmedabad, Bengaluru, Bareilly, Chennai, Delhi, Guwahati, Hyderabad, Jaipur, Jhansi, Kolkata, Lucknow, Nagpur & Pune.

卐 **ISBN :** 978-93-25796-79-9

卐 **PRICE :** ₹ 250.00

PO No : TXT-XX-XXXXXXX-X-XX

Published by Arihant Publications (India) Ltd.

For further information about the books published by Arihant, log on to www.arihantbooks.com or e-mail at info@arihantbooks.com

Follow us on    

Contents

Watch Free Learning Videos

Subscribe **arihant** You Tube Channel

- ☑ Video Solutions of CBSE Sample Papers
- ☑ Chapterwise Important MCQs
- ☑ CBSE Updates

Syllabus

CBSE Term II Class XI

Accounting for Bills of Exchange

- Bill of exchange and Promissory Note: Definition, Specimen, Features, Parties.
- Difference between Bill of Exchange and Promissory Note
- Terms in Bill of Exchange:
  - i. Term of Bill
  - ii. Accommodation bill (concept)
  - iii. Days of Grace
  - iv. Date of maturity
  - v. Discounting of bill
  - vi. Endorsement of bill
  - vii. Bill after due date
  - viii. Negotiation
  - ix. Bill sent for collection
  - x. Dishonour of bill
- Accounting Treatment

Note: excluding accounting treatment for accommodation bill

Trial balance and Rectification of Errors

- Trial balance: objectives and preparation

(**Scope:** Trial balance with balance method only)

- Errors: types-errors of omission, commission, principles, and compensating; their effect on Trial Balance.
- Detection and rectification of errors; preparation of suspense account.

After going through this Unit, the students will be able to:

- acquire the knowledge of using bills of exchange and promissory notes for financing business transactions.
- understand the meaning and distinctive features of these instruments and develop the skills of their preparation.
- state the meaning of different terms used in bills of exchange and their implication in accounting.
- explain the method of recording of bill transactions.
- state the need and objectives of preparing trial balance and develop the skill of preparing trial balance.
- appreciate that errors may be committed during the process of accounting.
- understand the meaning of different types of errors and their effect on trial balance.
- develop the skill of identification and location of errors and their rectification and preparation of suspense account.

PART B: FINANCIAL ACCOUNTING - II

Unit 3: Financial Statements of Sole Proprietorship

Financial Statements

Meaning, objectives and importance; Revenue and Capital Receipts; Revenue and Capital Expenditure; Deferred Revenue expenditure.

Trading and Profit and Loss Account: Gross Profit, Operating profit and Net profit. Preparation.

Balance Sheet: need, grouping and marshalling of assets and liabilities. Preparation.

Adjustments in preparation of financial statements with respect to closing stock, outstanding expenses, prepaid expenses, accrued income, income received in advance, depreciation, bad debts, provision for doubtful debts, provision for discount on debtors, Abnormal loss, goods taken for personal use/staff welfare, interest on capital and managers commission.

Preparation of Trading and Profit and Loss account and Balance Sheet of a sole proprietorship with adjustments.

Incomplete Records

Features, reasons and limitations.

Ascertainment of Profit/Loss by Statement of Affairs method.

- state the meaning of financial statements
- purpose of preparing financial statements.
- state the meaning of gross profit, operating profit and net profit and develop the skill of preparing trading and profit and loss account.
- explain the need for preparing balance sheet.
- understand the technique of grouping and marshalling of assets and liabilities.
- appreciate that there may be certain items other than those shown in trial balance which may need adjustments while preparing financial statements.
- develop the understanding and skill to do adjustments for items and their presentation in financial statements like depreciation, closing stock, provisions, abnormal loss etc.
- develop the skill of preparation of trading and profit and loss account and balance sheet.
- state the meaning of incomplete records and their uses and limitations.
- develop the understanding and skill of computation of profit / loss using the statement of affairs method.

Unit 4: Computers in Accounting

- Introduction to computer and accounting information system {AIS}: Introduction to computers (elements, capabilities, limitations of computer system)

Scope:

(i) *The scope of the unit is to understand accounting as an information system for the generation of accounting information and preparation of accounting reports.*

(ii) *It is presumed that the working knowledge of any appropriate accounting software will be given to the students to help them learn basic accounting operations on computers.*

- state the meaning of a computer, describe its components, capabilities and limitations.
- state the meaning of accounting information system.
- appreciate the need for use of computers in accounting for preparing accounting reports.
- develop the understanding of comparing the manual and computerized accounting process and appreciate the advantages and limitations of automation.
- understand the different kinds of accounting software.

PART C: PROJECT WORK

The project work would be divided into two parts i.e. Term I (10 marks) and Term II (10 marks) for the purpose of assessment and will be covered as detailed below.

Comprehensive project of any sole proprietorship business. This may state with journal entries and their ledger postings, preparation of Trial balance. Trading and Profit and Loss Account and Balance Sheet. Expenses, incomes and profit (loss), assets and liabilities are to be depicted using pie chart / bar diagram.

CBSE Circular

Exam Scheme Term I & II

केन्द्रीय माध्यमिक शिक्षा बोर्ड

(शिक्षा मंत्रालय, भारत सरकार के अधीन एक स्वायत संगठन)

CENTRAL BOARD OF SECONDARY EDUCATION

(An Autonomous Organisation under the Ministryof Education, Govt. of India)

CBSE/DIR (ACAD)/2021

Date: July 05, 2021
Circular No: Acad-51/2021

All the Heads of Schools affiliated to CBSE

Subject: Special Scheme of Assessment for Board Examination Classes X and XII for the Session 2021-22

COVID 19 pandemic caused almost all CBSE schools to function in a virtual mode for most part of the academic session of 2020-21. Due to the extreme risk associated with the conduct of Board examinations during the second wave in April 2021, CBSE had to cancel both its class X and XII Board examinations of the year 2021 and results are to be declared on the basis of a credible, reliable, flexible and valid alternative assessment policy. This, in turn, also necessitated deliberations over alternative ways to look at the learning objectives as well as the conduct of the Board Examinations for the academic session 2021-22 in case the situation remains unfeasible.

CBSE has also held stake holder consultations with Government schools as well as private independent schools from across the country especially schools from the remote rural areas and a majority of them have requested for the rationalization of the syllabus, similar to last year in view of reduced time permitted for organizing online classes. The Board has also considered the concerns regarding differential availability of electronic gadgets, connectivity and effectiveness of online teaching and other socio-economic issues specially with respect to students from economically weaker section and those residing in far flung areas of the country. In a survey conducted by CBSE, it was revealed that the rationalized syllabus notified for the session 2020-21 was effective for schools in covering the syllabus and helped learners in achieving learning objectives in a less stressful manner.

In the above backdrop and in line with the Board's continued focus on assessing stipulated learning outcomes by making the examinations competencies and core concepts based, student-centric, transparent, technology-driven, and having advance provision of alternatives for different future scenarios, the following schemes are introduced for the Academic Session for Class X and Class XII 2021-22.

केन्द्रीय माध्यमिक शिक्षा बोर्ड

(शिक्षा मंत्रालय, भारत सरकार के अधीन एक स्वायत संगठन)

CENTRAL BOARD OF SECONDARY EDUCATION

(An Autonomous Organisation under the Ministryof Education, Govt. of India)

Special Scheme for 2021-22

A. Academic session to be divided into 2 Terms with approximately 50% syllabus in each term:

The syllabus for the Academic session 2021-22 will be divided into 2 terms by following a systematic approach by looking into the interconnectivity of concepts and topics by the Subject Experts and the Board will conduct examinations at the end of each term on the basis of the bifurcated syllabus. This is done to increase the probability of having a Board conducted classes X and XII examinations at the end of the academic session.

B. The syllabus for the Board examination 2021-22 will be rationalized similar to that of the last academic session to be notified in July 2021. For academic transactions, however, schools will follow the curriculum and syllabus released by the Board vide Circular no. F.1001/CBSE-Acad/Curriculum/2021 dated 31 March 2021. Schools will also use alternative academic calendar and inputs from the NCERT on transacting the curriculum.

C. Efforts will be made to make Internal Assessment/ Practical/ Project work more credible and valid as per the guidelines and Moderation Policy to be announced by the Board to ensure fair distribution of marks.

Details of Curriculum Transaction

- Schools will continue teaching in distance mode till the authorities permit in-person mode of teaching in schools.

- **Classes IX-X: Internal Assessment** (throughout the year-irrespective of Term I and II) would include the *3 periodic tests, student enrichment, portfolio and practical work/ speaking listening activities/ project.*

- **Classes XI-XII: Internal Assessment** (throughout the year-irrespective of Term I and II) would include end of topic or unit tests/ exploratory activities/ practicals/ projects.

- Schools would create a student profile for all assessment undertaken over the year and retain the evidences in digital format.

- CBSE will facilitate schools to upload marks of Internal Assessment on the CBSE IT platform.

- Guidelines for Internal Assessment for all subjects will also be released along with the rationalized term wise divided syllabus for the session 2021-22.The Board would also provide additional resources like sample assessments, question banks, teacher training etc. for more reliable and valid internal assessments.

केन्द्रीय माध्यमिक शिक्षा बोर्ड

(शिक्षा मंत्रालय, भारत सरकार के अधीन एक स्वायत संगठन)

CENTRAL BOARD OF SECONDARY EDUCATION

(An Autonomous Organisation under the Ministryof Education, Govt. of India)

Term I Examinations:

- At the end of the first term, the Board will organize **Term I Examination** in a flexible schedule to be conducted between November-December 2021 with a window period of 4-8 weeks for schools situated in different parts of country and abroad. Dates for conduct of examinations will be notified subsequently.

- The Question Paper will have Multiple Choice Questions (MCQ) including case-based MCQs and MCQs on assertion-reasoning type. Duration of test will be **90 minutes** and it will cover only the rationalized syllabus of **Term I only** (i.e. approx. 50% of the entire syllabus).

- Question Papers will be sent by the CBSE to schools along with marking scheme.

- The exams will be conducted under the supervision of the External Center Superintendents and Observers appointed by CBSE.

- The responses of students will be captured on OMR sheets which, after scanning may be directly uploaded at CBSE portal or alternatively may be evaluated and marks obtained will be uploaded by the school on the very same day. The final direction in this regard will be conveyed to schools by the Examination Unit of the Board.

- Marks of the **Term I** Examination will contribute to the final overall score of students.

Term II Examination/ Year-end Examination:

- At the end of the second term, the Board would organize **Term II or Year-end Examination** based on the rationalized syllabus of Term II only (i.e. approximately 50% of the entire syllabus).

- This examination would be held around **March-April 2022** at the examination centres fixed by the Board.

- The paper will be of **2 hours duration** and have questions of different formats (case-based/ situation based, open ended- short answer/ long answer type).

- In case the situation is not conducive for normal descriptive examination **a 90 minute MCQ based exam** will be conducted at the end of the Term II also.

- Marks of the Term II Examination would contribute to the final overall score.

केन्द्रीय माध्यमिक शिक्षा बोर्ड

(शिक्षा मंत्रालय, भारत सरकार के अधीन एक स्वायत संगठन)

CENTRAL BOARD OF SECONDARY EDUCATION

(An Autonomous Organisation under the Ministryof Education, Govt. of India)

Assessment / Examination as per different situations

A. In case the situation of the pandemic improves and students are able to come to schools or centres for taking the exams.

Board would conduct Term I and Term II examinations at schools/centres and the theory marks will be distributed equally between the two exams.

B. In case the situation of the pandemic forces complete closure of schools during November-December 2021, but Term II exams are held at schools or centres.

Term I MCQ based examination would be done by students online/offline from home - in this case, the weightage of this exam for the final score would be reduced, and weightage of Term II exams will be increased for declaration of final result.

C. In case the situation of the pandemic forces complete closure of schools during March-April 2022, but Term I exams are held at schools or centres.

Results would be based on the performance of students on Term I MCQ based examination and internal assessments. The weightage of marks of Term I examination conducted by the Board will be increased to provide year end results of candidates.

D. In case the situation of the pandemic forces complete closure of schools and Board conducted Term I and II exams are taken by the candidates from home in the session 2021-22.

Results would be computed on the basis of the Internal Assessment/Practical/Project Work and Theory marks of Term-I and II exams taken by the candidate from home in Class X / XII subject to the moderation or other measures to ensure validity and reliability of the assessment.

In all the above cases, data analysis of marks of students will be undertaken to ensure the integrity of internal assessments and home based exams.

Dr. Joseph Emmanuel
Director (Academics)

PART A

Financial Accounting-I

CHAPTER 01

Accounting for Bills of Exchange

In this Chapter...

- Meaning of Bills of Exchange
- Promissory Note
- Accounting Treatment of Bills of Exchange and Promissory Note
- Dishonour of Bill

Meaning of Bills of Exchange

According to Section 5 of the Negotiable Instruments Act, 1881, "A bill of exchange is an instrument in writing, containing an unconditional order, signed by the maker directing a certain person to pay a certain sum of money only to or to the order of a certain person or to the bearer of the instrument." A bill of exchange is generally drawn by the creditor upon his debtor. It has to be accepted by the drawee (debtor) or someone on his behalf.

Features of Bills of Exchange

- It must be in writing.
- It is an order to make payment.
- The order to make payment is unconditional.
- The maker of the bill of exchange must sign it.
- The payment to be made must be certain.
- The date on which payment is to be made must also be certain.
- It must be payable to a certain person.
- The amount mentioned in the bill of exchange is payable either on demand or on the expiry of a fixed period of time.
- It must be stamped as per the requirement of law.

Parties to a Bills of Exchange

There are three parties to a bills of exchange

1. **Drawer** The maker of the bill of exchange is the drawer i.e., the person who draws the bill. He is the person who has granted credit to the person on whom the bill of exchange is drawn.

2. **Drawee** The person upon whom the bill of exchange is drawn for his acceptance is a drawee. Drawee is the person to whom credit has been granted.

3. **Payee** He is the person to whom the payment is to be made i.e., the person in whose favour the bill is made. Payee may be third person or the drawer himself.

Types of Bills of Exchange

There are two types of bills of exchange

1. **Trade Bill** A trade bill is the bills of exchange drawn and accepted for a trade transaction i.e., purchases and sales of goods. In other words, bills which are drawn in the ordinary course of business are known as trade bills. These bills can be further categorised as follows

   (i) **Bills at Sight or Demand Bill** In bills of exchange, 'at sight' and 'on presentment' means payable on demand. The instruments in which no time for payment is mentioned are known as bills at sight. Such instruments may be presented for payment at anytime.

   (ii) **Bills after Date** Where a bill is payable at a fixed period after date, the period begins from the date of drawing the bill. 3 days of grace are allowed on such bills. For example, bills of exchange dated 1st January, 2021 is payable 2 months after the date and it is accepted on 15th January, 2021. The due date of the bill will be 4th March, 2021.

   (iii) **Bills after Sight** In bills of exchange, 'after sight' means accepting. Where a bill is payable at a fixed period after sight, the period begins from the date of acceptance. 3 days of grace are allowed on such bills. For example, Bills of exchange dated 1st January, 2021 is payable 2 months after sight and it is accepted on 15th January, 2021. The due date of the bill will be 18th March, 2021.

2. **Accommodation Bill** These bills are drawn to help the other party i.e., bills drawn for mutual benefit are known as accommodation bills. It is accepted by the drawee to accommodate the drawer. Here, the drawee is called the **accommodating party** and the drawer is called the **accommodated party**.

   For example, Suppose X needs finance for 2 months. In that case, he may ask his friend Y to accept his bill. The bills of exchange may then be taken by X to his bank and get it discounted. Thus, X will be able to make use of funds. When the 2 months period expires, X will send the requisite amount to Y and Y will meet the bill. Thus, X is able to raise money for his use with the help of an accommodation bill.

Specimen of Bills of Exchange

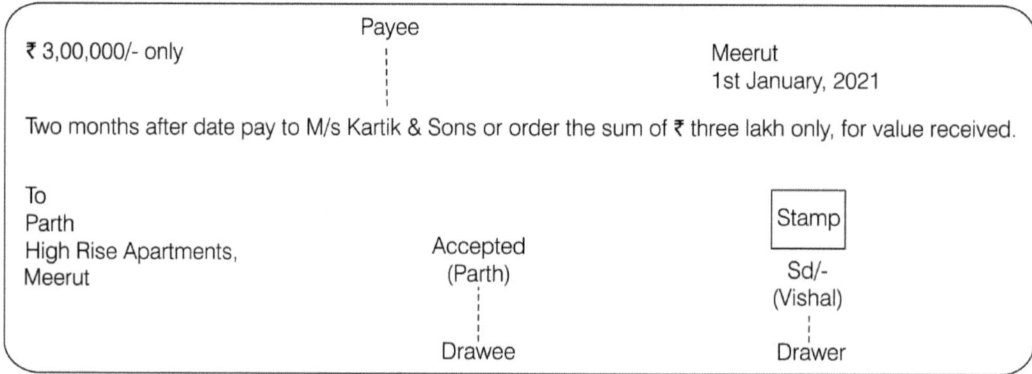

Promissory Note

According to Section 4 of the Negotiable Instruments Act, 1881, "A promissory note is defined as an instrument in writing (not being a bank note or a currency note), containing an unconditional undertaking signed by the maker, to pay a certain sum of money only to or to the order of a certain person or to the bearer of the instrument."

A promissory note does not require any acceptance because the maker of the promissory note himself promises to make the payment.

Features of Promissory Note

- It must be in writing.
- The sum payable must be certain.
- It must be payable to a certain person.
- It must contain an unconditional promise to pay.
- It must be signed by the maker.
- It should be properly stamped.

Parties to a Promissory Note

There are two parties to a promissory note

1. **Maker or Drawer** The person who makes or draws the promissory note to pay a certain amount is called a maker. He is the person who has availed the credit. He is also called the promisor.
2. **Payee** The person in whose favour the promissory note is drawn, i.e. the person to whom the payment is to be made is called the payee. He is also called the promisee.

Specimen of a Promissory Note

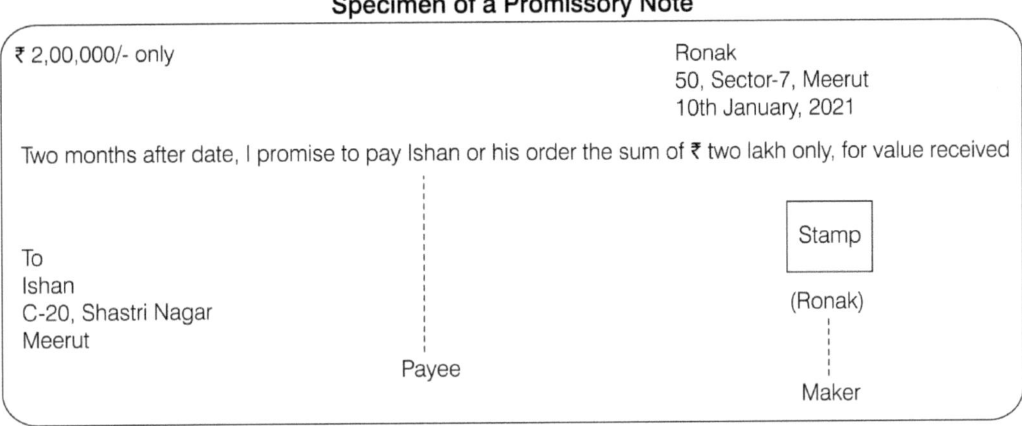

Terms Related to Accounting of Bills of Exchange/Promissory Note

Following are the important terms related to accounting of bills of exchange or promissory note

1. **Term of a Bill/Note** It is referred to as the period between the date on which a bill/note is drawn and the date on which it becomes due.
2. **Days of Grace** Days of grace are three extra days added to the period of bill/note.
3. **Due Date of a Bill/Note** It is the date on which the payment of the bill/note is due, i.e. the date on which the term of a bill/note expires.
4. **Date of Maturity of a Bill/Note** The date which comes after adding three days of grace to the due date of a bill/note, is called the date of maturity.
5. **Holder** Holder of a negotiable instrument (i.e., bill of exchange, promissory note or cheque) is a person entitled in his own name to the possession thereof and to receive or recover the amount due thereon from the parties to it.

Calculation of Due Date of a Bill/Note

The calculation of due date of a bill/note in various cases is calculated as follows

Cases	Due Date
When the bill/note is made payable on a specific date.	The specific date will be the due date.
When the bill/note is made payable at a stated number of month(s) after date.	That date on which the term of the bill/note shall expire will be the due date. Calculation of due date will be in terms of calendar months, ignoring the number of days in a month.
	For example, A bill dated 1st January, 2021 is payable 3 months after date.
	The date of maturity will be 4th April, 2021 (3 months from 1st January, 2021 is 1st April, 2021 adding 3 days of grace, the due date will be 4th April, 2021)

Cases	Due Date
When the bill/note is made payable at a stated number of days after date.	That date which comes after adding stated number of days to the date of bill/note, shall be the due date. The date of bill is excluded.
	For example, A bill dated 1st January, 2020 is payable after 60 days. The date of maturity will be 4th March, 2020 (30 days of January + 29 days of February + 1 day of March + 3 days of grace)
When the due date is a public holiday.	The preceding business day will be the due date.
	For example, Suppose the date of maturity is 15th August, 2021 (Independence Day) it being a public holiday, then the maturity date will be 14th August, 2021.
When the due date is an emergency/unforseen holiday.	The next working day will be the due date of maturity.

Accounting Treatment of Bills of Exchange and Promissory Note

For accounting purposes, no distinction is made between bills of exchange and promissory note. The entries passed in both the cases are the same.

Basic accounting treatment of bills of exchange can be studied in respect of the following cases

- When the bill is retained till the date of maturity.
- When the bill is sent to bank for collection.
- When the bill is discounted with bank.
- When the bill is endorsed or negotiated in favour of a creditor.

When the Bill is Retained Till the Date of Maturity

In this case, the drawer retains the bill with him till the date of its maturity. The drawer receives the money from the drawee on the maturity date.

Journal Entries

Transactions	Books of Creditor/Drawer		Books of Debtor/Acceptor/Drawee	
Sales/Purchases of Goods	Debtor's A/c	Dr	Purchases A/c	Dr
	To Sales A/c		To Creditor's A/c	
	(Being goods sold on credit)		(Being goods purchased on credit)	
Receiving/Accepting the Bill	Bills Receivable A/c	Dr	Creditor's A/c	Dr
	To Debtor's A/c		To Bills Payable A/c	
	(Being bills receivable drawn)		(Being bills payable accepted)	
Collection of the Bill	Cash/Bank A/c	Dr	Bills Payable A/c	Dr
	To Bills Receivable A/c		To Cash/Bank A/c	
	(Being payment received against bills receivable)		(Being payment made against bills payable)	

When the Bill is Sent to Bank for Collection

At times, the bill is sent to the bank with instruction that the bank should keep the bill till maturity and collect its amount from the acceptor on that date. This process is known as '**bill sent for collection**'. The bank credits the net proceed to the customer's account, after charging for the service.

Journal Entries

Transactions	Books of Creditor/Drawer	Books of Debtor/Acceptor/Drawee
Sales/Purchases of Goods	Debtor's A/c　Dr 　To Sales A/c (Being goods sold on credit)	Purchases A/c　Dr 　To Creditor's A/c (Being goods purchased on credit)
Receiving/Accepting the Bill	Bills Receivable A/c　Dr 　To Debtor's A/c (Being bills receivable drawn)	Creditor's A/c　Dr 　To Bills Payable A/c (Being bills payable accepted)
Sending the Bill for Collection	Bill Sent for Collection A/c　Dr 　To Bills Receivable A/c (Being bill sent to bank for collection)	—
On Receiving from the Bank, Advice that the Bill has been Collected	Bank A/c　Dr 　To Bill Sent for Collection A/c (Being amount of bill collected by the bank)	Bills Payable A/c　Dr 　To Bank A/c (Being bill met on due date)

When the Bill is Discounted with Bank

In case, a holder of the bill is in need of money, he may discount it through the bank i.e., the holder of the bill takes amount from a bank against the bill before the due date. This process is known as **discounting of the bill**. The bank charges an amount for this purpose and it is termed as '**discounting charges**'.

The charges depend upon the rate of interest and the remaining period of the bill i.e., from the date of discounting till the due date. The bank gets the amount from the drawee on the due date.

Journal Entries

Transactions	Books of Creditor/Drawer	Books of Debtor/Acceptor/Drawee
Sales/Purchases of Goods	Debtor's A/c　Dr 　To Sales A/c (Being goods sold on credit)	Purchases A/c　Dr 　To Creditor's A/c (Being goods purchased on credit)
Receiving/Accepting the Bill	Bills Receivable A/c　Dr 　To Debtor's A/c (Being bills receivable drawn)	Creditor's A/c　Dr 　To Bills Payable A/c (Being bills payable accepted)
Discounting the Bill	Cash/Bank A/c　Dr Discount Charges A/c　Dr 　To Bills Receivable A/c (Being bills receivable discounted with he bank)	—
On Maturity of the Bill	—	Bills Payable A/c　Dr 　To Cash/Bank A/c (Being bill met on due date)

When the Bill is Endorsed or Negotiated

Transfer of bills of exchange or promissory note to another person is referred to as **endorsement or negotiation**. The person receiving it becomes entitled to receive the payment. The bill can be initially endorsed by the drawer by putting his signatures at the back of the bill along with the name of the party to whom it is being transferred.

The person who endorses the bill is called the **endorser**. The person to whom the bill is endorsed is called **endorsee**. A bill can be endorsed multiple times before its presentation.

Journal Entries

Transactions	Books of Creditor/ Drawer/ Endorser	Books of Debtor/ Acceptor/ Drawee	Books of Endorsee

Sales/Purchases of Goods	Debtor's A/c Dr
	  To Sales A/c
	(Being goods sold on credit)
		Purchases A/c Dr
		  To Creditor's A/c
		(Being goods purchased on credit)
			—

Receiving/Accepting the Bill	Bills Receivable A/c Dr
	  To Debtor's A/c
	(Being bills receivable drawn)
		Creditor's A/c Dr
		  To Bills Payable A/c
		(Being bills payable accepted)
			—

Endorsing the Bill	Creditor's A/c Dr
	  To Bills Receivable A/c
	(Being bills receivable endorsed to a creditor)
		—	Bills Receivable A/c Dr
			  To Endorser
			(Being the receipt of a duly endorsed bill)

On Maturity of the Bill	—	Bills Payable A/c Dr
		  To Bank A/c
		(Being bill met on due date)
			Cash/Bank A/c Dr
			  To Bills Receivable A/c
			(Being bill collected on due date)

Dishonour of Bill

When the drawee or acceptor of the bill fails to make the payment on the date of maturity, a bill is said to have been dishonoured. In case a bill is dishonoured, it is advisable that the holder of the bill present the bill to a **notary public** and get the dishonour of the bill noted. **Noting** authenticates the fact of dishonour and serves as a legal proof in the court of law. For providing this service, a fees is charged by notary public which is called **noting charges**.

The journal entries related to dishonour of a bill and noting charges are given below

Journal Entries on Dishonour of a Bill
In the Books of Drawer

S.No.	Case	Entry

(i)	**When the Bill is Retained till Maturity**	Drawee's A/c Dr
		  To Bills Receivable A/c (with the amount of bill)
		  To Cash or Bank A/c (with noting charges paid)
		(Being the amount of dishonoured bill and noting charges debited to the drawee)

(ii)	**When the Bill is Sent to the Bankers for Collection**	Drawee's A/c Dr
		  To Bill Sent for Collection A/c (with the amount of bill)
		  To Cash or Bank A/c (with noting charged paid)
		(Being the amount of dishonoured bill and noting charges debited to the drawee)

(iii)	**When the Bill is Discounted**	Drawee's A/c Dr To Cash or Bank A/c (With the amount of bill and noting charges) (Being the amount of dishonoured bill and noting charges debited to the drawee)
(iv)	**When the Bill is Endorsed**	Drawee's A/c Dr To Endorsee's A/c (with the amount of bill and noting charges) (Being the amount of dishonoured bill and noting charges debited to the drawee)

In the Books of Drawee

Bills Payable A/c	Dr
Noting Charges A/c	Dr
To Drawer's A/c	
(Being the amount of dishonoured bill and noting charges credited to the drawer)	

Note
- *When the bill is dishonoured, in all the circumstances drawee or acceptor account is debited when entries are passed in the books of drawer and drawer's account is always credited and bills payable account is always debited, when entries are passed in the books of drawee.*
- *It may be noticed that whosoever pays the noting charges, ultimately these have to be borne by the drawee. This is because he is responsible for the dishonour of the bill and hence, he has to bear these expenses. For recording the noting charges in his books, the drawee opens noting charges account. He debits the noting charges account and credits the drawer's account.*

Solved Examples

Example 1. On 1st January, 2021, S purchased goods from P for ₹ 16,000 and immediately drew a promissory note in favour of P payable after 3 months. On the date of maturity of the promissory note, the Government of India declared holiday under the Negotiable Instrument Act, 1881. Since, P was unaware about the provision of the law regarding the date of maturity of the bill, she handed over the bill to her lawyer, who duly presented the bill and received the payment. The amount of the bill was handed over by the lawyer to P immediately. Record the necessary journal entries in the books of P and S.

Ans.

In the Books of P
JOURNAL

Date	Particulars		LF	Amt (Dr)	Amt (Cr)
2021 Jan 1	S	Dr		16,000	
	To Sales A/c				16,000
	(Being goods sold to S on credit)				
Jan 1	Bills Receivable A/c	Dr		16,000	
	To S				16,000
	(Being received S's promissory note)				
April 5	Bank A/c	Dr		16,000	
	To Bills Receivable A/c				16,000
	(Being amount received in respect of promissory note due)				

In the Books of S
JOURNAL

Date	Particulars		LF	Amt (Dr)	Amt (Cr)
2021 Jan 1	Purchases A/c	Dr		16,000	
	To P				16,000
	(Being goods purchased from P on credit)				
Jan 1	P	Dr		16,000	
	To Bills Payable A/c				16,000
	(Being promissory note sent to P)				
Apr 5	Bills Payable A/c	Dr		16,000	
	To Bank A/c				16,000
	(Being payment made to meet the promissory note due this day)				

Note *Since the due date of the promissory note i.e., 4th April has been declared as emergency holiday, the due date will be one day later i.e., 5th April.*

Example 2. On 1st October, 2021, Y sells goods to Z for ₹ 24,000. On that date, Z accepted a bill drawn upon him by Y at 2 months for ₹ 24,000. Y decides to retain the bill till due date and sends the bill to the banker for collection. In due course, Y receives the information from the bank that the bill has been duly met. Pass journal entries in the books of Y and Z.

Ans.

In the Books of Y
JOURNAL

Date	Particulars		LF	Amt (Dr)	Amt (Cr)
2021 Oct 1	Z Dr			24,000	
	To Sales A/c				24,000
	(Being goods sold to Z)				
Oct 1	Bills Receivable A/c Dr			24,000	
	To Z				24,000
	(Being acceptance received)				
Dec 4	Bill Sent for Collection A/c Dr			24,000	
	To Bills Receivable A/c				24,000
	(Being bill sent to bank for collection)				
Dec 4	Bank A/c Dr			24,000	
	To Bill Sent for Collection A/c				24,000
	(Being the amount of bill collected by the bank)				

In the Books of Z
JOURNAL

Date	Particulars		LF	Amt (Dr)	Amt (Cr)
2021 Oct 1	Purchases A/c Dr			24,000	
	To Y				24,000
	(Being goods purchased from Y)				
Oct 1	X Dr			24,000	
	To Bills Payable A/c				24,000
	(Being acceptance given)				
Dec 4	Bills Payable A/c Dr			24,000	
	To Bank A/c				24,000
	(Being bill met on due date)				

Example 3. Vishal sold goods for ₹ 7,000 to Manju on 5th January, 2021 and drew upon her bills of exchange payable after 2 months. Manju accepted Vishal's draft and handed over the same to Vishal after acceptance. Vishal immediately discounted the bill with his bank @ 12% per annum. On the due date, Manju met her acceptance. Journalise the above transactions in the books of Vishal and Manju.   **(NCERT)**

Ans.

In the Books of Vishal
JOURNAL

Date	Particulars		LF	Amt (Dr)	Amt (Cr)
2021 Jan 5	Manju Dr			7,000	
	To Sales A/c				7,000
	(Being goods sold to Manju)				
Jan 5	Bills Receivable A/c Dr			7,000	
	To Manju				7,000
	(Being acceptance received)				

Date	Particulars		LF	Amt (Dr)	Amt (Cr)
Jan 5	Bank A/c	Dr		6,860	
	Discounting Charges A/c (WN)	Dr		140	
	To Bills Receivable A/c				7,000
	(Being bill discounted with the bank @ 12% per annum)				

Working Note

$$\text{Calculation of Discount} = 7,000 \times \frac{12}{100} \times \frac{2}{12} = ₹\ 140$$

In the Books of Manju
JOURNAL

Date	Particulars		LF	Amt (Dr)	Amt (Cr)
2021					
Jan 5	Purchases A/c	Dr		7,000	
	To Vishal				7,000
	(Being goods purchased from Vishal)				
Jan 5	Vishal	Dr		7,000	
	To Bills Payable A/c				7,000
	(Being acceptance given)				
Mar 8	Bills Payable A/c	Dr		7,000	
	To Bank A/c				7,000
	(Being bills payable paid on maturity)				

Example 4. On 1st January, X sold goods worth ₹ 1,00,000 to Y and drew a bill on Y at 3 months for the amount. Y accepted the bill and returned it to X who endorsed the bill a month after the acceptance, in favour of a creditor Z in full settlement of his debt for ₹ 1,02,000. The bill is duly honoured at maturity. Pass the necessary journal entries in the books of X, Y and Z.

Ans.

In the Books of X
JOURNAL

Date	Particulars		LF	Amt (Dr)	Amt (Cr)
Jan 1	Y	Dr		1,00,000	
	To Sales A/c				1,00,000
	(Being the goods sold to Y on credit)				
Jan 1	Bills Receivable A/c	Dr		1,00,000	
	To Y				1,00,000
	(Being the acceptance of the bill received from Y)				
Feb 1	Z	Dr		1,02,000	
	To Bills Receivable A/c				1,00,000
	To Discount Received A/c				2,000
	(Being a bill of ₹ 1,00,000 endorsed to Z in full settlement of ₹ 1,02,000)				

In the Books of Y
JOURNAL

Date	Particulars		LF	Amt (Dr)	Amt (Cr)
Jan 1	Purchases A/c	Dr		1,00,000	
	To X				1,00,000
	(Being goods purchased on credit from X)				
Jan 1	X	Dr		1,00,000	
	To Bills Payable A/c				1,00,000
	(Being the acceptance of the bill given to X)				
Apr 4	Bills Payable A/c	Dr		1,00,000	
	To Bank A/c				1,00,000
	(Being the bill discharged)				

In the Books of Z
JOURNAL

Date	Particulars		LF	Amt (Dr)	Amt (Cr)
Feb 1	Bills Receivable A/c	Dr		1,00,000	
	Discount Allowed A/c	Dr		2,000	
	To X				1,02,000
	(Being the receipt of a duly endorsed bill)				
Apr 4	Bank A/c	Dr		1,00,000	
	To Bills Receivable A/c				1,00,000
	(Being the bill collected on due date)				

Example 5. P draws on Q three bills of exchange for ₹ 15,000, ₹ 12,000 and ₹ 9,000 respectively for goods sold to him on 1st February, 2021. These bills were for 1 month, 2 months and 3 months, respectively. The first bill was endorsed to his creditor R. The second bill was discounted with his bank on 4th February, 2021 @ 12% per annum and the third bill was sent to his bank for collection on 30th April. On the due dates, all the bills were duly met by Q. The bank sent the collection advice for the third bill after deducting ₹ 75 as collection charges. Pass the journal entries in the books of P and Q.

Ans.

In the Books of P
JOURNAL

Date	Particulars		LF	Amt (Dr)	Amt (Cr)
2021					
Feb 1	Q	Dr		36,000	
	To Sales A/c				36,000
	(Being goods sold on credit)				
Feb 1	Bills Receivable (No. 1) A/c	Dr		15,000	
	Bills Receivable (No. 2) A/c	Dr		12,000	
	Bills Receivable (No. 3) A/c	Dr		9,000	
	To Q				36,000
	(Being the acceptances received)				
Feb 1	R	Dr		15,000	
	To Bills Receivable (No. 1) A/c				15,000
	(Being the bill endorsed in favour of creditor, R)				

Date	Particulars		LF	Amt (Dr)	Amt (Cr)
Feb 4	Bank A/c	Dr		11,760	
	Discounting Charges A/c (WN)	Dr		240	
	To Bills Receivable (No. 2) A/c				12,000
	(Being the bill discounted with the bank)				
Apr 30	Bill Sent for Collection A/c	Dr		9,000	
	To Bills Receivable (No. 3) A/c				9,000
	(Being the bill sent to the bank for collection)				
May 4	Bank A/c	Dr		8,925	
	Bank Charges A/c	Dr		75	
	To Bill Sent for Collection A/c				9,000
	(Being the bill collected by the bank and collection charges deducted)				

Working Note

$$\text{Calculation of Discount} = 12,000 \times \frac{12}{100} \times \frac{2}{12} = ₹\ 240$$

In the Books of Q
JOURNAL

Date	Particulars		LF	Amt (Dr)	Amt (Cr)
2021 Feb 1	Purchases A/c	Dr		36,000	
	To P				36,000
	(Being the goods purchased on credit)				
Feb 1	P	Dr		36,000	
	To Bills Payable (No. 1) A/c				15,000
	To Bills Payable (No. 2) A/c				12,000
	To Bills Payable (No. 3) A/c				9,000
	(Being the acceptances given)				
Mar 4	Bills Payable (No. 1) A/c	Dr		15,000	
	To Cash A/c				15,000
	(Being the bill met on maturity)				
Apr 4	Bills Payable (No. 2) A/c	Dr		12,000	
	To Cash A/c				12,000
	(Being the bill met on maturity)				
May 4	Bills Payable (No. 3) A/c	Dr		9,000	
	To Cash A/c				9,000
	(Being the bill met on maturity)				

Example 6. On 1st January, 2021, X sold goods to Y for ₹ 20,000 less 2% cash discount. Y paid 50% price immediately and X drew a bill on Y for two months for the balance. This bill is duly accepted by Y. The bill was dishonoured on the due date and X paid ₹ 100 as noting charges. Y paid the amount due to X by cheque after ten days. Pass entries in the books of both the parties.

Ans.

In the Books of X
JOURNAL

Date	Particulars		LF	Amt (Dr)	Amt (Cr)
2021					
Jan 1	Y	Dr		20,000	
	To Sales A/c				20,000
	(Being goods sold to Y)				
Jan 1	Cash A/c	Dr		9,800	
	Discount Allowed A/c (10,000 × 2%)	Dr		200	
	To Y (20,000 × 50%)				10,000
	(Being cash received from Y and discount allowed at 2%)				
Jan 1	Bills Receivable A/c	Dr		10,000	
	To Y				10,000
	(Being acceptance received for 2 months)				
Mar 4	Y	Dr		10,100	
	To Bills Receivable A/c				10,000
	To Cash A/c				100
	(Being bill dishonoured and noting charges paid)				
Mar 14	Bank A/c	Dr		10,100	
	To Y				10,100
	(Being amount received)				

In the Books of Y
JOURNAL

Date	Particulars		LF	Amt (Dr)	Amt (Cr)
2021					
Jan 1	Purchases A/c	Dr		20,000	
	To X				20,000
	(Being goods purchased from X)				
Jan 1	X	Dr		10,000	
	To Cash A/c				9,800
	To Discount Received A/c				200
	(Being cash paid to X and discount received @ 2%)				
Jan 1	X	Dr		10,000	
	To Bills Payable A/c				10,000
	(Being acceptance given for 2 months)				
Mar 4	Bills Payable A/c	Dr		10,000	
	Noting Charges A/c	Dr		100	
	To X				10,100
	(Being bill dishonoured and noting charges paid by X)				
Mar 14	X	Dr		10,100	
	To Bank A/c				10,100
	(Being amount paid)				

Example 7. On 1st January, 2021, Shieba sold goods to Vishal for ₹ 10,000 and drew upon him bills of exchange of 2 months. Vishal accepted the bill and returned it to Shieba. On the date of maturity the bill was dishonoured by Vishal. Record the necessary entries in all the cases listed below in the books of Shieba.

   (i) When the bill is kept by Shieba till its maturity.
  (ii) When the bill is discounted by Shieba for ₹ 200.
 (iii) When the bill is endorsed to Lal Chand by Shieba.
 (iv) When the bill is sent to bank for collection.
      Noting charges were ₹ 100.

Ans.

In the Books of Shieba
JOURNAL

Date	Particulars		LF	Amt (Dr)	Amt (Cr)
	Entry in All the Cases				
2021 Jan 1	Vishal	Dr		10,000	
	To Sales A/c				10,000
	(Being goods sold to Vishal)				
Jan 1	Bills Receivable A/c	Dr		10,000	
	To Vishal				10,000
	(Being Vishal's acceptance received)				
	Additional Entry in Case (i)				
Mar 4	Vishal	Dr		10,100	
	To Bills Receivable A/c				10,000
	To Cash A/c				100
	(Being Vishal dishonoured his acceptance)				
	Additional Entry in Case (ii)				
Jan 1	Bank A/c	Dr		9,800	
	Discount A/c	Dr		200	
	To Bills Receivable A/c				10,000
	(Being bill receivable discounted with bank)				
Mar 4	Vishal	Dr		10,100	
	To Bank A/c				10,100
	(Being discounted bill dishonoured by Vishal)				
	Additional Entry in Case (iii)				
Jan 1	Lal Chand	Dr		10,000	
	To Bills Receivable A/c				10,000
	(Being Vishal's acceptance endorsed in favour of Lal Chand)				
Mar 4	Vishal	Dr		10,100	
	To Lal Chand				10,100
	(Being endorsed bill dishonoured by Vishal)				
	Additional Entry in Case (iv)				
Jan 1	Bank for Collection A/c	Dr		10,000	
	To Bills Receivable A/c				10,000
	(Being bills receivable sent to bank for collection)				
Mar 4	Vishal	Dr		10,100	
	To Bank A/c				100
	To Bank for Collection A/c				10,000
	(Being bills receivable dishonoured and noting charges paid by bank)				

Chapter Practice

PART 1
Objective Questions

• Multiple Choice Questions

1. A bills of exchange is drawn by a ....
   (a) shareholder   (b) debtor   (c) creditor   (d) foreigner

Ans. (c) A bill is drawn by creditor on his debtor. He is known as maker or drawer of the bill.

2 The party who is ordered to pay the amount is known as ....
   (a) Payee   (b) Drawee   (c) Drawer   (d) All of these

Ans. (b) Drawee or acceptor is the purchaser on whom the bill is drawn and is liable to pay the amount mentioned in the bill.

3 Which of the following is a type of bills of exchange?
   (a) Trade bill   (b) Accommodation bill   (c) Promissory note   (d) Both (a) and (b)

Ans. (d) Both (a) and (b)

4 Which of the following Act defines the bills of exchange?
   (a) Indian Partnership Act, 1932   (b) Indian Companies Act, 2013
   (c) Indian Negotiable Instrument Act, 1881   (d) None of these

Ans. (c) Indian Negotiable Instrument Act, 1881

5 "Sometimes the purchaser of the goods himself writes a note, signs it and gives it to the seller of the goods." This type of instrument is known as
   (a) Credit note   (b) Promissory note   (c) Debit note   (d) All of these

Ans. (b) Promissory note

6. On 12th July, 2021, A draws a bill on B for ₹ 50,000 for 1 month and 15th August is a public holiday. What will be the maturity date of the bill?
   (a) 13th August, 2021   (b) 16th August, 2021   (c) 14th August, 2021   (d) 15th August, 2021

Ans. (c) The date of maturity is 15th August, 2021, it being a public holiday, so the preceding day will be considered as the maturity date, i.e. 14th August, 2021.

7. Which among the following will be the journal entry in the books of drawer for sending the bill for collection?

   (a) Bill Sent for Collection A/c   Dr
        To Drawee
   (b) Bill Sent for Collection A/c   Dr
        To Bills Receivable A/c
   (c) Drawee A/c   Dr
        To Bill Sent for Collection A/c
   (d) None of the above

Ans. (b) Bill Sent for Collection A/c   Dr
        To Bills Receivable A/c

8. A draws a bill on X for ₹ 1,20,000 for 3 months. A got the bill discounted at a rate of 12%. The amount of discount will be

(a) ₹ 3,600   (b) ₹ 2,400   (c) ₹ 1,200   (d) ₹ 2,600

Ans. (a) Discount $= 1,20,000 \times \dfrac{3}{12} \times \dfrac{12}{100} = ₹\ 3,600$

9. A bill of ₹ 12,000 was discounted by A with the banker for ₹ 11,880. At maturity, the bill returned dishonoured, with noting charges ₹ 20. How much amount will the bank deduct from A's bank balance at the time of such dishonour?

(a) ₹ 12,000   (b) ₹ 11,880   (c) ₹ 12,020   (d) ₹ 11,900

Ans. (c) Bill Amount + Noting Charges = 12,000 + 20 = ₹ 12,020

10. X draws a bill on Y for ₹ 10,000. The bill is duly accepted by Y. On due date, bill was dishonoured and X paid ₹ 200 as noting charges. Which of the undermentioned journal entries reflect correct entry at the time of dishonour in books of X?

(a) Y		Dr	10,200	
	To Bills Receivable A/c			10,200
(b) Y		Dr	10,200	
	To Cash A/c			10,200
(c) Y		Dr	10,200	
	To Bills Receivable A/c			10,000
	To Cash A/c			200
(d) Bills Receivable A/c		Dr	10,200	
	To Y			10,200

Ans. (c)

Y	Dr	10,200	
To Bills Receivable A/c			10,000
To Cash A/c			200

11. Match the items given in column I with their respective treatment at the time of dishonour of bill in the books of drawer.

Column I	Column II	
A. When bill is discounted	(i) Drawee's A/c To Endorsee's A/c	Dr
B. When the bill is retained till maturity	(ii) Drawee's A/c To Bill Sent for Collection A/c To Cash or Bank A/c	Dr
C. When the bill is endorsed	(iii) Drawee's A/c To Bills Receivable A/c To Cash or Bank A/c	Dr
D. When the bill is sent to the bank for collection	(iv) Drawee's A/c To Cash or Bank A/c	Dr

Codes

	A	B	C	D
(a)	(i)	(ii)	(iv)	(iii)
(c)	(iv)	(iii)	(i)	(ii)

	A	B	C	D
(b)	(iv)	(i)	(ii)	(iii)
(d)	(iii)	(iv)	(i)	(ii)

Ans. (c) (iv) (iii) (i) (ii)

12. A draws a bill on B for ₹ 1,50,000. A endorsed it to C in full settlement of ₹ 1,51,500. Noting charges of ₹ 600, as the bill returned dishonoured. A wants to pay the amount to C at 2% discount. The amount to be paid by A to C will be

(a) ₹ 1,37,000   (b) ₹ 1,38,470   (c) ₹ 1,49,058   (d) ₹ 1,51,500

Ans. (c) Amount to be paid by A to C

$$\text{Discount @ 2\% to C} = (1,51,500 + 600) \times \frac{2}{100} = ₹\ 3,042$$

Final Amount paid by A to C $= 1,52,100 - 3,042 = ₹\ 1,49,058$

13. Which of the following statements are correct?

(i) Three days added for ascertaining the date of maturity of bills of exchange are called grace days.

(ii) The person in whose favour an endorsement of bills of exchange is made is called endorsee.

(iii) The fee charged for getting the bill noted is called noting charges.

Alternatives

(a) (ii) and (iii) are correct   (b) (i) and (ii) are correct

(c) (i) and (iii) are correct   (d) All are correct

Ans. (d) All are correct

14. When a bill is drawn to settle a trade debt, it is known as

(a) Proper bill   (b) Exchange bill   (c) Trade bill   (d) Accommodation bill

Ans. (c) Trade bill

15. "I owe you ₹ 50,000," it is a

(a) promissory note   (b) bill of exchange   (c) acknowledgement of debt   (d) None of these

Ans (c) It is neither a promissory note nor a bill of exchange. It is merely an acknowledgement of debt without any promise to pay.

• Assertion-Reasoning MCQs

Direction (Q. Nos. 1 to 3) *There are two statements marked as Assertion (A) and Reason (R). Read the statements and choose the appropriate option from the options given below.*

(a) Assertion (A) is correct, but Reason (R) is wrong   (b) Both Assertion (A) and Reason (R) are correct

(c) Assertion (A) is wrong, but Reason (R) is correct   (d) Both Assertion (A) and Reason (R) are wrong

1. **Assertion** (A) Promissory note does not require any acceptance.

Reason (R) Drawer of the promissory note himself promises to make the payment.

Ans. (b) A promissory note does not require acceptance because it is already a valuable instrument.

2. **Assertion** (A) A bill given to a creditor is said to be bills payable.

Reason (R) In case of a bills of exchange, the drawer and the payee can be the same person.

Ans. (b) Both Assertion (A) and Reason (R) are correct.

3. **Assertion** (A) When the bill has been discounted with bank and it is dishonoured, then noting charges will be debited in books of drawer.

Reason (R) Noting charges is an expense for drawer.

Ans. (d) Noting charges will always be debited in books of drawee as it is an expense for him.

• Case Based MCQs

1. **Direction** *Read the following case study and answer the question no. (i) to (iv) on the basis of the same.*

Rakesh runs a boutique in Karol bagh, Delhi. 80% of his transactions are on credit. Therefore, to avoid any default on part of buyers, he always use bills of exchange.

On 1st February, 2021, Ritika purchased goods worth ₹ 40,000 on credit. Ritika requested him to drew three bills of exchange instead of one. Therefore, he drew on her, three bills of exchange for ₹ 15,000, ₹ 13,000 and ₹ 12,000 respectively. These bills were for 1 month, 2 months and 3 months respectively. The first bill was endorsed to his creditor, Anuj.

The second bill was discounted with his bank on 4th February, 2021 @ 12% p.a. and the third bill was sent to bank for collection on 30th April, 2021. On the due dates, all bills were duly met by Ritika. Bank sent the collection advice for the third bill after deducting ₹ 75 as collection charges.

(i) Which of the aforementioned journal entry will be passed in books of Rakesh for discounting 2nd bill with the bank?

(a)	Bank A/c	Dr	12,740	
	To Bills Receivable (No.2)			12,740
(b)	Bank A/c	Dr	12,740	
	Discounting Charges A/c	Dr	260	
	To Bills Receivable (No.2)			13,000
(c)	Bank A/c	Dr	13,000	
	To Bills Receivable A/c (No.2)			13,000
(d)	Bank A/c	Dr	11,440	
	Discounting Charges A/c	Dr	1,560	
	To Bills Receivable (No.2) A/c			13,000

Ans. (b) Calculation of Discount $= 13,000 \times \dfrac{12}{100} \times \dfrac{2}{12} = ₹\ 260$

(ii) Which of the following journal entry shows the correct treatment for third bill on its due date?

(a)	Bank A/c	Dr	11,925	
	To Bill Sent for Collection A/c			11,925
(b)	Bank A/c	Dr	11,925	
	Bank Charges A/c	Dr	75	
	To Bill Sent for Collection A/c			12,000
(c)	Bank A/c	Dr	12,000	
	To Bill Sent for Collection A/c			12,000
(d)	Bank A/c	Dr	11,925	
	Bank Charges A/c	Dr	75	
	To Bills Receivable (No.3) A/c			12,000

Ans. (b)

Bank A/c	Dr	11,925	
Bank Charges A/c	Dr	75	
To Bill Sent for Collection A/c			12,000

(iii) Which of the undermentioned journal entry will be passed in the books of Ritika if Rakesh send third bill to bank for collection?

(a)	Bill Sent for Collection A/c	Dr	12,000	
	To Bills Receivable (No.3) A/c			12,000
(b)	Bills Payable A/c (No.3)	Dr	12,000	
	To Bill Sent for Collection A/c			12,000
(c)	Bill Sent for Collection A/c	Dr	12,000	
	To Rakesh A/c			12,000
(d)	Nil			

Ans. (d) Journal entry will not be passed in the books of Ritika.

(iv) The person to whom bill is endorsed is called ………. .

(a) Endorser   (b) Endorsee
(c) Acceptor   (d) Acceptee

Ans. (b) Endorsee

2. Direction *Read the following case study and answer the question no. (i) to (iv) on the basis of the same.*

Shri Ram Jewellers in Chandni chowk deals in crafting timeless pieces of handmade gold jewellery since 1950. CEO Mohit Gupta has decided to sell goods on credit to their old customers as a gesture for their customer loyalty over years. But to avoid any default on part of their customers, they decided to draw bill of exchange.

On 1st April, 2021, Rohan Kapoor purchased gold ring for ₹ 60,000. On the same date, Mohit drew a bill of the same amount for 3 months. The bill was accepted by Rohan. Mohit discounted the bill with his bank on 4th April, 2021 @ 18% p.a. On the due date, the bill was dishonoured and noting charges ₹ 850 were paid by the bank. Rohan agreed to pay ₹ 60,500 in full settlement after 10 days of dishonour of the bill.

(i) Which of the following journal entry will be passed in the books of Mohit Gupta upon dishonour of bill?

(a)	Rohan	Dr	60,850	
	To Bank A/c			60,850
(b)	Rohan	Dr	58,150	
	To Bank A/c			58,150
(c)	Rohan	Dr	60,850	
	To Bills Receivable A/c			60,000
	To Bank A/c			850
(d)	Bills Receivable A/c	Dr	60,850	
	To Rohan			60,000
	To Bank			850

Ans. (a) Amount due from Rohan = 850 + 60,000 = ₹ 60,850.

(ii) Consider the following statements about bills of exchange.

(i) Bills of exchange is a legal document under Negotiable Instrument Act, 1881.

(ii) Bills of exchange must contain an unconditional promise to pay.

Which of the following is incorrect?

(a) Only (i) (b) Only (ii)
(c) Both (i) and (ii) (d) None of these

Ans. (b) Bills of exchange contains an unconditional order to pay.

(iii) Which of the aforementioned journal entry will be passed in books of Mohit upon receiving the payment?

(a)	Bills Receivable A/c	Dr	60,000	
	To Rohan			60,000
(b)	Rohan	Dr	60,000	
	To Bills Payable A/c			60,000
(c)	Bank A/c	Dr	60,500	
	To Rohan			60,500
(d)	No Entry Required			

Ans. (c) Bank A/c   Dr   60,500

                To Rohan   60,500

(iv) "Mohit drew a bill of the same amount for 3 months". In this case, Mohit is ....

(a) drawer (b) drawee (c) Either (a) or (b) (d) None of these

Ans. (a) drawer

PART 2
Subjective Questions

• Short Answer (SA) Type Questions

1. Define bills of exchange and briefly explain parties to a bills of exchange.

Ans. According to Indian Negotiable Instrument Act, 1881, "A bills of exchange is an instrument in writing, an unconditional order signed by the maker directing to pay a certain sum of money only to or to the order of a certain person or to the bearer of the instrument". Parties to bills of exchange are as follows
  (i) **Drawer** He is a person who sold goods on credit to someone. He writes or draws the bill.
  (ii) **Drawee** He is the debtor who purchases the goods on credit and accepts bill. He is liable to pay the amount mentioned in the bill.
  (iii) **Payee** The person to whom the payment is to be made is called payee. The drawee himself or any other person may be the payee of the bill.

2. State any four essential features of bills of exchange.   (NCERT)

Ans. The essential features of bills of exchange are (any four)
  (i) It must be in writing.
  (ii) It is an order to make payment.
  (iii) The order to make payment is unconditional.
  (iv) The maker of the bills of exchange must sign it.
  (v) The payment to be made must be certain.
  (vi) The date on which payment is to be made must also be certain.
  (vii) It must be payable to a certain person.
  (viii) It must be stamped as per the requirement of law.

3. Bills of exchange must contain 'an unconditional promise to pay'. Do you agree with the statement? (NCERT)

Ans. No, I do not agree with this statement. According to Section 5 of the Negotiable Instrument Act, 1881, "Bills of exchange is an instrument in writing containing an unconditional order, signed by the maker directing a certain person to pay a certain sum of money only to or to the order of a certain person or to the bearer of the instrument". Therefore, bills of exchange is an order by the drawer (creditor) to the drawee (debtor) without any condition. Hence, the bills of exchange does not contain an unconditional promise to pay rather it contains an unconditional order to pay.

4. On 1st January, 2021, P sold goods to Q for ₹ 1,00,000. On the same date P draws a bill on Q for ₹ 1,00,000 due after three months. Q accepted the bill and returned it to P. P retained the bill till the due date and Q meets the bill on due date. Pass journal entries in the books of both the parties.

Ans.
In the Books of P (Drawer)
JOURNAL

Date	Particulars		LF	Amt (Dr)	Amt (Cr)
2021 Jan 1	Q To Sales A/c (Being goods sold to Q on credit)	Dr		1,00,000	1,00,000
Jan 1	Bill Receivable A/c To Q (Being bill Receivable form Q)	Dr		1,00,000	1,00,000
Apr 4	Bank A/c To bills Receivable A/c (Being the amount of the the bill received on due date)	Dr		1,00,000	1,00,000

In the Books of Q (Acceptor)
JOURNAL

Date	Particulars		LF	Amt (Dr)	Amt (Cr)
2021					
Jan 1	Purchases A/c	Dr		1,00,000	
	To P				1,00,000
	(Being goods purchased from P on credit)				
Jan 1	P	Dr		1,00,000	
	To Bills Payable A/c				1,00,000
	(Being acceptance given to P)				
Apr 4	Bills Payable A/c	Dr		1,00,000	
	To Bank A/c				1,00,000
	(Being the amount of the bill paid on due date)				

5. On 1st January, 2020, Rao sold goods worth ₹ 20,000 to Reddy. Half of the payment was made immediately and for the remaining half, Rao drew a bill of exchange upon Reddy payable after 30 days. Reddy accepted the bill and returned it to Rao. On the due date, Rao presented the bill to Reddy and received the payment. Journalise the above transactions in the books of Rao and prepare Rao's account in the books of Reddy.

Ans.

In the Books of Rao
JOURNAL

Date	Particulars		LF	Amt (Dr)	Amt (Cr)
2020					
Jan 1	Reddy	Dr		20,000	
	To Sales A/c				20,000
	(Being goods sold to Reddy on credit)				
Jan 1	Cash A/c	Dr		10,000	
	Bills Receivable A/c	Dr		10,000	
	To Reddy				20,000
	(Being half of the amount received and acceptance for remaining half amount received)				
Feb 2	Cash A/c	Dr		10,000	
	To Bills Receivable A/c				10,000
	(Being cash received on due date)				

In the Books of Reddy
Rao's Account

Dr   Cr

Date	Particulars	JF	Amt (₹)	Date	Particulars	JF	Amt (₹)
2020				2020			
Jan 1	To Cash A/c		10,000	Jan 1	By Purchases A/c		20,000
Jan 1	To Bills Payable A/c		10,000				
			20,000				20,000

6. Kapil purchased goods for ₹ 21,000 from Gaurav on 1st February, 2021 and accepted the bills of exchange drawn by Gaurav for the same amount. The bill was payable after a month. On 25th February, 2021, Gaurav sent the bill to his bank for collection. The bill was duly presented by the bank. Kapil dishonoured the bill and the bank paid ₹ 100 as noting charges. Record the necessary journal entries for the above transactions in the books of Gaurav.   **(NCERT, Modified)**

Ans.

In the Books of Gaurav
JOURNAL

Date	Particulars		LF	Amt (Dr)	Amt (Cr)
2021 Feb 1	Kapil	Dr		21,000	
	To Sales A/c				21,000
	(Being goods sold to Kapil)				
Feb 1	Bills Receivable A/c	Dr		21,000	
	To Kapil				21,000
	(Being acceptance received from Kapil)				
Feb 25	Bill Sent for Collection A/c	Dr		21,000	
	To Bills Receivable A/c				21,000
	(Being bills sent to the bank for collection)				
Mar 4	Kapil	Dr		21,100	
	To Bill Sent for Collection A/c				21,000
	To Bank A/c				100
	(Being bills dishonoured on due date and noting charges paid)				

7. Lipakshi sold goods worth ₹ 19,000 to Ipshita on 2nd March, 2021. ₹ 4,000 were paid by Ipshita immediately and for the balance, she accepted a bills of exchange drawn upon her by Lipakshi payable after 3 months. Lipakshi discounted the bill immediately with her bank @10% p.a. On the due date, Ipshita dishonoured the bill and the bank paid ₹ 30 as noting charges.

Record the necessary journal entries in the books of Lipakshi.

Ans.

In the Books of Lipakshi
JOURNAL

Date	Particulars		LF	Amt (Dr)	Amt (Cr)
2021 Mar 2	Ipshita	Dr		19,000	
	To Sales A/c				19,000
	(Being goods sold to Ipshita)				
Mar 2	Cash A/c	Dr		4,000	
	Bills Receivable A/c	Dr		15,000	
	To Ipshita				19,000
	(Being ₹ 4,000 cash and acceptance for ₹ 15,000 received)				
Mar 2	Bank A/c	Dr		14,625	
	Discounting Charges A/c	Dr		375	
	To Bills Receivable A/c				15,000
	(Being bill discounted by bank)				
Jun 5	Ipshita	Dr		15,030	
	To Bank A/c				15,030
	(Being bill dishonoured on due date and noting charges paid)				

Note *Computation of discount = 15,000 × 10% × 3/12 = ₹ 375*

8. On 1st January, 2021, Khushi drew a bill on Sarthak for ₹ 1,00,000 payable after 3 months. Sarthak accepted the bill and returned it to Khushi. After 10 days, Khushi endorsed the bill to her creditor, Smita. On the due date, the bill was dishonoured and Smita paid ₹ 2,000 as noting charges.

Record the transactions in the journal of Sarthak and Smita.

Ans.

In the Books of Sarthak (Drawee)
JOURNAL

Date	Particulars		LF	Amt (Dr)	Amt (Cr)
2021 Jan 1	Khushi	Dr		1,00,000	
	To Bills Payable A/c				1,00,000
	(Being acceptance given)				
Apr 4	Bills Payable A/c	Dr		1,00,000	
	Noting Charges A/c	Dr		2,000	
	To Khushi				1,02,000
	(Being bill dishonoured)				

In the Books of Smita
JOURNAL

Date	Particulars		LF	Amt (Dr)	Amt (Cr)
2021 Jan 11	Bills Receivable A/c	Dr		1,00,000	
	To Khushi				1,00,000
	(Being bill received from Khushi)				
Apr 4	Khushi	Dr		1,02,000	
	To Bills Receivable A/c				1,00,000
	To Cash A/c				2,000
	(Being bill dishonoured and noting charges paid ₹ 2,000)				

• Long Answer (LA) Type Questions

1 Explain briefly the procedure of calculating the date of maturity of bills of exchange. Give example. (**NCERT**)

Ans. In arriving at the maturity date (i.e. the date on which bills of exchange or promissory note becomes due for payment) 3 days, known as days of grace must be added to the date on which the period of credit expires. However, when the date of maturity is a public holiday, the maturity date will be the preceding business day. Also when an emergency holiday is declared under the Negotiable Instruments Act, 1881, which happens to be the date of maturity of bills of exchange, then the date of maturity will be the next working day immediately after the holiday.

For example,

Date of the Bill	Period
(i) 1st January, 2021	2 months
(ii) 23rd November, 2021	2 months
(iii) 23rd May, 2021	60 days

Emergency Holiday - 25th July, 2021

  (i) The due date will be — 1st March, 2021 + 3 days of grace = 4th March, 2021

 (ii) The due date will be — 23rd January + 3 days of grace = 26th January.
     Since, due date is falling on 26th January, 2021 which is a public holiday, the due date will be the preceding day, i.e. 25th January, 2021.

(iii) The due date will be — 8 days of May + 30 days of June + 22 days of July + 3 days of grace = 25th July
     Since, due date is falling on 25th July which is declared as an emergency holiday, the due date will be 26th July, 2021.

2. Distinguish between bills of exchange and a promissory note.

Ans. The differences between bills of exchange and promissory note are as follows

Basis	Bills of Exchange	Promissory Note
Drawer	It is drawn by the creditor.	It is drawn by the debtor.
Order or Promise and Parties	It contains an order to make payment. There can be three parties to it viz. the drawer, the drawee and the payee.	It contains a promise to make payment. There are only two parties to it *viz.* the drawer and the payee.
Acceptance	It requires acceptance by the drawee or someone else on his behalf.	It does not require any acceptance.
Payee	Drawer and payee can be the same party.	Drawer cannot be the payee of it.
Notice	In case of its dishonour, due notice of dishonour is to be given by the holder to the drawer.	No notice needs to be given in case of its dishonour.
Copies	In case of foreign bill, three copies are made, otherwise only one copy is prepared.	Only one copy is prepared whether, it is foreign or local.
Liability	The liability of the drawer arises only if the acceptor does not pay.	The promisor has the primary liability to pay.
Stamps	Stamps are not required to be fixed, on the bills payable on demand. However, on the other bills, stamps are require to be fixed.	Stamps have to be fixed in any case.

3. On 1st January, 2020, A sold goods for ₹ 60,000 to S. 50% of the payment was made immediately by S on which A allowed a cash discount of 2%. For the balance, S drew a promissory note in favour of A payable after 22 days. Since, the date of maturity of bill was a public holiday, A presented the bill on a day, as per the provisions of Negotiable Instrument Act which was met by S. State the date on which the bill was presented by A for payment and journalise the above transactions in the books of A and S.

Ans.

In the Books of A
JOURNAL

Date	Particulars		LF	Amt (Dr)	Amt (Cr)
2020 Jan 1	S	Dr		60,000	
	To Sales A/c				60,000
	(Being goods sold to S on credit)				
Jan 1	Bank A/c	Dr		29,400	
	Discount Allowed A/c ($30,000 \times 2\%$)	Dr		600	
	To S ($60,000 \times 50\%$)				30,000
	(Being 50% of ₹ 60,000 received from S after allowing a cash discount of 2%)				
Jan 1	Bills Receivable A/c	Dr		30,000	
	To S				30,000
	(Being received a promissory note from S for the balance)				
Jan 25	Bank A/c	Dr		30,000	
	To Bills Receivable A/c				30,000
	(Being amount received in respect of promissory note due this day)				

In the Books of S
JOURNAL

Date	Particulars		LF	Amt (Dr)	Amt (Cr)
2020 Jan 1	Purchases A/c To A (Being goods purchased from A on credit)	Dr		60,000	60,000

Jan 1	A
	    To Bank A/c
	    To Discount Received A/c
	(Being 50% of ₹ 60,000 paid to A and received a cash discount of 2%)
		Dr		30,000	29,400
					600

Jan 1	A To Bills Payable A/c (Being a promissory note sent to A)	Dr		30,000	30,000
Jan 25	Bills Payable A/c To Bank A/c (Being payment made to meet the promissory note due this day)	Dr		30,000	30,000

Note *Since the due date of the promissory note i.e., 26th January, falls on a public holiday, due date will be one day earlier i.e., 25th January.*

4. Anil drew a 3 months bill for ₹ 10,000 upon Sunil. The bill was endorsed in favour of Vimal who endorsed it in favour of Kamal who in turn endorsed it in favour of Anil to discharge his own acceptance. Prepare journal in the books of Anil, Sunil, Vimal and Kamal.

Ans.

In the Books of Anil
JOURNAL

Date	Particulars		LF	Amt (Dr)	Amt (Cr)
	Bills Receivable A/c To Sunil (Being the acceptance of the bill received from Sunil)	Dr		10,000	10,000
	Vimal To Bills Receivable A/c (Being the bill endorsed in favour of Vimal)	Dr		10,000	10,000
	Bills Receivable A/c (New) To Bills Receivable A/c (Old) (Being the receipt of a duly endorsed bill towards the payment of an old bill)	Dr		10,000	10,000

In the Books of Sunil
JOURNAL

Date	Particulars		LF	Amt (Dr)	Amt (Cr)
	Anil To Bills Payable A/c (Being the acceptance of the bill given to Anil)	Dr		10,000	10,000

In the Books of Vimal
JOURNAL

Date	Particulars		LF	Amt (Dr)	Amt (Cr)
	Bills Receivable A/c	Dr		10,000	
	To Anil				10,000
	(Being the receipt of a duly endorsed bill)				
	Kamal	Dr		10,000	
	To Bills Receivable A/c				10,000
	(Being the endorsed bill endorsed in favour of Kamal)				

In the Books of Kamal
JOURNAL

Date	Particulars		LF	Amt (Dr)	Amt (Cr)
	Bills Receivable A/c	Dr		10,000	
	To Vimal				10,000
	(Being the receipt of a duly endorsed bill)				
	Bills Payable A/c (Old)	Dr		10,000	
	To Bills Receivable A/c (New)				10,000
	(Being own acceptance discharged by endorsing an endorsed bill)				

Note *Since the question is silent with regard to payment of bill on maturity, therefore no journal entries are passed to that effect.*

5. From the following information, complete the following journal entries.

In the Books of Nonu
JOURNAL

Date	Particulars		LF	Amt (Dr)	Amt (Cr)
2021 Feb 1	....	Dr		72,000	
	To .... A/c				72,000
	(Being goods worth ₹ 72,000 sold to Monu on credit)				
Feb 1	....	Dr		30,000	
	Bills Receivable (No. 2) A/c	Dr		24,000	
	....	Dr		...	
	To Monu				...
	(Being the acceptances received from monu for 3 bills for 1 month, 2 months and 3 months respectively)				
Feb 1	Sonu	Dr		...	
	To Bills Receivable (No. 1) A/c				...
	(Being the 1st bill endorsed in favour of creditor Sonu)				
Feb 4	....	Dr		...	
	....	Dr		...	
	To Bills Receivable (No. 2) A/c				24,000
	(Being the 2nd bill discounted with the bank @ 12% pa on 4th February)				
Apr 30	....	Dr		18,000	
	To Bills Receivable (No. 3) A/c				18,000
	(Being the 3rd bill sent to the bank for collection on 30th April)				
May 4	....	Dr		...	
	....	Dr		...	
	To Bills Sent for Collection A/c				18,000
	(Being the bill collected by the bank and 150 collection charges deducted)				

In the books of Monu
JOURNAL

Date	Particulars		LF	Amt (Dr)	Amt (Cr)
2021 Feb 1	.... A/c .... (Being the goods purchased from Nonu on credit)	Dr		72,000	72,000

Feb 1	Nonu
	    To Bills Payable (No. 1) A/c
	    To Bills Payable (No. 2) A/c
	    To Bills Payable (No. 3) A/c
	(Being the acceptances given for 3 bills)
		Dr		72,000	30,000
					24,000
					18,000

Mar 4	.... To Cash A/c (Being the 1st bill met on maturity)	Dr		30,000	30,000
Apr 4	.... To Cash A/c (Being the 2nd bill met on maturity)	Dr		24,000	24,000
May 4	.... To Cash A/c (Being the 3rd bill met on maturity)	Dr		18,000	18,000

Ans.

In the Books of Nonu
JOURNAL

Date	Particulars		LF	Amt (Dr)	Amt (Cr)
2021 Feb 1	Monu To Sales A/c (Being goods worth ₹ 72,000 sold to Monu on credit)	Dr		72,000	72,000
Feb 1	Bills Receivable (No. 1) A/c Bills Receivable (No. 2) A/c Bills Receivable (No. 3) A/c To Monu (Being the acceptances received from Monu for 3 bills for 1 month, 2 months and 3 months respectively)	Dr Dr Dr		30,000 24,000 18,000	72,000
Feb 1	Sonu To Bills Receivable (No. 1) A/c (Being the 1st bill endorsed in favour of creditor Sonu)	Dr		30,000	30,000
Feb 4	Bank A/c Discounting Charges A/c To Bills Receivable (No. 2) A/c (Being the 2nd bill discounted with the bank @ 12% p.a. on 4th Feb)	Dr Dr		23,520 480	24,000
Apr 30	Bills Sent for Collection A/c To Bills Receivable (No. 3) A/c (Being the 3rd bill sent to the bank for collection on 30th April)	Dr		18,000	18,000
May 4	Bank A/c Bank Charges A/c To Bills Sent for Collection A/c (Being the bill collected by the bank and 150 collection charges deducted)	Dr Dr		17,850 150	18,000

In the Books of Monu
JOURNAL

Date	Particulars		LF	Amt (Dr)	Amt (Cr)
2021 Feb 1	**Purchases** A/c	Dr		72,000	
	To **Nonu**				72,000
	(Being the goods purchased from Nonu on credit)				
Feb 1	Nonu	Dr		72,000	
	To Bills Payable (No. 1) A/c				30,000
	To Bills Payable (No. 2) A/c				24,000
	To Bills Payable (No. 3) A/c				18,000
	(Being the acceptances given for 3 bills)				
Mar 4	**Bills Payable (No. 1) A/c**	Dr		30,000	
	To Cash A/c				30,000
	(Being the 1st bill met on maturity)				
Apr 4	**Bills Payable (No. 2) A/c**	Dr		24,000	
	To Cash A/c				24,000
	(Being the 2nd bill met on maturity)				
May 4	**Bills Payable (No. 3) A/c**	Dr		18,000	
	To Cash A/c				18,000
	(Being the 2rd bill met on maturity)				

Working Note

$$\text{Calculation of discount} = 24,000 \times \frac{12}{100} \times \frac{2}{12} = ₹\ 480$$

6. On 1st February, 2020, John purchased goods for ₹ 25,000 from Jimmi. He immediately made a payment of ₹ 5,000 by cheque and for the balance accepted the bill of exchange drawn upon him by Jimmi. The bill of exchange was payable after 40 days.

Five days before the maturity of the bill, Jimmi sent the same to his bank for collection. The bank duly presented the bill to John on the due date who met the bill. The bank informed the same to Jimmi.

Pass necessary journal entries in the books of John and Jimmi and prepare John's account in the books of Jimmi and Jimmi's account in the books of John.

Ans.

In the Books of Jimmi (Drawer)
JOURNAL

Date	Particulars		LF	Amt (Dr)	Amt (Cr)
2020 Feb 1	John	Dr		25,000	
	To Sales A/c				25,000
	(Being goods sold to John on credit)				
Feb 1	Bank A/c	Dr		5,000	
	Bills Receivable A/c	Dr		20,000	
	To John				25,000
	(Being cheque and acceptance received from John)				

Date	Particulars		LF	Amt (Dr)	Amt (Cr)
Mar 10	Bills Sent for Collection A/c	Dr		20,000	
	To Bills Receivable A/c				20,000
	(Being bill sent to bank for collection)				
Mar 15	Bank A/c	Dr		20,000	
	To Bills Sent for Collection A/c				20,000
	(Being bill was met on maturity)				

Dr John's Account **Cr**

Date	Particulars	Amt (₹)	Date	Particulars	Amt (₹)
2020			2020		
Feb 1	To Sales A/c	25,000	Feb 1	By Bank A/c	5,000
			Feb 1	By Bills Receivable A/c	20,000
		25,000			25,000

In the Books of John (Drawee)
JOURNAL

Date	Particulars		LF	Amt (Dr)	Amt (Cr)
2020					
Feb 1	Purchases A/c	Dr		25,000	
	To Jimmi				25,000
	(Being goods purchased from Jimmi on credit)				
Feb 1	Jimmi	Dr		25,000	
	To Bank A/c				5,000
	To Bills Payable A/c				20,000
	(Being bills payable and cheque paid to Jimmi)				
Mar 15	Bills Payable A/c	Dr		25,000	
	To Cash A/c				25,000
	(Being cash paid on maturity)				

Dr Jimmi's Account **Cr**

Date	Particulars	Amt (₹)	Date	Particulars	Amt (₹)
2020			2020		
Feb 1	To Bank A/c	5,000	Feb 1	By Purchases A/c	25,000
Feb 1	To Bills Payable A/c	20,000			
		25,000			25,000

7. A bill for ₹ 13,500 is drawn by Vishal on Rakesh and accepted by the latter payable at Union Bank of India. Show what journal entries would be recorded in the books of both the parties under each of the following circumstances, if the bill is met on maturity

  (i) The bill is retained till the due date.

 (ii) The bill is discounted with SBI, for ₹ 13,140.

(iii) The bill is endorsed by Vishal in favour of his creditors Harshit & Co in full settlement of their debt of ₹ 13,560.

(iv) The bill is sent to bank for collection.

Ans.

In the Books of Vishal
JOURNAL

Date	Particulars		LF	Amt (Dr)	Amt (Cr)
	Entry in All Cases				
	Bills Receivable A/c	Dr		13,500	
	To Rakesh				13,500
	(Being the bill drawn and accepted by Rakesh)				
	Additional Entry in Case (i)				
	Cash or Bank A/c	Dr		13,500	
	To Bills Receivable A/c				13,500
	(Being the bill realised on due date)				
	Additional Entry in Case (ii)				
	Bank A/c	Dr		13,140	
	Discounting Charges A/c	Dr		360	
	To Bills Receivable A/c				13,500
	(Being the bill discounted with SBI for ₹ 13,140)				
	Additional Entry in Case (iii)				
	Harshit & Co.	Dr		13,560	
	To Bills Receivable A/c				13,500
	To Discount Received A/c				60
	(Being the bill endorsed in favour of creditors Harshit & Co. in settlement of their debt)				
	Additional Entries in Case (iv)				
	(a) **When the Bill is Sent for Collection**				
	Bill Sent for Collection A/c	Dr		13,500	
	To Bills Receivable A/c				13,500
	(Being the bill sent for collection)				
	(b) **When Bill is Collected**				
	Bank A/c	Dr		13,500	
	To Bill Sent for Collection A/c				13,500
	(Being the bill collected at maturity)				

In the Books of Rakesh
JOURNAL

Date	Particulars		LF	Amt (Dr)	Amt (Cr)
	Vishal	Dr		13,500	
	To Bills Payable A/c				13,500
	(Being the bill accepted)				
	Bills Payable A/c	Dr		13,500	
	To Bank A/c				13,500
	(Being the bill duly met on maturity)				

8. On 1st January, 2020, A sold goods to B for ₹ 40,000 less 2% cash discount. B paid 50% price immediately and A drew a bill on B for two months for the balance. This bill is duly accepted by B.

The bill was dishonoured on the due date and A paid ₹ 200 as noting charges. B paid the amount due to A by cheque after ten days. Pass entries in the books of both the parties.

Ans.

In the Books of A
JOURNAL

Date	Particulars		LF	Amt (Dr)	Amt (Cr)
2020 Jan 1	B	Dr		40,000	
	To Sales A/c				40,000
	(Being goods sold to B)				
Jan 1	Cash A/c	Dr		19,600	
	Discount Allowed A/c	Dr		400	
	To B				20,000
	(Being cash received from B and discount allowed at 2%)				
Jan 1	Bills Receivable A/c	Dr		20,000	
	To B				20,000
	(Being acceptance received for 2 months)				
Mar 4	B	Dr		20,200	
	To Bill Receivable A/c				20,000
	To Cash A/c				200
	(Being bill dishonoured and noting charges paid)				
Mar 14	Bank A/c	Dr		20,200	
	To B				20,200
	(Being amount received)				

In the Books of B
JOURNAL

Date	Particulars		LF	Amt (Dr)	Amt (Cr)
2020 Jan 1	Purchases A/c	Dr		40,000	
	To A				40,000
	(Being goods purchased from A)				
Jan 1	A	Dr		20,000	
	To Cash A/c				19,600
	To Discount Received A/c				400
	(Being cash paid to A and discount received at 2%)				
Jan 1	A	Dr		20,000	
	To Bills Payable A/c				20,000
	(Being acceptance given for 2 months)				
Mar 4	Bills Payable A/c	Dr		20,000	
	Noting Charges A/c	Dr		200	
	To A				20,200
	(Being bill dishonoured and noting charges paid by A)				
Mar 14	A	Dr		20,200	
	To Bank A/c				20,200
	(Being amount paid)				

9. On 1st January, 2020, A drew a bill on B for ₹ 30,000 payable after 3 months. B accepted the bill and returned it to A. After 10 days, A endorsed the bill to his creditor C. On the due date, the bill was dishonoured and C paid ₹ 600 as noting charges. Record the transactions in the books of A, B and C.

Ans.

In the Books of A
JOURNAL

Date	Particulars		LF	Amt (Dr)	Amt (Cr)
2020 Jan 1	Bills Receivable A/c To B (Being acceptance received)	Dr		30,000	 30,000
Jan 11	C To Bills Receivable A/c (Being bill endorsed to C)	Dr		30,000	 30,000
Apr 4	B To C (Being bill dishonoured and noting charges paid by C)	Dr		30,600	 30,600

In the Books of B
JOURNAL

Date	Particulars		LF	Amt (Dr)	Amt (Cr)
2020 Jan 1	A To Bills Payable A/c (Being acceptance given)	Dr		30,000	 30,000
Apr 4	Bills Payable A/c Noting Charges A/c To A (Being bill dishonoured)	Dr Dr		30,000 600	 30,600

In the Books of C
JOURNAL

Date	Particulars		LF	Amt (Dr)	Amt (Cr)
2020 Jan 11	Bills Receivable A/c To A (Being bill received from A)	Dr		30,000	 30,000
Apr 4	A To Bills Receivable To Cash A/c (Being bill dishonoured and noting charges paid)	Dr		30,600	 30,000 600

10. On 2nd February, 2020, A purchased from B goods for ₹ 17,500. A paid ₹ 2,500 immediately and for the balance gave a promissory note to B, payable after 60 days. B endorsed the promissory note in favour of his creditor C for the full settlement of a debt of ₹ 15,400. On the due date of the bill, C presented the bill to A, which the latter dishonoured and C paid ₹ 50 as noting charges. On the same date, C informed B about the dishonour of the bill and B immediately settled his debt to C by cheque for ₹ 15,050 which includes noting charges. A settled B's claim by cheque for the same amount. Record the necessary journal entries in the books of B, C and A for the above transactions and prepare A's and C's accounts, in the books of B, B's account in the books of A and also B's account in the books of C.

Ans.

In the Books of B
JOURNAL

Date	Particulars		LF	Amt (Dr)	Amt (Cr)
2020 Feb 2	A	Dr		17,500	
	To Sales A/c				17,500
	(Being goods sold to Verma)				
Feb 2	Bank A/c	Dr		2,500	
	Bills Receivable A/c	Dr		15,000	
	To A				17,500
	(Being received ₹ 2,500 in cash and a promissory note for the balance)				
Feb 2	C	Dr		15,400	
	To Bills Receivable A/c				15,000
	To Discount Received A/c				400
	(Being promissory note endorsed to Gupta in full settlement of ₹ 15,400)				
Apr 6	A	Dr		15,050	
	To C (15,000 + 50)				15,050
	(Being promissory note dishonoured by A and noting charges paid by C being ₹ 50)				
Apr 6	C	Dr		15,050	
	To Bank A/c				15,050
	(Being amount paid to C)				
Apr 6	Bank A/c	Dr		15,050	
	To A				15,050
	(Being amount received from A)				

Note *Discount of ₹ 400 has not been debited in the entry for dishonour because full payment has been made to C on the date of dishonour itself.*

Dr				**A's Account**				Cr
Date	Particulars	JF	Amt (₹)	Date	Particulars	JF	Amt (₹)
2020				2020			
Feb 2	To Sales A/c		17,500	Feb 2	By Bank A/c		2,500
Apr 6	To C		15,050	Feb 2	By Bills Receivable A/c		15,000
				Apr 6	By Bank A/c		15,050
			32,550				32,550

Dr				**C's Account**				Cr
Date	Particulars	JF	Amt (₹)	Date	Particulars	JF	Amt (₹)
2020				2020			
Feb 2	To Bills Receivable A/c		15,000	Feb 2	By Balance b/d		15,400
Feb 2	To Discount Received A/c		400	Apr 6	By A		15,050
Apr 6	To Bank A/c		15,050				
			30,450				30,450

In the Books of A
JOURNAL

Date	Particulars		LF	Amt (Dr)	Amt (Cr)
2020					
Feb 2	Purchases A/c	Dr		17,500	
	To B				17,500
	(Being goods purchased from B)				
Feb 2	B	Dr		17,500	
	To Bank A/c				2,500
	To Bills Payable A/c				15,000
	(Being paid ₹ 2,500 in cash and a promissory note for the balance)				
Apr 6	Bills Payable A/c	Dr		15,000	
	Noting Charges A/c	Dr		50	
	To B				15,050
	(Being promissory note dishonoured and noting charges due)				
Apr 6	B	Dr		15,050	
	To Bank A/c				15,050
	(Being payment made to B)				

Dr   **B's Account**   Cr

Date	Particulars	JF	Amt (₹)	Date	Particulars	JF	Amt (₹)
2020				2020			
Feb 2	To Bank A/c		2,500	Feb 2	By Purchases A/c		17,500
Feb 2	To Bills Payable A/c		15,000	Apr 6	By Bills Payable A/c		15,000
Apr 6	To Bank A/c		15,050	Apr 6	By Noting Charges A/c		50
			32,550				32,550

In the Books of C
JOURNAL

Date	Particulars		LF	Amt (Dr)	Amt (Cr)
2020					
Feb 2	Bills Receivable A/c	Dr		15,000	
	Discount Allowed A/c	Dr		400	
	To B				15,400
	(Being promissory note received from B in full settlement of ₹ 15,400)				
Apr 6	B	Dr		15,050	
	To Bills Receivable A/c				15,000
	To Cash A/c				50
	(Being promissory note dishonoured and noting charges paid)				
Apr 6	Bank A/c	Dr		15,050	
	To B				15,050
	(Being amount received from B)				

Dr					B's Account			Cr
Date	**Particulars**	**JF**	**Amt (₹)**	**Date**	**Particulars**	**JF**	**Amt (₹)**	
2020				2020				
Feb 2	To Balance b/d		15,400	Feb 2	By Bills Receivable A/c		15,000	
Apr 6	To Bills Receivable A/c		15,000	Feb 2	By Discount Allowed A/c		400	
Apr 6	To Cash A/c		50	Apr 6	By Bank A/c		15,050	
			30,450				30,450	

11. Arun sold goods to Bala for ₹ 16,000 and drew a bill on Bala for three months who duly accepted the same. Arun endorsed the bill to Charan. Charan endorsed it to his creditor Dharam. Dharam discounted the bill at 15% per annum. On the date of maturity, the bill was dishonoured and bank paid noting charges amounting ₹ 100.

Show the necessary journal entries in the books of all the parties.

Ans.
In the Books of Arun
JOURNAL

Date	Particulars		LF	Amt (Dr)	Amt (Cr)
	Bala	Dr		16,000	
	To Sales A/c				16,000
	(Being goods sold to Bala)				
	Bills Receivable A/c	Dr		16,000	
	To Bala				16,000
	(Being the acceptance received)				
	Charan	Dr		16,000	
	To Bills Receivable A/c				16,000
	(Being the bill endorsed to Charan)				
	Bala (16,000 + 100)	Dr		16,100	
	To Charan				16,100
	(Being the bill dishonoured and noting charges receivable from Bala and payable to Charan)				

In the Books of Bala
JOURNAL

Date	Particulars		LF	Amt (Dr)	Amt (Cr)
	Purchases A/c	Dr		16,000	
	To Arun				16,000
	(Being the goods purchased from Arun)				
	Arun	Dr		16,000	
	To Bills Payable A/c				16,000
	(Being the acceptance given)				
	Bills Payable A/c	Dr		16,000	
	Noting Charges A/c	Dr		100	
	To Arun				16,100
	(Being the bills payable dishonoured and noting charges payable to Arun)				

In the Books of Charan
JOURNAL

Date	Particulars		LF	Amt (Dr)	Amt (Cr)
	Bills Receivable A/c	Dr		16,000	
	To Arun				16,000
	(Being bill received from Arun)				
	Dharam	Dr		16,000	
	To Bills Receivable A/c				16,000
	(Being the bill endorsed to Dharam)				
	Arun	Dr		16,100	
	To Dharam				16,100
	(Being bill dishonoured and noting charges receivable from Arun and payable to Dharam)				

In the Books of Dharam
JOURNAL

Date	Particulars		LF	Amt (Dr)	Amt (Cr)
	Bills Receivable A/c	Dr		16,000	
	To Charan				16,000
	(Being the bill received from Charan)				
	Bank A/c	Dr		15,400	
	Discounting Charges A/c (WN)	Dr		600	
	To Bills Receivable A/c				16,000
	(Being the bill discounted from bank)				
	Charan	Dr		16,100	
	To Bank A/c				16,100
	(Being the bill dishonoured and noting charges paid by the bank)				

Working Note

$$\text{Discount amount} = 16,000 \times \frac{15}{100} \times \frac{3}{12} = ₹\ 600$$

12. On 1st July, 2021, Ashu draws on Vishu who owed him ₹ 25,000, two bills, one for ₹ 15,000 for three months and another for ₹ 10,000 for two months. Vishu accepts these bills. Ashu endorses on 3rd July the first bill to his creditor Krish in full settlement of his account of ₹ 15,500 and discounts the second bill on 4th July with his banker @ 12% per annum. The first bill is duly paid at maturity but the second bill is dishonoured and ₹ 150 are paid as noting charges. On 15th September, Vishu paid due amount to Ashu.

Give journal entries to record these transactions in the books of Ashu and Vishu.

Ans.

In the Books of Ashu
JOURNAL

Date	Particulars		LF	Amt (Dr)	Amt (Cr)
2021					
July 1	Bills Receivable A/c (No. I)	Dr		15,000	
	Bills Receivable A/c (No. II)	Dr		10,000	
	To Vishu				25,000
	(Being two acceptances received from Vishu)				
July 3	Krish	Dr		15,500	
	To Bills Receivable A/c (No. I)				15,000
	To Discount Received A/c				500
	(Being first bill endorsed to Krish in full settlement of his account of ₹ 15,500)				

Date	Particulars		LF	Amt (Dr)	Amt (Cr)
July 4	Bank A/c	Dr		9,800	
	Discounting Charges A/c $\left[10,000 \times \dfrac{12}{100} \times \dfrac{2}{12}\right]$	Dr		200	
	To Bills Receivable A/c (No. II)				10,000
	(Being second bill discounted at 12% per annum)				
Sep 4	Vishu	Dr		10,150	
	To Bank (10,000 + 150)				10,150
	(Being second bill dishonoured and noting charges paid by the bank)				
Sep 15	Bank A/c	Dr		10,150	
	To Vishu				10,150
	(Being the amount received)				

In the Books of Vishu
JOURNAL

Date	Particulars		LF	Amt (Dr)	Amt (Cr)
2021					
July 1	Ashu	Dr		25,000	
	To Bills Payable A/c (No. I)				15,000
	To Bills Payable A/c (No. II)				10,000
	(Being the two acceptance given to Ashu)				
Sep 4	Bills Payable A/c (No. II)	Dr		10,000	
	Noting Charges A/c	Dr		150	
	To Ashu				10,150
	(Being the second bill dishonoured and noting charges payable)				
Sep 15	Ashu	Dr		10,150	
	To Bank A/c				10,150
	(Being amount paid)				
Oct 4	Bills Payable A/c (No. I)	Dr		15,000	
	To Bank A/c				15,000
	(Being the amount of first bill paid on due date)				

Chapter Test

Multiple Choice Questions

1. Which of the following is a disadvantage of bills of exchange?
   (a) No reminder to debtor   (b) Valid evidence of debt   (c) Certainty as to payment   (d) Time consuming process

2. In which of the following circumstances, days of grace are not allowed?
   (a) Bills at sight   (b) Bills after date   (c) Bills after sight   (d) Bills at date

3. Due date of a promissory note, dated 31st March, 2021 payable 90 days after date, is
   (a) 27th June, 2021   (b) 28th June, 2021   (c) 29th June, 2021   (d) 2nd July, 2021

4. When the bills are sent for collection, the sender of the bills opens a new account, i.e.,
   (a) bill sent for collection account   (b) bank account
   (c) discounting account   (d) None of these

5. Give journal entry for dishonour of a bill on maturity in the books of drawee, if noting charges are also payable on this bill and this bill was previously discounted from bank by the drawer.

   (a) Bills Payable A/c   Dr
       Noting Charges A/c   Dr
         To Drawer

   (b) Bills Payable A/c   Dr
         To Drawer
         To Noting Charges A/c

   (c) Bills Receivable A/c   Dr
       Noting Charges A/c   Dr
         To Drawer

   (d) Drawer   Dr
         To Bills Payable A/c
         To Noting Charges A/c

Short Answer (SA) Type Questions

1. Define promissory note and mention about parties to a promissory note.

2. Differentiate between trade bills and accommodation bills on any four basis.

3. Suresh owed ₹ 78,000 to Naresh. On 5th June, 2020, he accepted a bill for ₹ 75,000 for one month drawn by Naresh in full settlement of his debt. Naresh allowed ₹ 3,000 as discount. Naresh endorsed the bill to his creditor Mahesh immediately. The bill was duly met on the due date. Pass journal entries in the books of all the three parties.

4. A bill for ₹ 27,000 is drawn by Amit on Vineet and accepted by a latter payable at Canara Bank. Show what journal entries would be recorded in the books of Amit under each of the following circumstances, if the bill is met on maturity
   (i) The bill is endorsed by Amit in favour of his creditors Rakshit & Co in full settlement of their debt of ₹ 27,120.
   (ii) The bill is sent to bank for collection.

Long Answer (LA) Type Questions

1. On 1st January, 2021, X drew a bill on Y for ₹ 15,000 payable after 3 months. Y accepted the bill and returned it to X. After 10 days, X endorsed the bill to his creditor Z. On the due date, the bill was dishonoured and Z paid ₹ 300 as noting charges. Record the transactions in the books of X, Y and Z.

2. Asha sold goods worth ₹ 19,000 to Nisha on 2nd March, 2021. ₹ 4,000 were paid by Nisha immediately and for the balance, she accepted the bills of exchange drawn upon her by Asha payable after 3 months. Asha discounted the bill immediately with her bank. On the due date, Nisha dishonoured the bill and the bank paid ₹ 30 as noting charges. Record the necessary journal entries in the books of Asha and Nisha.

3. Paul purchased goods for ₹ 42,000 from Kevin on 1st February, 2020 and accepted the bills of exchange drawn by Kevin for the same amount. The bill was payable after a month. On 25th February, 2020, Kevin sent the bill to his bank for collection. The bill was duly presented by the bank. Paul dishonoured the bill and the bank paid ₹ 200 as noting charges. Record the necessary journal entries for the above transactions in the books of Paul and Kevin.

4. Vikram sold goods for ₹ 15,000 to Anjali on 5th July, 2020 and drew upon her bills of exchange payable after 2 months. Anjali accepted Vikram's draft and handed over the same to Vikram after acceptance. Vikram immediately discounted the bill with his bank @ 10% per annum. On the due date, Anjali met her acceptance. Journalise the above transactions in the books of Vikram and Anjali.

Answers

Multiple Choice Questions

1. (d)   *2. (a)*   *3. (d)*   *4. (a)*   *5. (a)*

For Detailed Solutions

Scan the code

CHAPTER 02

Trial Balance

In this Chapter...
- Meaning of Trial Balance
- Balance Method of Preparing Trial Balance

Meaning of Trial Balance

Trial balance is a statement which incorporates the balances of ledger accounts. It consists of debit column which records debit balances of ledger accounts and credit column which records credit balances of ledger accounts. If the total of the debit column equals to that of the credit column, then this proves the arithmetical accuracy of the accounts maintained. So, on the basis of the above discussion, it can be concluded that trial balance is a statement prepared with the help of ledger balances, at the end of a specific period, to find out whether debit total agrees with the credit total.

Objectives of Preparing a Trial Balance

The trial balance is prepared to fulfil the following objectives
- To ascertain the arithmetical accuracy of ledger accounts
- To help in identifying errors.
- To help in the preparation of financial statements (trading account, profit and loss account and balance sheet).

Balance Method of Preparing Trial Balance

Balance method is the most commonly used method of preparing trial balance as it facilitates the preparation of final accounts. Under this method, trial balance is prepared by showing the balances of all ledger accounts (including cash and bank accounts) and then totalling up the debit and credit columns of the trial balance to assure their correctness. The account balances are used because the balance summarises the net effect of all transactions relating to an account and helps in preparing the financial statements. Trial balance can be prepared under this method, only when all the ledger accounts have been balanced.

Steps to Prepare a Trial Balance

Step 1   The balances of each account in the ledger are ascertained.

Step 2   List each account and place its balance in the debit or credit column (if an account has a zero balance, it may be included in the trial balance with zero in the column for its normal balance).

Step 3   Compute the total of debit balances column.

Step 4   Compute the total of credit balances column.

Step 5   Verify that the sum of the debit balances equal the sum of credit balances. If they do not tally, it indicates that there are some errors. So, one must check the correctness of the balances of all accounts.

Format of Trial Balance

An illustrative trial balance indicating list of various accounts with their respective balances (i.e., debit or credit) is shown as below

Trial Balance
as on ......

Name of Accounts	LF	Debit Balance (₹)	Credit Balance (₹)
Capital			...
Land and Buildings		...	
Plant and Machinery		...	
Equipment		...	
Furniture and Fixtures		...	
Cash in Hand		...	
Cash at Bank		...	
Debtors		...	
Bills Receivable		...	
Stock of Raw Materials		...	
Stock of Finished Goods		...	
Purchases		...	
Carriage Inwards		...	
Carriage Outwards		...	
Sales			...
Sales Return		...	
Purchases Return			...
Interest Paid		...	
Commission/Discount Received			...
Salaries		...	
Long-term Loan			...
Bills Payable			...
Creditors			...
Advances from Customers			...
Drawings		...	
Total		...	...

Limitations of Trial Balance

Limitations of a trial balance are as follows
- Trial balance only confirms that the total of all debit balances matches the total of all credit balances.
- A trial balance gives only condensed information of each account.
- Trial balance total may agree inspite of errors. There are certain errors which are not disclosed by a trial balance.

  These are
  - (a) Errors of complete omission
  - (b) Errors of principle
  - (c) Compensating errors
  - (d) Incorrect amount entered in the journal
  - (e) Posting to the wrong account but on the correct side
  - (f) An entry posted twice in the ledger

Rules for Preparing the Trial Balance from the Given List of Ledger Balances

Following rules should be taken into care
- The balances of all assets accounts, expenses and losses accounts, drawings, cash and bank balances, purchases, sales return are placed in the debit column of the trial balance.
- The balances of all liabilities accounts, income and profit accounts, capital, sales, purchases return are placed in the credit column of the trial balance.
- Generally, closing stock does not appear in the trial balance. It is usually given outside the trial balance as an additional information or adjustment.

  In case, it appears in the trial balance, it means that it has already been adjusted through purchases.

Example 1. Given below is a ledger extract relating to the business of Viren & Co as on 31st March, 2021. You are required to prepare the trial balance by balance method.

Dr   **Cash Account**   Cr

Date	Particulars	JF	Amt (₹)	Date	Particulars	JF	Amt (₹)
	To Capital A/c		1,00,000		By Furniture A/c		30,000
	To Veer		2,50,000		By Salaries A/c		25,000
	To Sales A/c		5,000		By Arjun		2,10,000
					By Purchases A/c		10,000
					By Capital A/c		5,000
					By Balance c/d		75,000
			3,55,000				3,55,000

Dr   **Furniture Account**   Cr

Date	Particulars	JF	Amt (₹)	Date	Particulars	JF	Amt (₹)
	To Cash A/c		30,000		By Balance c/d		30,000
			30,000				30,000

Dr   **Salaries Account**   Cr

Date	Particulars	JF	Amt (₹)	Date	Particulars	JF	Amt (₹)
	To Cash A/c		25,000		By Balance c/d		25,000
			25,000				25,000

Dr   **Arjun's Account**   Cr

Date	Particulars	JF	Amt (₹)	Date	Particulars	JF	Amt (₹)
	To Cash A/c		2,10,000		By Purchases A/c (Credit purchases)		2,50,000
	To Purchases Return A/c		5,000				
	To Balance c/d		35,000				
			2,50,000				2,50,000

Dr   **Purchases Account**   Cr

Date	Particulars	JF	Amt (₹)	Date	Particulars	JF	Amt (₹)
	To Cash A/c		10,000		By Balance c/d		2,60,000
	To Arjun (as per purchases book-credit purchases)		2,50,000				
			2,60,000				2,60,000

Dr | **Purchases Return Account** | | | | | | Cr

Date	Particulars	JF	Amt (₹)	Date	Particulars	JF	Amt (₹)
	To Balance c/d		5,000		By Arjun (as per purchases return book)		5,000
			5,000				5,000

Dr | **Veer's Account** | | | | | | Cr

Date	Particulars	JF	Amt (₹)	Date	Particulars	JF	Amt (₹)
	To Sales A/c (Credit sales)		3,00,000		By Sales Return A/c By Cash A/c By Balance c/d		1,000 2,50,000 49,000
			3,00,000				3,00,000

Dr | **Sales Account** | | | | | | Cr

Date	Particulars	JF	Amt (₹)	Date	Particulars	JF	Amt (₹)
	To Balance c/d		3,05,000		By Cash A/c		5,000
					By Veer (as per sales book-credit sales)		3,00,000
			3,05,000				3,05,000

Dr | **Sales Return Account** | | | | | | Cr

Date	Particulars	JF	Amt (₹)	Date	Particulars	JF	Amt (₹)
	To Veer (as per sales return book)		1,000		By Balance c/d		1,000
			1,000				1,000

Dr | **Capital Account** | | | | | | Cr

Date	Particulars	JF	Amt (₹)	Date	Particulars	JF	Amt (₹)
	To Cash A/c To Balance c/d		5,000 95,000		By Cash A/c		1,00,000
			1,00,000				1,00,000

Students should keep in mind that balancing amount on the credit side signifies debit balance and balancing amount on the debit side signifies credit balance.

Ans.

Trial Balance
as on 31st March, 2021

Name of Accounts	LF	Debit Balance (₹)	Credit Balance (₹)
Cash A/c		75,000	—
Furniture A/c		30,000	—
Salaries A/c		25,000	
Arjun's A/c		—	35,000
Purchases A/c		2,60,000	—
Purchases Return A/c		—	5,000
Veer's A/c		49,000	—
Sales A/c		—	3,05,000
Sales Return A/c		1,000	—
Capital A/c		—	95,000
Total		**4,40,000**	**4,40,000**

Example 2. From the following list of balances extracted from the books of Shri Sahiram. Prepare a trial balance as on 31st March, 2021.

Name of Accounts	Amt (₹)	Name of Accounts	Amt (₹)
Stock on 1st April, 2020	48,000	Discount Received	20,000
Purchases	2,57,500	Long-term Borrowings	1,70,000
Sales	3,61,800	Provision for Doubtful Debts	5,000
Carriage Inwards	300	Provision for Depreciation on Machinery	5,000
Carriage Outwards	120	Bad Debts	600
Return Inwards	23,500	Stationery	420
Return Outwards	2,000	Insurance	340
Debtors	32,000	Wages and Salaries	18,500
Creditors	17,400	Investment	30,000
Leasehold Premises	1,60,000	Interest on Investment	2,700
Equipment	2,00,000	Cash and Bank Balance	1,240
Repairs to Equipment	2,000	Premises	60,000
Depreciation	8,000	Furniture and Fixtures	14,000
Bills Receivable	840	Miscellaneous Expenses	520
Bills Payable	480	Miscellaneous Income	140
Bank Overdraft	1,50,000	Loan from Axis Bank	25,000
Interest on Overdraft	640	Interest on above Loan	3,000
Purchases Return	50,000	Capital	96,000
Discount Allowed	4,000	Proprietor's Withdrawals (Drawings)	6,000
Salaries	10,000	Computers	9,000
		Goodwill	15,000
		Stock on 31st March, 2021 (not adjusted)	31,000

Ans.

Trial Balance
as on 31st March, 2021

Name of Accounts	LF	Debit Balance (₹)	Credit Balance (₹)
Stock on 1st April, 2020		48,000	—
Purchases		2,57,500	—
Sales		—	3,61,800
Carriage Inwards		300	—
Carriage Outwards		120	—
Return Inwards		23,500	—
Return Outwards		—	2,000
Debtors		32,000	—
Creditors		—	17,400
Leasehold Premises		1,60,000	—
Equipment		2,00,000	—
Repairs to Equipment		2,000	—
Depreciation		8,000	—
Bills Receivable		840	—
Bills Payable		—	480
Bank Overdraft		—	1,50,000
Interest on Overdraft		640	—
Purchases Return		—	50,000
Discount Allowed		4,000	—
Salaries		10,000	—

Name of Accounts	LF	Debit Balance (₹)	Credit Balance (₹)
Discount Received		—	20,000
Long-term Borrowings		—	1,70,000
Provisions for Doubtful Debts		—	5,000
Provision for Depreciation on Machinery		—	5,000
Bad Debts		600	—
Stationery		420	—
Insurance		340	—
Wages and Salaries		18,500	—
Investment		30,000	—
Interest on Investment		—	2,700
Cash and Bank Balance		1,240	—
Premises		60,000	—
Furniture and Fixtures		14,000	—
Miscellaneous Expenses		520	—
Miscellaneous Income		—	140
Loan from Axis Bank		—	25,000
Interest on above Loan		3,000	—
Capital		—	96,000
Proprietor's Withdrawals (Drawings)		6,000	—
Computers		9,000	—
Goodwill		15,000	—
Total		9,05,520	9,05,520

Closing stock will not be shown in trial balance because it has not yet been adjusted.

Chapter Practice

Objective Questions

• Multiple Choice Questions

1. Trial balance is

    (a) an account   (b) a statement   (c) ledger   (d) Both (a) and (b)

Ans. (b) a statement

2. Which of the following statements is/are true about trial balance?

    (a) Trial balance is prepared with the help of all accounts and cash book

    (b) Trial balance is prepared only at the end of financial or calendar year

    (c) Both (a) and (b)

    (d) None of the above

Ans. (a) Trial balance is prepared with the help of all accounts and cash book

3. Identify the incorrect objective of preparing trial balance.

    (a) To prepare financial statements

    (b) To locate errors

    (c) To communicate accounting information to the users

    (d) To ascertain arithmetical accuracy of ledger accounts

Ans. (c) Extract of trial balance is not a part of financial statements but only helps to prepare them. Financial statements include profit and loss account, trading account and balance sheet which are available to users to ascertain financial position of business.

4. Format of a trial balance is

    (a) Name of Accounts, LF, Debit Balance, Credit Balance

    (b) Name of Accounts, JF, Debit Balance, Credit Balance

    (c) Name of Accounts, Voucher no., Debit Balance, Credit Balances

    (d) Name of Accounts, Voucher no., LF, JF, Debit and Credit Balances

Ans. (a) Name of Accounts, LF, Debit Balance, Credit Balance

5. Identify the incorrect characteristic of trial balance.

    (a) It shows balances of all ledger accounts and cash book

    (b) It shows final position of all accounts

    (c) It is a part of double entry system of book-keeping

    (d) It can be prepared anytime

Ans. (c) Trial balance is not a part of double entry system of book-keeping. It is a result of double entry system of book-keeping.

6. Trial balance is prepared

    (a) monthly   (b) quarterly   (c) half yearly   (d) on any date

Ans. (d) Trial balance is normally prepared at the end of an accounting year. However, it is at discretion of an organisation. Thus, it can be prepared monthly, quarterly, half yearly, annually or at any time.

7. Balance method of trial balance shows
   (a) total of debit and credit of all ledger accounts separately
   (b) final balance of all ledger accounts
   (c) total of debit and credit balance separately and then in separate column, final balance of all ledger accounts
   (d) None of the above

Ans. (b) Balance method is the most widely used method which shows balances of all ledger accounts and then totalling up of credit and debit balances is done to ascertain accuracy.

8. Identify the error that do not affect trial balance.
   (a) Error of commission   (b) Error of principle   (c) Error of partial omission   (d) All of these

Ans. (b) Error of principle arise due to incorrect application of principles of accounting. It is a two sided error, therefore it does not affect the trial balance.

9. If closing stock is shown in trial balance, it means
   (a) it is adjusted against opening stock
   (b) it is adjusted against purchases
   (c) Both (a) and (b)
   (d) None of these

Ans. (b) Usually, closing stock is shown outside trial balance as an additional information. However, if it appears in trial balance, it means that it has already been adjusted through purchases by debiting closing sock and crediting purchases account.

10. Balance of purchase is shown
   (a) in debit column of trial balance
   (b) in credit column of trial balance
   (c) as an adjustment at end
   (d) None of these

Ans. (a) Purchase is an expense, therefore it's balance will be shown in debit column of trial balance.

11. Balance of bad debts is shown
   (a) in debit column of trial balance
   (b) in credit column of trial balance
   (c) as an adjustment at end
   (d) by adjusting it with debtors

Ans. (a) Bad debts is a loss and accounts of all expenses and losses have debit balances. Therefore, it will be shown in debit column of trial balance.

12. Sundry creditors worth ₹ 50,000 will be shown
   (a) in debit column of trial balance
   (b) in credit column of trial balance
   (c) as an adjustment at end
   (d) None of these

Ans. (b) All liabilities are shown in credit column of trial balance. Therefore, sundry creditors worth ₹ 50,000 will be shown in credit column of trial balance.

13. Interest received worth ₹ 1,000 and sales worth ₹ 5,00,000 are shown
   (a) in debit column and credit column respectively of trial balance
   (b) in credit column and debit column respectively of trial balance
   (c) in credit column of trial balance
   (d) in debit column of trial balance

Ans. (c) Interest received and sales are income, therefore, they are shown in credit column of trial balance.

14. A trader has prepared the trial balance and total doesn't tie. Which approach the trader should follow?
   (a) Firstly, he should recheck all the ledger
   (b) He should recheck the total of trial balance
   (c) He should open the suspense account
   (d) All of these

Ans. (d) All of these

15. What will be the effect on trial balance if ₹ 2,000 received as rent and correctly entered in the cash book but not posted to rent account?
   (a) Debit side of trial balance will exceed by ₹ 2,000
   (b) Debit side of trial balance will decrease by ₹ 2,000
   (c) Credit side of trial balance will decrease by ₹ 2,000
   (d) Credit side of trial balance will exceed by ₹ 2,000

Ans. (a) In this situation, one account has been posted correctly, i.e., cash account but one account has been left to be posted i.e., rent account.

• Assertion-Reasoning MCQs

Direction *(Q. Nos. 1 to 5) There are two statements marked as Assertion (A) and Reason (R). Read the statements and choose the appropriate option from the options given below.*

(a) Assertion (A) is correct, but Reason (R) is wrong
(b) Both Assertion (A) and Reason (R) are correct
(c) Assertion (A) is wrong, but Reason (R) is correct
(d) Both Assertion (A) and Reason (R) are wrong

1. Assertion (A) Rent received is shown in credit column of trial balance.

   Reason (R) All incomes and profits are shown in credit column of trial balance.

Ans. (b) Both Assertion (A) and Reason (R) are correct

2. Assertion (A) Owner's wife loan to the business is shown in debit column of trial balance.

   Reason (R) All assets are shown in credit column of trial balance.

Ans. (d) All liabilities are shown in credit column of trial balance. Therefore, owner's wife loan to the business will be shown in credit column of trial balance whereas all assets are shown in debit column of trial balance.

3. Assertion (A) Trial balance is not a conclusive proof of accuracy of accounts.

   Reason (R) Error of commission do not affect trial balance.

Ans. (a) Trial balance is not a conclusive proof of the accuracy of the books of accounts since some errors are not disclosed by the trial balance. Most of the errors of commission like error of casting, error of carrying forward, etc affect trial balance.

4. Assertion (A) Furniture and fixtures is shown in debit column of trial balance.

   Reason (R) All assets are shown in debit column of trial balance.

Ans. (b) Both Assertion (A) and Reason (R) are correct

5. Assertion (A) Trial balance total may agree inspite of errors.

   Reason (R) Various errors like errors of principle, errors of partial omission are not disclosed by trial balance.

Ans. (a) Two sided errors are not disclosed by trial balance. Therefore, it agrees even if these errrors are made. Error of partial omission is one sided errror that can be easily disclosed by trial balance.

• Case Based MCQs

1. Direction *Read the following case study and answer the question no. (i) to (iv) on the basis of the same.*
Mr Gupta is a sole proprietor who lives near Darya ganj and deals in sanitary ware. He started his business on 1st April, 2021 with capital of ₹ 1,40,000. His daughter, Reena who is in class 11th of ABC school prepares his trial balance as on 31st March, 2022. Mr. Gupta is a penny pincher who does not want to appoint a CA to prepare his financial statements. Following is extract of trial balance prepared by Reena.

Name of Accounts	LF	Debit Balance (₹)	Credit Balance (₹)
Cash in Hand		10,000	—
Machinery		—	50,000
Mr Gupta's Wife Loan		30,000	—
Drawings		—	15,000
Purchases		25,000	—
Return Inwards		—	500
Return Outwards		600	—
Sundry Expenses		100	—
Rent		1,200	—
Debtors		1,140	—
Creditors		—	10,000
Total		**68,040**	**75,500**

(i) Reena has shown machinery in credit balance of trial balance. According to you, where it should be shown?

(a) In credit balance
(b) In debit balance
(c) As an adjustment
(d) Should be adjusted against cash

Ans. (b) All accounts of assets are shown in debit column of trial balance. As machinery is an assset, it will be shown in debit column of trial balance.

(ii) Identify the item(s) that has/have been shown incorrectly by Reena.

(I) Mr Gupta's wife loan
(II) Cash-in-hand
(III) Drawings
(IV) Purchases

Alternatives

(a) Only (I)
(b) Only (II)
(c) Both (I) and (III)
(d) Both (IV) and (II)

Ans. (c) Mr Gupta's wife loan is a liability. Therefore, it will be shown in credit column of trial balance. Drawings have a debit balance and are shown in debit column of trial balance.

(iii) Reena has omitted to show balance of discount allowed and discount received. Can you identify where both will be shown?

(a) In debit and credit column respectively
(b) In credit and debit column respectively
(c) Both will be shown in debit column
(d) Both will be shown in credit column

Ans. (a) Accounts of expenses have debit balance and are shown in the debit column of trial balance. Therefore, discount allowed will be shown in debit column of trial balance. Accounts of gains have credit balance and are shown in credit column of trial balance. Therefore, discount received will be shown in credit column of trial balance.

(iv) According to rules for preparing trial balance, liabilities and drawings are shown in

(a) debit column of trial balance
(b) credit column of trial balance
(c) debit and credit column respectively
(d) credit and debit column respectively

Ans. (d) Drawings have a debit balance and are shown in debit column of trial balance. All liabilities have credit balance and are shown in credit column of trial balance.

2. Direction *Read the following case study and answer the question no. (i) to (iv) on the basis of the same.*

Manuj Jindal, dropout UPSC aspirant has now started his own Edtech Company "MJ Enterprises", where he sell UPSC, RBI and SEBI exam courses books. To maintain his books of accounts, he hired his friend Sahil, who has just passed IPCC group II.

After preparing following trial balance, Sahil discovered that some transactions were not recorded.

Trial Balance
as on ......

Name of Accounts	LF	Debit Balance (₹)	Credit Balance (₹)
Furniture		2,00,000	—
Capital		—	2,00,000
Drawings		1,00,000	—
Debtors		1,80,000	—
Creditors		—	1,95,000
Purchases		2,00,000	—
Sales		—	5,00,000
Bank		60,000	—
Cash in Hand		85,000	—
Rent		70,000	—
Total		8,95,000	8,95,000

Following transactions were not recorded
(i) Books worth ₹ 5,000 purchased on credit.
(ii) Manuj withdraws ₹ 10,000 for personal use.
(iii) Purchased from M/s Kamran Furniture costing ₹ 20,000.

(i) Which journal entry reflects the correct accounting treatment of transaction "Manuj withdraws ₹ 10,000 for personal use"?

(a) Drawings A/c   Dr   10,000
        To Cash A/c   10,000
(b) Manuj A/c   Dr   10,000
        To Cash A/c   10,000
(c) Capital A/c   Dr   10,000
        To Cash A/c   10,000
(d) MJ Enterprises A/c   Dr   10,000
        To Cash A/c   10,000

Ans. (a) Drawings A/c   Dr   10,000
                To Cash A/c   10,000

(ii) Which of the following will be the amount of purchases shown in trial balance?

(a) ₹ 2,15,000   (b) ₹ 2,25,000   (c) ₹ 1,95,000   (d) ₹ 2,05,000

Ans. (d) Purchases = 2,00,000 + 5,000 = ₹ 2,05,000

(iii) What will be the amount of cash to be shown in trial balance?

(a) ₹ 75,000   (b) ₹ 85,000   (c) ₹ 55,000   (d) ₹ 45,000

Ans. (a) Cash = 85,000 − 10,000 = ₹ 75,000

(iv) What will be the total of trial balance after taking into consideration unrecorded transactions?

(a) ₹ 9,80,000   (b) ₹ 9,20,000   (c) ₹ 10,50,000   (d) ₹ 12,00,000

Ans. (b) ₹ 9,20,000

Trial Balance
as on...

Name of Accounts	LF	Debit Balance (₹)	Credit Balance (₹)
Furniture (2,00,000+20,000)		2,20,000	—
Capital		—	2,00,000
Drawings (1,00,000 + 10,000)		1,10,000	—
Debtors		1,80,000	—
Creditors (1,95,000 + 20,000 + 5,000)		—	2,20,000
Purchases (2,00,000 + 5,000)		2,05,000	—
Sales		—	5,00,000
Bank		60,000	—
Cash (85,000 − 10,000)		75,000	—
Rent		70,000	—
Total		9,20,000	9,20,000

Subjective Questions

• Short Answer (SA) Type Questions

1. State whether the balance of the following accounts should be placed in the debit or the credit columns of the trial balance.

   (i) Plant and machinery   (ii) Discount allowed   (iii) Bank overdraft

   (iv) Sales   (v) Interest paid   (vi) Bad debts

Ans.   (i) **Debit** Plant and machinery is an asset which has a debit balance. Therefore, it will be shown in debit column of trial balance.

    (ii) **Debit** Discount allowed is an expense which has a debit balance. Therefore, it will be shown in debit column of trial balance.

   (iii) **Credit** Bank overdraft is a liability which has a credit balance. Therefore, it will be shown in credit column of trial balance.

   (iv) **Credit** Sales account always has a credit balance which is shown in the credit column of trial balance.

    (v) **Debit** Interest paid always has a debit balance which is shown in the debit column of trial balance.

   (vi) **Debit** Bad debts is a loss which has a debit balance. Therefore, it will be shown in debit column of trial balance.

2. State the limitations of trial balance.

Ans.   (i) Trial balance only confirm that the total of all debit balances matches the total of all credit balances.

    (ii) A trial balance gives only condensed information of each account.

   (iii) Trial balance total may agree inspite of errors. There are certain errors which are not disclosed by a trial balance.

3. Ramesh's CA extracted the following trial balance as on 31st March, 2020

Trial Balance
as on 31st March, 2020

Name of Accounts	LF	Debit Balance (₹)	Credit Balance (₹)
Furniture		—	30,000
Machinery		—	40,000
Debtors		2,00,000	—
Goodwill		—	10,000
Creditors		1,00,000	—
Discount Received		—	2,000
Capital		—	1,00,000
Bank Loan		—	1,18,000
Total		3,00,000	3,00,000

State the errors committed in the above trial balance along with reasons.

Ans.   (i) Furniture and machinery are assets, therefore their balances should appear in debit columns.

    (ii) Goodwill is also an asset. Thus, it's balance should be shown in debit column.

   (iii) Creditors are liability for the firm. Thus, they should be shown under credit column.

4. State whether the balances of the following accounts should be placed in debit or credit column of trial balance and also state the reasons

Bank overdraft   Commission received

Motor cycle   Rates, taxes and insurance

Salaries   Repairing charges

Ans. Bank overdraft and commission received will be shown under credit column of trial balance as they are liability and income respectively.

Motor cycle, rates, taxes and insurance, salaries and repairing charges will be shown under debit column of trial balance as motor cycle is an asset and rest of them are expenses.

5. What will be the effect of the following on trial balance?

   (i) Rent received ₹ 2,000 entered in cash book but not posted to rent account.

   (ii) Purchase return of ₹ 20,000 has been wrongly posted to the debit side of sales return account but correctly entered in the customers account.

   (iii) Discount received ₹ 1,000 entered in cash book but not posted to discount received account.

Ans.   (i) Debit side of trial balance will exceed by ₹ 2,000.

   (ii) Debit side of trial balance will increase by ₹ 20,000.

   (iii) Debit column of trial balance will increase by ₹ 1,000.

6. Write a note on balance method for preparing trial balance.

Ans. Balance method is the most commonly used method for preparing trial balance. Under this method, the balance of all the accounts (including cash and bank accounts) are incorporated in the trial balance. The debit and credit columns of the trial balance are totalled and they must be equal.

This method can be used to prepare trial balance only when all the ledger accounts have been balanced. The account balances are used because the balance summarises the net effect of all transactions relating to an account and helps in the preparation of financial statements.

7. State any four functions of a trial balance.

Or Describe the purpose for the preparation of a trial balance.   **(NCERT)**

Or What are the objectives or functions or importance of a trial balance?

Ans The objectives, functions or purpose of a trial balance are

   (i) **Ascertain the Arithmetical Accuracy of the Ledger Accounts** The trial balance ensures the arithmetical accuracy of the ledger accounts.

   When the debit and credit balances in the trial balance are equal, it is assumed that the posting to the ledger accounts is arithmetically correct i.e., all debits and corresponding credits have been properly recorded in the ledger.

   (ii) **Helps in Locating Errors** A trial balance helps in the detection or location of errors. However, all the errors are not disclosed, but only arithmetical errors are disclosed.

   (iii) **Summary of the Ledger Accounts** Trial balance offers a summary of the ledger. It enables us to know the assets, liabilities, expenses, incomes, etc.

   (iv) **Helps in the Preparation of Final Accounts** Trial balance is considered as the connecting link between accounting records and the preparation of financial statements. As trial balance is a list of summary of all ledger accounts, it provides a basis for preparation of final accounts (trading and profit and loss account and balance sheet).

8. Prepare the trial balance with following information.

Capital	₹ 3,00,000	Cash at Bank	₹ 70,000
Cash	₹ 1,80,000	Debtors	₹ 4,00,000
Creditors	₹ 2,00,000	Bank Loan	₹ 1,00,000
Sales	₹ 2,00,000	Purchases	₹ 1,50,000

Ans.

Trial Balance

as on ...

Name of Accounts	LF	Debit Balance (₹)	Credit Balance (₹)
Capital		—	3,00,000
Cash		1,80,000	—
Creditors		—	2,00,000
Sales		—	2,00,000
Cash at Bank		70,000	—
Debtors		4,00,000	—
Bank Loan		—	1,00,000
Purchases		1,50,000	—
Total		8,00,000	8,00,000

9. The following trial balance has been prepared by an unexperienced accountant. Redraft it in a correct form.

Name of Accounts	LF	Debit Balance (₹)	Credit Balance (₹)
Cash in Hand		4,000	—
Machinery		25,000	—
Purchases		66,000	—
Sundry Debtors		24,000	—
Carriage Inwards		2,000	—
Carriage Outwards		—	1,000
Wages		18,000	—
Rent and Taxes		5,000	—
Sundry Creditors		—	15,500
Discount Allowed		—	1,000
Return Outwards		2,500	
Return Inwards		—	10,000
Capital		30,000	—
Drawings		—	6,000
Bank Loan		10,000	—
Interest on Loan		1,500	—
Opening Stock		—	26,000
Sales		—	1,30,000
Discount Received		1,500	—
Total		**1,89,500**	**1,89,500**

Ans.

Trial Balance

as on …

Name of Accounts	LF	Debit Balance (₹)	Credit Balance (₹)
Cash in Hand		4,000	—
Machinery		25,000	—
Purchases		66,000	—
Sundry Debtors		24,000	—
Carriage Inwards		2,000	—
Carriage Outwards		1,000	—
Wages		18,000	—
Rent and Taxes		5,000	—
Sundry Creditors		—	15,500
Discount Allowed		1,000	—
Return Outwards		—	2,500
Return Inwards		10,000	—
Capital		—	30,000
Drawings		6,000	—
Bank Loan		—	10,000
Interest on Loan		1,500	—
Opening Stock		26,000	—
Sales		—	1,30,000
Discount Received		—	1,500
Total		**1,89,500**	**1,89,500**

10. From the ledger balances, prepare trial balance.

Capital	₹ 20,000	Goodwill	₹ 10,000
Rent Outstanding	₹ 1,410	Interest Received	₹ 1,000
Amount Due to Ram	₹ 10,000	Discount Received	₹ 1,520
Drawings	₹ 3,000	Amount due from Priya	₹ 40,000
Sales	₹ 19,070		

Ans.

Trial Balance

as on ...

Name of Accounts	LF	Debit Balance (₹)	Credit Balance (₹)
Capital		—	20,000
Rent Outstanding		—	1,410
Goodwill		10,000	—
Interest Received		—	1,000
Amount due to Ram		—	10,000
Drawings		3,000	—
Sales		—	19,070
Discount Received		—	1,520
Amount due from Priya		40,000	—
Total		53,000	53,000

11. Prepare a correct trial balance from the following trial balance in which there are certain mistakes.

Trial Balance

as on ...

Name of Accounts	LF	Debit Balance (₹)	Credit Balance (₹)
Cost of Goods Sold		75,000	—
Closing Stock		—	20,000
Debtors		—	30,000
Creditors		—	15,000
Fixed Assets		25,000	—
Opening Stock		30,000	—
Expenses		—	10,000
Sales		—	1,00,000
Capital		45,000	—
Total		1,75,000	1,75,000

Ans. Errors in trial balance which are identified above are as follows

   (i) Closing stock will appear in debit column of trial balance.

   (ii) Since, cost of goods sold is given, opening stock will not be taken as it is already included in cost of goods sold.

   (iii) Debtors and expenses will come in debit column of trial balance.

   (iv) Capital will appear in credit column of trial balance as it is a liability for business.

Corrected Trial Balance

as on...

Name of Accounts	LF	Debit Balance (₹)	Credit Balance (₹)
Cost of Goods Sold		75,000	—
Closing Stock		20,000	—
Debtors		30,000	—
Creditors		—	15,000
Fixed Assets		25,000	—
Expenses		10,000	—
Sales		—	1,00,000
Capital		—	45,000
Total		1,60,000	1,60,000

Note *Cost of Goods Sold = Opening Stock + Purchase + Direct Expenses – Closing Stock*

12. Mention the rules that are taken into consideration while preparing trial balance.

Ans. Following rules should be taken into care

   (i) The balances of all assets accounts, expenses and losses accounts, drawings, cash and bank balances, purchases and sales return are placed in debit column of the trial balance.

   (ii) The balances of all liabilities accounts, income and profit accounts, capital, sales, purchases return are shown in credit column of trial balance.

(iii) Normally, closing stock does not appear in the trial balance. It is usually given outside the trial balance as an adjustment. In case, it appears in the trial balance, it means that it has already been adjusted through purchases.

(iv) The amount due from all debtors is shown collectively under the head 'Sundry Debtors'.

(v) The amount due to all creditors is shown collectively under the head 'Sundry Creditors'.

• Long Answer (LA) Type Questions

1. Following balances were extracted from the books of Shri A Jadeja on 31st March, 2021. You are required to prepare a trial balance. The amount required to balance the trial balance should be entered as capital.

Name of Accounts	Amt (₹)	Name of Accounts	Amt (₹)
Purchases	2,12,500	Drawings	9,625
Stock (1st April, 2020)	30,000	Return Inwards	4,375
Sales	1,31,250	Premises	6,60,000
Sundry Debtors	29,750	Sundry Creditors	20,125
Discount Received	4,375	Discount Allowed	3,500
Carriage Outwards	875	Carriage Inwards	1,750
Cash in Hand	4,375	Cash at Bank	21,875
Machinery	1,55,625	General Expenses	2,625
Provision for Depreciation on Machinery	30,250	Bad Debts Written-off	3,065
		Provision for Doubtful Debts	2,975

Ans.

Trial Balance
as on 31st March, 2021

Name of Accounts	LF	Debit Balance (₹)	Credit Balance (₹)
Purchases		2,12,500	—
Stock		30,000	—
Sales		—	1,31,250
Sundry Debtors		29,750	—
Discount Received		—	4,375
Carriage Outwards		875	—
Cash in Hand		4,375	—
Machinery		1,55,625	—
Provision for Depreciation on Machinery		—	30,250
Drawings		9,625	—
Return Inwards		4,375	—
Premises		6,60,000	—
Sundry Creditors		—	20,125
Discount Allowed		3,500	—
Carriage Inwards		1,750	—
Cash at Bank		21,875	—
General Expenses		2,625	—
Bad Debts written-off		3,065	—
Provision for Doubtful Debts		—	2,975
Capital (Balancing figure)		—	9,50,965
Total		11,39,940	11,39,940

2. Following is the trial balance of Anuj Jindal as on 31st March, 2020.

Trial Balance
as on 31st March, 2020

Name of Accounts	LF	Debit Balance (₹)	Credit Balance (₹)
Capital		—	6,40,000
Fixed Assets		3,60,000	—
Drawings		1,20,000	—
Debtors		4,80,000	—

Name of Accounts	LF	Debit Balance (₹)	Credit Balance (₹)
Creditors		—	3,60,000
Purchases		14,20,000	—
Sales		—	21,00,000
Bank Balance		90,000	—
Cash in Hand		60,000	—
Salaries		3,30,000	—
Rent		2,40,000	—
Total		31,00,000	31,00,000

Having prepared trial balance, it was discovered that following transactions remained unrecorded.

(i) Goods were sold on credit amounting to ₹ 80,000   (ii) Paid to creditors ₹ 44,000 by cheque

(iii) Goods worth ₹ 14,000 were returned to the supplier   (iv) Paid salary ₹ 30,000 by cheque

You are required to pass journal entries for the above mentioned transactions. Also, redraft the trial balance.

Ans.

In the books of Anuj Jindal
JOURNAL

Date	Particulars		LF	Amt (Dr)	Amt (Cr)
	Debtors A/c	Dr		80,000	
	To Sales A/c				80,000
	(Being the goods sold on credit)				
	Creditors A/c	Dr		44,000	
	To Bank A/c				44,000
	(Being the creditors paid by cheque)				
	Creditors A/c	Dr		14,000	
	To Purchases Return A/c				14,000
	(Being the goods returned to suppliers)				
	Salaries A/c	Dr		30,000	
	To Bank A/c				30,000
	(Being the salaries paid by cheque)				

Trial Balance
as on 31st March, 2020

Name of Accounts	LF	Debit Balance (₹)	Credit Balance (₹)
Capital		—	6,40,000
Fixed Assets		3,60,000	—
Drawings		1,20,000	—
Debtors (WN1)		5,60,000	—
Creditors (WN2)		—	3,02,000
Purchases		14,20,000	—
Sales (WN3)		—	21,80,000
Bank Balance (WN4)		16,000	—
Cash in Hand		60,000	—
Salaries (WN5)		3,60,000	—
Rent		2,40,000	—
Purchase Returns		—	14,000
Total		31,36,000	31,36,000

Working Notes

1. Debtors = 4,80,000 + 80,000 = ₹ 5,60,000

2. Creditors = 3,60,000 − 44,000 − 14,000 = ₹ 3,02,000

3. Sales = 21,00,000 + 80,000 = ₹ 21,80,000

4. Bank balance = 90,000 − 44,000 − 30,000 = ₹ 16,000

5. Salaries = 3,30,000 + 30,000 = ₹ 3,60,000

3. Following is the trial balance of Sudhir Chaudhary as on 31st March, 2021.

Name of Accounts	LF	Debit Balance (₹)	Credit Balance (₹)
Capital		—	10,00,000
Plant and Machinery		13,40,000	—
Furniture		2,40,000	—
Cash in Hand		60,000	—
Bank Overdraft		—	1,10,000
Purchases		22,40,000	—
Sales		—	34,80,000
Debtors		10,20,000	—
Creditors		—	5,00,000
Rent		1,76,000	—
General Expenses		14,000	—
Total		**50,90,000**	**50,90,000**

Following transactions were entered into but were not recorded in the books of accounts

(i) Goods worth ₹ 30,000 were purchased on credit.

(ii) Received a cheque of ₹ 48,000 from a debtor in full settlement of his account of ₹ 50,000.

(iii) Goods amounting to ₹ 6,000 were returned by a customer.

(iv) Paid rent for the month ₹ 16,000 by cheque.

You are required to pass journal entries for the above mentioned transactions and post them into the ledger. Also, redraft the trial balance.

Ans.

JOURNAL

Date	Particulars		LF	Amt (Dr)	Amt (Cr)
	Purchases A/c	Dr		30,000	
	To Creditors A/c				30,000
	(Being the goods purchased on credit)				
	Bank A/c	Dr		48,000	
	Discount Allowed A/c	Dr		2,000	
	To Debtors A/c				50,000
	(Being the amount received from debtors and discount allowed)				
	Sales Return A/c	Dr		6,000	
	To Debtors A/c				6,000
	(Being the goods returned by a debtor)				
	Rent A/c	Dr		16,000	
	To Bank A/c				16,000
	(Being the rent paid by cheque)				

Dr   **Purchases Account**   **Cr**

Date	Particulars	JF	Amt (₹)	Date	Particulars	JF	Amt (₹)
	To Balance b/d		22,40,000		By Balance c/d		22,70,000
	To Creditors A/c		30,000				
			22,70,000				22,70,000

Dr   **Creditors Account**   **Cr**

Date	Particulars	JF	Amt (₹)	Date	Particulars	JF	Amt (₹)
	To Balance c/d		5,30,000		By Balance b/d		5,00,000
					By Purchases A/c		30,000
			5,30,000				5,30,000

Dr   **Bank Account**   **Cr**

Date	Particulars	JF	Amt (₹)	Date	Particulars	JF	Amt (₹)
	To Debtors A/c		48,000		By Balance b/d		1,10,000
	To Balance c/d		78,000		By Rent A/c		16,000
			1,26,000				1,26,000

Dr   **Discount Allowed Account**   **Cr**

Date	Particulars	JF	Amt (₹)	Date	Particulars	JF	Amt (₹)
	To Debtors A/c		2,000		By Balance c/d		2,000
			2,000				2,000

Dr   **Debtors Account**   **Cr**

Date	Particulars	JF	Amt (₹)	Date	Particulars	JF	Amt (₹)
	To Balance b/d		10,20,000		By Bank A/c		48,000
					By Discount Allowed A/c		2,000
					By Sales Return A/c		6,000
					By Balance c/d		9,64,000
			10,20,000				10,20,000

Dr   **Sales Return Account**   **Cr**

Date	Particulars	JF	Amt (₹)	Date	Particulars	JF	Amt (₹)
	To Debtors A/c		6,000		By Balance c/d		6,000
			6,000				6,000

Dr   **Rent Account**   **Cr**

Date	Particulars	JF	Amt (₹)	Date	Particulars	JF	Amt (₹)
	To Balance b/d		1,76,000		By Balance c/d		1,92,000
	To Bank A/c		16,000				
			1,92,000				1,92,000

Trial Balance
as on 31st March, 2021

Name of Accounts	LF	Debit Balance (₹)	Credit Balance (₹)
Capital		—	10,00,000
Plant and Machinery		13,40,000	—
Furniture		2,40,000	—
Cash in Hand		60,000	—
Bank Overdraft		—	78,000
Purchases		22,70,000	—
Discount Allowed		2,000	—
Sales		—	34,80,000
Debtors		9,64,000	—
Creditors		—	5,30,000
Sales Return		6,000	—
Rent		1,92,000	—
General Expenses		14,000	—
Total		**50,88,000**	**50,88,000**

Multiple Choice Questions

1. When closing stock is given outside the trial balance it should be recorded in
(a) trading account (debit side) and balance sheet (asset side)   (b) trading account (credit side) and balance sheet (asset side)
(c) trading account (credit side)   (d) balance sheet (asset side)

2. Which of the following errors cannot be disclosed by trial balance?
(a) Error of omission   (b) Error of principle   (c) Both (a) and (b)   (d) None of these

3. Errors of comission do not permit
(a) correct totalling of balance sheet   (b) correct totalling of trial balance
(c) trial balance to agree   (d) None of these

4. (i) It shows final position of accounts and helps in preparation of financial statements.
(ii) It verifies arithmetical accuracy of posting entries from journal to the ledger.
In the above statements, what does 'It' refers to?
(a) Cash book   (b) Trial balance   (c) Trial and errror statement   (d) None of these

5. Which is not a trial balance method?
(a) Balance method   (b) Total method   (c) Balance cum total method   (d) Grand total method

Short Answer (SA) Type Questions

1. Trial Balance is a link between the ledger and final accounts. Explain. Also give any two advantages of trial balance.

2. From the following list of balances extracted from the books of Shri Mohan Prasad, prepare a trial balance as at 31st March, 2020.

Name of Accounts	Amt (₹)	Name of Accounts	Amt (₹)
Opening Stock	22,000	Investments	30,000
Purchases	2,57,500	Interest on Investments	2,700
Sales	3,61,800	Cash and Bank Balance	1,240
Carriage Inwards	300	Premises	60,000
Carriage Outwards	120	Fixtures	14,000
Return Inwards	8,500	Miscellaneous Expenses	520
Return Outwards	2,000	Miscellaneous Income	140
Debtors	32,000	Loan from PNB	25,000
Creditors	17,400	Interest on PNB Loan	3,000
Bad Debts	600	Capital	70,000
Stationary	420	Proprietor's Withdrawal	6,000
Insurance	340	Computers	9,000
Wages and Salaries	18,500	Goodwill	15,000
		Closing Stock (not adjusted)	31,000

3. From the following information, draw up a trial balance in the books of Shri Manmohan as on 31st March, 2020. Capital ₹ 1,12,000, purchases ₹ 28,800, discount allowed ₹ 960, carriage inwards ₹ 6,960, carriage outwards ₹ 1,840, sales ₹ 48,000, return inwards ₹ 240, return outwards ₹ 560, rent and taxes ₹ 960, plant and machinery ₹ 64,560, stock on 1st April, 2019 ₹ 12,400, sundry debtors ₹ 16,160, sundry creditors ₹ 9,600, investments ₹ 2,880, commission received ₹ 1,440, cash in hand ₹ 80, cash at bank ₹ 8,080, motor cycle ₹ 27,680 and stock on 31st March, 2020 (not adjusted) ₹ 16,400.

4. What are the methods for preparation of trial balance? Moreover, write in detail about the method of preparation of trial balance which is mostly used in practice.

Long Answer (LA) Type Question

1. Following is the trial balance of Anoop Kumar on 31st March, 2020.

Trial Balance
as on 31st March, 2020

Name of Accounts	LF	Debit Balance (₹)	Credit Balance (₹)
Cash at Bank		10,000	—
Fixed Assets		12,500	—
Capital		—	38,600
Purchases		22,500	—
Sales		—	10,250
Discount Allowed		250	—
Return Inwards		500	—
Return Outwards		—	700
Wags and Salaries		5,000	—
Debtors		1,340	—
Creditors		—	4,700
Drawings		1,000	—
Discount Received		—	350
Bills Receivable		1,170	—
Bills Payable		—	2,160
Rent		1,500	—
Interest Paid		1,000	—
Total		**56,760**	**56,760**

Having prepared trial balance, it was discovered that following transactions remained unrecorded.

  (i) Goods sold on credit amounting to ₹ 80,000   (ii) Paid to creditors ₹ 2,000 by cheque

(iii) Goods worth ₹ 1,000 were returned to a supplier

You are required pass journal entries for the above mentioned transactions and post them into ledger. Also, redraft the trial balance.

Answers

Multiple Choice Questions

1. (b)   *2. (c)*   *3. (c)*   *4. (b)*   *5. (d)*

For Detailed Solutions
Scan the code

CHAPTER 03

Rectification of Errors

In this Chapter...
- Meaning of Errors
- Rectification of Errors

Meaning of Errors

Errors are unintentional omission or commission of amounts and accounts in the process of recording transactions. These errors may be committed in the journal, ledger or trial balance or any financial statements.

Classification of Errors

Keeping in view the nature of errors, errors can be classified into the following four categories

1. **Errors of Commission** These are the errors which are committed due to wrong posting of transactions, wrong totalling or wrong balancing of the accounts, wrong casting of the subsidiary books or wrong recording of amount in the books of original entry. These errors affect the accuracy of trial balance.

   Errors of commission can be classified into the following

   (i) **Error of Recording** This error arises when any transaction is incorrectly recorded in the books of original entry.
   This error will not affect the trial balance.
   e.g., goods purchased from Ravi for ₹ 450, recorded as ₹ 540, in the purchase book.

   (ii) **Error of Casting** This error arises when a mistake is committed in totalling. This error affects the trial balance. e.g. sales book is totalled as ₹ 1,000 instead of ₹ 10,000.

   (iii) **Error of Carrying Forward** It is an error which arises when a mistake is committed in carrying forward a total of one page to the next page.

This error affects the trial balance. e.g. total of sales book is carried forward as ₹ 10,000 instead of ₹ 1,000

   (iv) **Error of Posting** When the information recorded in the books of original entry is incorrectly entered in the ledger, it is an error of posting.

   - Posting with wrong amount (this error will affect the trial balance). e.g. posting the total of purchase book ₹ 11,500 as ₹ 11,550 in the purchase account.

   - Posting to the wrong side but correct account (this error will affect the trial balance) e.g. goods sold to X for ₹ 550, entered to the credit of X's account instead of posting to the debit side of his account.

   - Posting twice in an account (this error will affect the trial balance).

   - Errors in posting to the wrong account but correct side (this error will not affect the trial balance).

2. **Errors of Omission** This kind of error arises when a transaction is partially or completely omitted to be recorded in the books of accounts. These can be of two types

   - Error of complete omission which does not affect the accuracy of trial balance. e.g. credit sales to Shyam for ₹ 10,000 omitted to be recorded in the books.

   - Error of partial omission which affect the accuracy of trial balance. e.g. credit sales recorded in the sales book but not posted into debtor's account.

3. **Errors of Principle** Transactions recorded in contravention of the accounting principles, are known as errors of principle. An error of principle may occur due to the incorrect classification of expenditure or receipt between capital and revenue as it may lead to under/over stating of income or assets or liabilities.

   This error does not affect the trial balance as amounts are placed on the correct side but in a wrong account. e.g. wages paid for installation of new machinery charged to wages account instead of machinery account.

4. **Compensating Errors** When two or more errors are committed in such a way that the net effect of these errors on the debits and credits of accounts is nil or nullified, such errors are called compensating errors. These errors do not affect the tallying of trial balance. e.g. The total of purchase book is posted in the ledger as ₹ 10,000 instead of ₹ 1,000 and at the same time Varsha's account is credited in the ledger as ₹ 10,000 instead of ₹ 1,000. As a result of these errors, there is an excess credit of ₹ 9,000 in Varsha's account and an excess debit of ₹ 9,000 in purchases account. Thus, these two errors nullify the effects of each other.

Searching of Errors

The following steps will be useful in searching errors

Step 1 The two columns of the trial balance should be totalled again. If in place of a number of accounts, only one account has been written in the trial balance, then the list of such accounts should be checked and totalled again.

Step 2 It should be seen that the cash and bank balances have been written in the trial balance.

Step 3 The exact difference in the trial balance should be determined. The ledger should be properly checked, it is possible that a balance equal to the difference has been omitted from the trial balance. The difference should also be halved; it is possible that balance equal to half the difference has been written in the wrong column.

Step 4 The ledger accounts should be balanced again.

Step 5 The totalling of subsidiary books should be checked again, especially if the difference is ₹ 1, ₹ 100, etc.

Step 6 If the difference is very big, the balance in various accounts should be compared with the corresponding accounts in the previous period. If the figures differ materially, the respective accounts should be checked again.

Step 7 Posting of the amounts equal to the difference or half the difference should be checked. It is possible that an amount has been omitted to be posted or has been posted on the wrong side.

Step 8 If there is still a difference in the trial balance, a complete checking will be necessary. The posting of all the entries including the opening entry should be checked. It may be better to begin with the nominal accounts.

Rectification of Errors

Rectification of errors is the procedure of rectifying the errors committed and to set right the accounting records.

There are various objectives or reasons for which the errors are rectified, they are as follows

- For the preparation of correct accounting records.
- For ascertainment of correct net profit or loss.
- For exhibiting true financial position of the organisation, by preparing the balance sheet with correct data.

Rectification of Errors which do not Affect the Trial Balance or Two-sided Errors

Two-sided errors are those errors that have been committed on both sides, i.e., debit and credit.

These are the errors which do not affect the trial balance or are not disclosed by trial balance and are committed in two or more accounts.

Examples of such errors are as follows
- Errors of complete omission
- Errors of recording in the books of original entry
- Errors of posting involving the posting to wrong account on correct side with correct amount
- Errors of principle
- Compensating errors

These errors can be rectified by recording a journal entry giving the correct debit and credit to the concerned accounts which were affected by the error.

The rectification process involves the following steps

Step 1 **Wrong Entry** Write the entry which has already been passed in the books, i.e., the wrong entry.

Step 2 **Reverse of Wrong Entry** Write the reverse of the wrong entry, to nullify the effect of wrong entry.

Step 3 **Correct Entry** Write the entry which should have been passed, i.e., the correct entry.

Step 4 **Rectifying Entry** Write the net effect of entry in step 2 and step 3.

Rectification of Errors affecting Trial Balance or One-sided Errors

One-sided errors are those errors, which have occurred in one-side 'debit or credit' of an account.

These are the errors which affects trial balance and affects only one account.

Examples of such errors are

- Error due to partial omission
- Error of casting
- Error in carrying forward
- Error in totalling or balancing of an account
- Errors of posting (other than an error of posting a correct amount in the wrong account but on the correct side)
- Omission of posting the total of a subsidiary book
- Omission of an account from trial balance
- Entering the balance of an account in the wrong column of the trial balance
- Wrong totalling of the trial balance

Rectification of One-sided Errors Depend on the Stage at which the Errors are Located

1. **Before Preparation of Trial Balance** This is a stage, when errors are located and rectified before the closing of accounts, i.e., before transferring the difference in the trial balance to the suspense account.

   Rectification of errors, at this stage, does not require passing of rectification entries, rectification can be done by giving an explanatory note.

   This can be done by debiting/crediting the 'respective account' with the required amount.

2. **After Preparing the Trial Balance but Before Final Accounts are Prepared** This is the stage, when errors are located and rectified after the closing of accounts, i.e., after transferring the difference in trial balance to suspense account but before the preparation of financial statements.

   When one-sided errors are located after the preparation of trial balance, rectifications are carried out by passing a journal entry with the help of respective account which is affected by the error and suspense account.

   Suspense account is used to complete the double entry, as only one account is debited/credited for rectification of one-sided error.

   It should be noted unless otherwise stated, errors are normally rectified before the preparation of final accounts, i.e., with the help of suspense account.

Suspense Account

Suspense account is an account used on a temporary basis for any transaction or balance that cannot be identified. Suspense account is used for rectifying the errors which affect the trial balance, the errors which do not affect the trial balance are not rectified with the help of suspense account.

The errors are rectified by passing their double entry in the debit side or credit side of the suspense account.

Following points should be kept in mind while rectifying one sided errors using suspense account

- For short debit in one account → Debit that account and credit the suspense account
- Excess credit in one account → Debit that account and credit the suspense account
- Short credit in one account → Credit that account and debit the suspense account
- Excess debit in one account → Credit that account and debit the suspense account

Preparation of Suspense Account

If the debit side of the trial balance exceeds the credit side, the difference is put on the credit side of the trial balance by opening suspense account. In this case, 'suspense account' will show a credit balance.

If the credit side of the trial balance exceeds the debit side, the difference is put on the debit side of trial balance.

In this case, 'suspense account' will show a debit balance. When the errors which affect the suspense account are located, they are rectified with the help of the suspense account. When all such errors are located and rectified, the suspense account stands balanced.

Treatment of Balance of Suspense Account

When the suspense account cannot be closed, i.e., when the errors affecting the trial balance are still to be located and rectified, the suspense account will show outstanding balance. The balance in the suspense account is taken to the balance sheet on the assets side, if there is a debit balance or to the liabilities side, if there is a credit balance.

Solved Examples

Example 1. Pass the rectifying entries.

   (i) Machinery purchased for ₹ 10,000 debited to purchases.

   (ii) A sum of ₹ 2,00,000 drawn by proprietor for his private travel was debited to travelling expenses account.

   (iii) Purchases return by Ram for ₹ 5,500 was not recorded in books.

   (iv) Credit purchase of ₹ 1,000 from Akshay was posted to credit of Veer's account.

Ans.

Rectification Entries in Journal

Date	Particulars		LF	Amt (Dr)	Amt (Cr)
(i)	Machinery A/c	Dr		10,000	
	To Purchases A/c				10,000
	(Being the machinery purchased for ₹ 10,000 debited to purchases, now rectified)				
(ii)	Drawings A/c	Dr		2,00,000	
	To Travelling Expenses A/c				2,00,000
	(Being the amount drawn by proprietor for his private travel was debited to travelling expenses account, now rectified)				
(iii)	Ram	Dr		5,500	
	To Purchases Return A/c				5,500
	(Being the purchases return by Ram for ₹ 5,500, now recorded)				
(iv)	Veer	Dr		1,000	
	To Akshay				1,000
	(Being the credit purchase of ₹1,000 from Akshay posted to credit of Veer's account, now rectified)				

Example 2. Rectify the following errors.

   (i) Purchases book was undercast by ₹ 4,000

   (ii) Purchases return was overcast by ₹ 66,500

   (iii) Sales return was undercast by ₹ 200

   (iv) Sales book was overcast by ₹ 500

Ans.

JOURNAL

Date	Particulars		LF	Amt (Dr)	Amt (Cr)
(i)	Purchases A/c	Dr		4,000	
	To Suspense A/c				4,000
	(Being the purchases book undercast, now rectified)				
(ii)	Purchase Return A/c	Dr		66,500	
	To Suspense A/c				66,500
	(Being the purchases return overcast, now rectified)				
(iii)	Sales Return A/c	Dr		200	
	To Suspense A/c				200
	(Being the sales return undercast, now rectified)				
(iv)	Sales A/c	Dr		500	
	To Suspense A/c				500
	(Being the sales book overcast, now rectified)				

Example 3. Pass the journal entries to rectify the following errors.
- (i) Credit purchase of goods ₹ 5,000 from Mohan & Co. was not recorded in books, although goods were taken into stock.
- (ii) Return of goods amounting to ₹ 500 by Mohan was entered in purchases return book.
- (iii) A purchases of goods from Ramesh amounting to ₹ 15,000 wrongly passed through sales book.
- (iv) A cheque for ₹ 1,000 received from Brijmohan was dishonoured and had been posted to the debit of sales return account.
- (v) Repairs made were debited to building account ₹ 7,300.
- (vi) Goods purchased from Rajeev for ₹ 540 recorded as ₹ 450 in the purchase book.
- (vii) ₹ 25,000 received from Shahrukh and Co. wrongly entered as received from Salman and Co.

Ans.

JOURNAL

Date	Particulars		LF	Amt (Dr)	Amt (Cr)
(i)	Purchases A/c	Dr		5,000	
	To Mohan and Co.				5,000
	(Being the credit purchases from Mohan and Co., now recorded)				
(ii)	Purchases Return A/c	Dr		500	
	Sales Return A/c	Dr		500	
	To Mohan				1,000
	(Being th return of goods worth ₹ 500 by Mohan entered wrongly in purchases return book, now rectified)				
(iii)	Purchases A/c	Dr		15,000	
	Sales A/c	Dr		15,000	
	To Ramesh				30,000
	(Being the purchases of goods from Ramesh worth ₹ 15,000 wrongly passed through sales book, now rectified)				
(iv)	Brijmohan	Dr		1,000	
	To Sales Return A/c				1,000
	(Being the cheque dishonoured posted to debit of sales return account, now rectified)				
(v)	Repairs A/c	Dr		7,300	
	To Building A/c				7,300
	(Being the repairs debited to building account, now rectified)				
(vi)	Purchases A/c	Dr		90	
	To Rajeev				90
	(Being the goods purchased from Rajeev for ₹ 540 recorded as ₹ 450, now rectified)				
(vii)	Salman and Co.	Dr		25,000	
	To Shahrukh and Co.				25,000
	(Being the amount received from Shahrukh & Co. wrongly entered as received from Salman and Co., now rectified)				

Example 4. Pass the journal entries to rectify the following errors and prepare suspense account afterwards to ascertain the difference in trial balance.

(i) Total of debit of expense account overcast by ₹ 200.

(ii) Sales account total undercast by ₹ 400.

(iii) One item of purchase of ₹ 100 has been posted from the day book to ledger as ₹ 1,000.

(iv) Sales return of ₹ 400 from a party not posted to sales return account though the party's account has been credited.

(v) Credit sales of ₹ 200 wrongly credited to sundry debtor's account.

Ans.

JOURNAL

Date	Particulars		LF	Amt (Dr)	Amt (Cr)
(i)	Suspense A/c	Dr		200	
	To Expenses A/c				200
	(Being the total of debit of expense account has been cast in excess by ₹ 200, now rectified)				
(ii)	Suspense A/c	Dr		400	
	To Sales A/c				400
	(Being the sales account totalled in short by ₹ 400, now rectified)				
(iii)	Supplier's/Creditor A/c	Dr		900	
	To Suspense A/c				900
	(Being one item of purchase of ₹ 100 has been posted from the day book to ledger as ₹ 1,000, now rectified)				
(iv)	Sales Return A/c	Dr		400	
	To Suspense A/c				400
	(Being the sales return of ₹ 400 from a party not posted to sales returns account though the party's account has been credited, now rectified)				
(v)	Sundry Debtors A/c	Dr		400	
	To Suspense A/c				400
	(Being the credit sales of ₹ 200 wrongly credited to sundry debtor's account, now rectified)				

Dr   **Suspense Account**   Cr

Date	Particulars	JF	Amt (₹)	Date	Particulars	JF	Amt (₹)
	To Expenses A/c		200		By Sundry Creditors/Suppliers A/c		900
	To Sales A/c		400		By Sales Return A/c		400
	To Difference in Trial Balance		1,100		By Sundry Debtors A/c		400
			1,700				1,700

Note *Suspense account exhibits a closing balance. This indicates that there are certain other errors which are not yet rectified.*

Example 5. Pass the journal entries to rectify the following errors and prepare suspense account afterwards to ascertain the difference in trial balance.

   (i) Sales book overcast by ₹ 4,000

  (ii) Purchases book undercast by ₹ 1,000

 (iii) Goods from Kamal purchased on credit for ₹ 5,000 was debited to his account.

 (iv) Discount allowed to customer for ₹ 2,500 credited to him as ₹ 5,200.

  (v) Cash paid to Mohan ₹ 7,000 credited to his account as ₹ 3,000.

 (vi) Goods returned by Rakesh ₹ 5,000 has been recorded in returns inward book only.

Ans.

JOURNAL

Date	Particulars		LF	Amt (Dr)	Amt (Cr)
(i)	Sales A/c	Dr		4,000	
	To Suspense A/c				4,000
	(Being the sales book overcasted by ₹ 4,000, now rectified)				
(ii)	Purchases A/c	Dr		1,000	
	To Suspense A/c				1,000
	(Being the purchases book undercasted by ₹ 1,000, now rectified)				
(iii)	Suspense A/c	Dr		10,000	
	To Kamal				10,000
	(Being the goods from Kamal on credit for ₹ 5,000 was debited to his account, now rectified)				
(iv)	Customer A/c	Dr		2,700	
	To Suspense A/c				2,700
	(Being the discount allowed to customer ₹ 2,500 credited to him as ₹ 5,200, rectified)				
(v)	Mohan	Dr		10,000	
	To Suspense A/c				10,000
	(Being the cash paid to Mohan ₹ 7,000 credited to his account as ₹ 3,000, rectified)				
(vi)	Suspense A/c	Dr		5,000	
	To Rakesh				5,000
	(Being the goods returned by Rakesh ₹ 5,000 has been recorded in returns inward book omitted to be posted to his account, rectified)				

Dr   **Suspense Account**   Cr

Particulars	Amt (₹)	Particulars	Amt (₹)
To Kamal	10,000	By Sales A/c	4,000
To Rakesh	5,000	By Purchases A/c	1,000
To Difference in Trial Balance	2,700	By Customer	2,700
		By Mohan	10,000
	17,700		17,700

Chapter Practice

PART 1

Objective Questions

• Multiple Choice Questions

1. Which error(s) does/do not affect the trial balance?

(a) Error of commission   (b) Error of principle   (c) Error of complete omission   (d) Both (b) and (c)

Ans. (d) Both (b) and (c)

2. Which of the following error(s) does/do affect trial balance?

(a) Error of principle   (b) Compensating errors

(c) Error of partial omission   (d) Error of complete omission

Ans. (c) Error of partial omission

3. Raghu wrongly treated capital expenditure worth ₹ 10,000 as revenue expenditure worth ₹ 10,000. Identify the error committed by Raghu.

(a) Error of principle   (b) Error of commission   (c) Error of omission   (d) Compensating error

Ans. (a) Treating a revenue expenditure as capital expenditure or vice-versa or treating a sale of a fixed asset as ordinary sale is error of principle.

4. Error in which effect of one error is nullified by the effect of another error is called …… error.

(a) error of commission   (b) compensating error   (c) error of omission   (d) None of these

Ans. (b) compensating error

5. If wages paid for installation of new machinery is debited to wages account, it is   **(NCERT)**

(a) an error of commission   (b) an error of principle   (c) a compensating error   (d) an error of omission

Ans. (b) an error of principle

6. ……… are not disclosed by trial balance. Therefore, trial balance total will still agree.

(a) One sided errors   (b) Partial sided errors   (c) Two sided errors   (d) Biased sided errors

Ans. (c) Two sided errors like errors of complete omission are not disclosed by trial balance.

7. Which of the following is not an error of commission?   **(NCERT)**

(a) Overcasting of sales book   (b) Credit sales to Ramesh ₹ 5,000 credited to his account

(c) Wrong balancing of machinery account   (d) Cash sales not recorded in cash book

Ans. (d) Cash sales not recorded in cash book is an error of omission.

8. Undercasting of sales book is corrected by …… sales account.

(a) debiting   (b) crediting   (c) both debit/credit   (d) None of these

Ans. (b) Suspense account will be made to debit and sales account will be made to credit with the same amount.

Suspense A/c   Dr

    To Sales A/c

9. Goods of ₹ 1,000 purchased on credit from Mr 'A' are recorded in purchases book for ₹ 10,000. Which type of error is this?

(a) Error of casting   (b) Error of recording   (c) Error of carrying forward   (d) Error of posting

Ans. (b) Error of recording

10. An item of ₹ 53 has been debited to a personal account as ₹ 35. It is an error of

(a) commission   (b) omission   (c) complete error   (d) principle

Ans. (a) commission

11. Which of the following statements is/are correct about suspense account?

(i) Suspense account is a temporary account opened to rectify one sided errors.

(ii) Debit balance of suspense account is taken to balance sheet on the assets side.

Alternatives

(a) Only (i)   (b) Only (ii)   (c) Both (i) and (ii)   (d) None of these

Ans. (c) Both (i) and (ii)

12. Preeti was paid cash ₹ 2,800 but Jyoti was debited by ₹ 2,000. In rectifying entry, suspense account will be

(a) debited by ₹ 2,800   (b) credited by ₹ 2,000   (c) credited by ₹ 800   (d) debited by ₹ 800

Ans. (c) Cash paid to Preeti wrongly debited to Jyoti, so Jyoti will be credited with ₹ 2,000 and Preeti will be debited with ₹ 2,800. Difference (2,800 − 2,000) = ₹ 800 will be put in credit side of suspense account.

13. Credit purchases from Rohan ₹ 9,000 was posted to the debit of Gobind as ₹ 10,000. In this case, suspense account will be debited with

(a) ₹ 9,000   (b) ₹ 10,000   (c) ₹ 19,000   (d) None of these

Ans. (c) This is the double amount error, in this Rohan will be credited with ₹ 9,000 and Gobind with ₹ 10,000 and suspense account will be debited with ₹ 19,000 (9,000 + 10,000).

14. Repairs were debited to building account for ₹ 20,000. Which journal entry reflects correct rectification of error done by Manoj Enterprises?

(a) Repairs A/c   Dr   20,000
       To Building A/c   20,000

(b) Repairs A/c   Dr   20,000
       To Suspense A/c   20,000

(c) Building A/c   Dr   20,000
       To Suspense A/c   20,000

(d) Building A/c   Dr   20,000
       To Repairs A/c   20,000

Ans. (a) Repairs A/c   Dr   20,000
       To Building A/c   20,000

15. Sales return book was overcast by ₹ 5,000. Which of the undermentioned options reflect correct rectifying entry for the above mistake?

(a) Suspense A/c   Dr   5,000
       To Sales Return A/c   5,000

(b) Sales Return A/c   Dr   5,000
       To Suspense A/c   5,000

(c) Debtors A/c   Dr   5,000
       To Sales Return A/c   5,000

(d) Sales Return A/c   Dr   5,000
       To Debtors A/c   5,000

Ans. (a) Suspense A/c   Dr   5,000
       To Sales Return A/c   5,000

16. Match the items given in column I with column II.

Column I	Column II
A. Old furniture sold recorded as sales of good	(i) Debit that account and credit the suspense account
B. Depreciation on computers not posted to depreciation account	(ii) Two sided error
C. Excess credit in one account	(iii) One sided error
D. Short credit in one account	(iv) Credit that account and debit the suspense account

Codes

	A	B	C	D			A	B	C	D
(a)	(ii)	(iii)	(i)	(iv)		(b)	(iv)	(i)	(ii)	(iii)
(c)	(iii)	(ii)	(iv)	(i)		(d)	(iii)	(i)	(ii)	(iv)

Ans. (a) (ii), (iii), (i), (iv)

• Assertion-Reasoning MCQs

Direction *(Q. Nos. 1 to 5) There are two statements marked as Assertion (A) and Reason (R). Read the statements and choose the appropriate option from the options given below.*

(a) Both Assertion (A) and Reason (R) are correct   (b) Both Assertion (A) and Reason (R) are wrong

(c) Assertion (A) is correct, but Reason (R) is wrong   (d) Assertion (A) is wrong, but Reason (R) is correct

1. Assertion (A) Trial balance is not a conclusive proof of accuracy of records.

     Reason (R) Errors of complete omission and compensating errors do not affect the agreement of trial balance.

Ans. (a) Both Assertion (A) and Reason (R) are correct

2. Assertion (A) Inspite of the fact that trial balance tallies, some errors may still be there in accounting records.

     Reason (R) Error of partial omission and error of casting do not affect the agreement of trial balance.

Ans. (c) Omitting to post the ledger account from the subsidiary books is an error of partial omission which will affect the trial balance. Mistake committed in totalling is error of casting which will affect the trial balance.

3. Assertion (A) Expectancy account is opened to rectify one sided errors.

     Reason (R) One sided errors cannot be rectified by recording a journal entry.

Ans. (d) Suspense account is opened to rectify one sided errors.

4. Assertion (A) Error of incorrectly recording transaction in the books of accounts is rectified by opening suspense account.

     Reason (R) Suspense account is opened to rectify one sided errors.

Ans. (d) Error of recording is a two sided error which will be rectified by passing rectifying journal entry.

5. Assertion (A) Purchase book overcast by ₹ 700 is rectified by opening suspense account.

     Reason (R) One sided errors cannot be rectified by recording a journal entry unless a suspense account is opened.

Ans. (a) Both Assertion (A) and Reason (R) are correct

• Case Based MCQs

1. Direction *Read the following case study and answer the question no. (i) to (iv) on the basis of the same.*

Tanvi Kaur, after completing her M.Com from Delhi School of Economics, decided to open her own boutique at Kamla Nagar. She buys clothes from Ramesh park in bulk and sell them in retail.

Due to wide knowledge of accounts, she is also handling books of accounts herself. On 31st March 2020, she prepared the trial balance and she was very elated as both sides were tallied. On the same day in afternoon, Neha, her friend who is a CA in PWC, visited her boutique to buy designer clothes. To Ensure accuracy of records, Tanvi requested her friend Neha to recheck the books of accounts. Neha happily agreed to check them at night. Next day, in the morning Neha informed Tanvi about two sided errors that were discovered by her.

Following two sided errors were discovered by Neha
(a) Credit sales to Priya ₹ 10,000 were recorded as ₹ 1,000.
(b) Purchases return of ₹ 25,000 to ABC Limited was not recorded.
(c) Purchased furniture for cash worth ₹ 1,00000 but debited to building account.
(d) Credit purchases from Rohan for ₹ 2,00,000 were not recorded.

(i) Which of the undermentioned options reflect correct rectification entry for 'Credit sales to Priya ₹ 10,000 were recorded as ₹ 1,000'?

(a) Priya	Dr 10,000	
To Suspense A/c		10,000
(b) Priya	Dr 9,000	
To Sales A/c		9,000
(c) Priya	Dr 9,000	
To Suspense A/c		9,000
(d) Priya	Dr 10,000	
To Sales A/c		10,000

Ans. (b) Priya   Dr 9,000

      To Sales A/c   9,000

(ii) Read the following statements carefully.

I Suspense account is temporary account which is opened to rectify errors that affect the trial balance.

II Posting twice in an account, error of partial omission, error in carrying forward, etc affect the agreement of trial balance.

In context of above two statements, which of them is incorrect?

(a) Only I   (b) Only II   (c) Both I and II   (d) None of these

Ans. (d) None of these

(iii) Which of the following journal entries reflect correct rectification entry for 'Purchases return of ₹ 25,000 to ABC Limited was not recored'?

(a)	ABC Limited	Dr 25,000	
	To Purchases Return A/c		25,000
(b)	Purchases Return A/c	Dr 25,000	
	To ABC Limited		25,000
(c)	ABC Limited	Dr 25,000	
	To Suspense A/c		25,000
(d)	Suspense A/c	Dr 25,000	
	To Purchases Return A/c		25,000

Ans. (a) ABC Limited   Dr 25,000

      To Purchases Return A/c   25,000

(iv) Which of the following options reflect correct rectification entry for 'Purchased furniture for cash worth ₹ 1,00,000 but debited to building account'?

(a) Furniture A/c	Dr 1,00,000	
To Building A/c		1,00,000
(b) Building A/c	Dr 1,00,000	
To Cash A/c		1,00,000
(c) Building A/c	Dr 1,00,000	
To Suspense A/c		1,00,000
(d) Suspense A/c	Dr 1,00,000	
To Furniture A/c		1,00,000

Ans. (a) Furniture A/c   Dr 1,00,000

      To Building A/c   1,00,000

2. **Direction** *Read the following case study and answer the question no. (i) to (iv) on the basis of the same.*

Niharika, a B.Com graduate from Dyal Singh College got job as an accountant at Anuj Furniture Enterprises, Kriti Nagar. She is very diligent girl who is working hard to earn her livelihood as she is sole bread earner of her family.

Anuj, CEO of Anuj Furniture Enterprises asked Niharika to make trial balance and then to prepare final accounts. She prepared all the subsidiary books and ledger accounts and then put in place final balances of them in format of trial balance. Unexpectedly, trial balance total didn't agree. At the same time, Anuj came to her cabin and Niharika shared her problem with him.

Anuj being a benevolent person asked her not to worry and called his brother Rahul, who is a CA in PWC. Rahul asked Niharika to mail him all accounting records. Then, she went home.

Next day, Rahul mailed Niharika all errors that she has committed while making trial balance.

Following errors were identified

(a) Purchases book under cast by ₹ 3,000.

(b) Goods withdrawn for personal use by Anuj worth ₹ 20,000 were not recorded in books.

(c) A credit sale of ₹ 16,500 credited to the sales account and also to the sundry debtors account.

(d) A cheque for ₹ 9,000 received from Ashok was dishonoured and posted to the debit of sales return account.

Niharika quickly rectified above errors and prepared a corrected trial balance.

(i) Which of the following options reflect correct rectification entry for 'A cheque for ₹ 9,000 received from Ashok was dishonoured and posted to the debit of sales return account'?

(a) Suspense A/c   Dr   9,000
     To Sales Return A/c   9,000

(b) Ashok   Dr   18,000
     To Sales Return A/c   9,000
     To Suspense A/c   9,000

(c) Ashok   Dr   9,000
     To Sales Return A/c   9,000

(d) Suspense A/c   Dr   18,000
     To Sales Return A/c   9,000
     To Ashok   9,000

Ans. (c) Ashok   Dr 9,000
     To Sales Return A/c   9,000

(ii) Read the following statements carefully.

I Error due to partial omission, error of casting, error in carrying forward and error of principle are one sided errors.

II Suspense account is used for rectifying the errors which do not affect trial balance while errors which affect trial balance are not rectified with the help of suspense account.

In the context of above two statements, which of them is correct?

(a) Only I   (b) Only II   (c) Both I and II   (d) None of these

Ans. (d) Error of principle is not a one sided error. Suspense account is used for rectifying errors which affect the trial balance.

(iii) Which of the undermentioned options reflect correct rectification entry for 'A credit sale of ₹ 16,500 credited to the sales account and also to the Sundry debtors account'?

(a) Sundry Debtors A/c   Dr   33,000
     To Suspense A/c   33,000

(b) Sundry Debtors A/c   Dr   16,500
     To Suspense A/c   16,500

(c) Suspense A/c   Dr   33,000
     To Sundry Debtors A/c   33,000

(d) Suspense A/c   Dr   16,500
     To Sundry Debtors A/c   16,500

Ans. (a) Sundry Debtors A/c   Dr 33,000

      To Suspense A/c   33,000

(iv) Which of the following options reflect correct rectification entry for 'Purchase book undercast by ₹ 3,000'?

(a) Purchases A/c		Dr	3,000	
To Suspense A/c				3,000
(b) Suspense A/c		Dr	3,000	
To Purchases A/c				3,000
(c) Purchases A/c		Dr	3,000	
To Creditors A/c				3,000
(d) Suspense A/c		Dr	3,000	
Purchase A/c		Dr	3,000	
To Creditors A/c				6,000

Ans. (a) Purchases A/c   Dr 3,000

      To Suspense A/c   3,000

PART 2
Subjective Questions

• Short Answer (SA) Type Questions

1. Write a short note on error of omission.

Ans. **Errors of Omission** This kind of error arises when a transaction is partially or completely omitted (left out) to be recorded in the books of accounts. These can be of two types

    (i) **Error of Complete Omission** When a transaction is completely omitted from being recorded in the books of original record, it is an error of complete omission. This error does not affect the trial balance.

    (ii) **Error of Partial Omission** When a transaction is partially omitted from being recorded in the books, it is an error of partial omission. This error affects the trial balance.

2. What is a suspense account? Is it necessary that a suspense account will balance off after rectification of the errors detected by the accountant? If not, then what happens to the balance still remaining in suspense account?   **(NCERT)**

Ans. Suspense account is an account which is opened on a temporary basis to balance the trial balance. No, it is not necessary that a suspense account will balance after rectification of errors detected by the accountant. Suspense account can remain unbalanced if all the errors are not detected. Balance remaining in the suspense account is transferred to the balance sheet on the assets side, if there is a debit balance or to the liabilities side if there is a credit balance.

3. Describe in brief about errors of commission.

Ans. When a transaction is recorded wrongly in the books of accounts, it is called error of commission. Errors of commission can be classified into the following

    (i) **Error of Recording** This error arises when any transaction is incorrectly recorded in the books of original entry. This error will not affect the trial balance.

    (ii) **Error of Casting** This error arises when a mistake is committed in totalling. This error affects the trial balance.

    (iii) **Error of Carrying Forward** It is an error which arises when a mistake is committed in carrying forward a total of one page to the next page. This error affects the trial balance.

    (iv) **Error of Posting** When the information recorded in the books of original entry are incorrectly entered in the ledger, it is an error of posting.

4. Rectify the following errors.

    (i) Cash received from Karim ₹ 6,000 posted to Nadeem.

    (ii) Cash sales to Radhika ₹ 15,000 was shown as receipt of commission in the cash book.

    (iii) Furniture purchased from M/s Rao, for ₹ 8,000 was entered into the purchases book.

Ans.

Rectification Entries in Journal

Date	Particulars	LF	Amt (Dr)	Amt (Cr)
(i)	Nadeem Dr		6,000	
	To Karim			6,000
	(Being cash received from Karim ₹ 6,000 posted to Nadeem account wrongly, now rectified)			
(ii)	Commission A/c Dr		15,000	
	To Sales A/c			15,000
	(Being the cash sales treated wrongly as commission, now rectified)			
(iii)	Furniture A/c Dr		8,000	
	To Purchases A/c			8,000
	(Being the furniture purchased wrongly recorded in purchases book, now rectified)			

5. Pass the necessary journal entries to rectify the following errors.

    (i) Credit sale of ₹ 1,700 to Raj was recorded as sales to Aryan.

    (ii) Credit sale of old machinery to Sohan for ₹ 1,700 was entered in the sales book for ₹ 7,100.

    (iii) Credit sales to Mohan ₹ 7,000 were not recorded.

Ans.

Rectification Entries in Journal

Date	Particulars	LF	Amt (Dr)	Amt (Cr)
(i)	Raj Dr		1,700	
	To Aryan			1,700
	(Being the credit sale of ₹ 1,700 to Raj recorded as sales to Aryan, now rectified)			
(ii)	Sales A/c Dr		7,100	
	To Sohan			5,400
	To Machinery A/c			1,700
	(Being the credit sale of machinery to Sohan for ₹ 1,700 entered in the sales book as ₹ 7,100, now rectified)			
(iii)	Mohan Dr		7,000	
	To Sales A/c			7,000
	(Being the goods sold to Mohan not recorded, now rectified)			

6. Rectify the following errors.

    (i) Credit sales to Mohan ₹ 7,000 were recorded as ₹ 700.

    (ii) Credit purchases from Rohan ₹ 9,000 were recorded as ₹ 900.

    (iii) Goods returned to Rakesh ₹ 4,000 were recorded as ₹ 400.

Ans.

Rectification Entries in Journal

Date	Particulars	LF	Amt (Dr)	Amt (Cr)
(i)	Mohan Dr		6,300	
	To Sales A/c			6,300
	(Being the goods sold to Mohan for ₹ 7,000 recorded as ₹ 700, now rectified)			
(ii)	Purchases A/c Dr		8,100	
	To Rohan			8,100
	(Being the goods purchased from Rohan on credit for ₹ 9,000 recorded as ₹ 900, now rectified)			
(iii)	Rakesh Dr		3,600	
	To Purchases Return A/c			3,600
	(Being the goods returned to Rakesh ₹ 4,000 recorded as ₹ 400, now rectified)			

7. Rectify the following errors.

  (i) A credit purchases of ₹ 3,120 from Vihan was passed in the books as ₹ 4,200.

  (ii) Goods (cost ₹ 2,500 sales price ₹ 3,000) distributed as free samples among prospective customers were not recorded.

  (iii) Wages paid to the firm's workmen for making additions to machinery amounting to ₹ 1,050 were debited to the wages account.

Ans.

Rectification Entries in Journal

Date	Particulars		LF	Amt (Dr)	Amt (Cr)
(i)	Vihan	Dr		1,080	
	To Purchases A/c				1,080
	(Being the rectification of purchases of ₹ 3,120 from Vihan passed as ₹ 4,200)				
(ii)	Free Samples A/c	Dr		2,500	
	To Purchases A/c				2,500
	(Being the goods distributed as free samples omitted to be recorded, now recorded)				
(iii)	Plant and Machinery A/c	Dr		1,050	
	To Wages A/c				1,050
	(Being the wages for additions to machinery wrongly treated as revenue expenditure, now rectified by capitalising the same)				

8. The following errors, affecting the account for the year 2020 were detected in the books of Raj Brothers, Meerut.

  (i) Sale of old furniture ₹ 300 treated as sale of goods.

  (ii) Receipt of ₹ 1,000 from A credited to B.

  (iii) Goods worth ₹ 200 bought from Z have remained unrecorded so far.

  (iv) Rent of proprietor, ₹ 1,200 debited to rent account.

Ans.

Rectification Entries in Journal

Date	Particulars		LF	Amt (Dr)	Amt (Cr)
(i)	Sales A/c	Dr		300	
	To Furniture A/c				300
	(Being the rectification of sales of furniture treated as sales of goods)				
(ii)	B	Dr		1,000	
	To A				1,000
	(Being the rectification of a receipt from A credited to B)				
(iii)	Purchases A/c	Dr		200	
	To Z				200
	(Being the purchases of goods from Z unrecorded)				
(iv)	Drawings A/c	Dr		1,200	
	To Rent A/c				1,200
	(Being the rectification of payment of rent of proprietor's residence treated as payment of office rent)				

9. Rectify the following errors.

  (i) Credit purchases from Rohan ₹ 9,000 were recorded in sales book.

  (ii) Goods returned to Rakesh ₹ 4,000 were recorded in the sales return book.

  (iii) Good returned from Mahesh ₹ 1,000 were recorded in purchases return book.

  (iv) Goods returned from Mahesh ₹ 2,000 were recorded in purchases book.

Ans.

Rectification Entries in Journal

Date	Particulars		LF	Amt (Dr)	Amt (Cr)
(i)	Sales A/c	Dr		9,000	
	Purchases A/c	Dr		9,000	
	To Rohan				18,000
	(Being the goods purchased from Rohan on credit were recorded in sales book, now rectified)				
(ii)	Rakesh	Dr		8,000	
	To Purchases Return A/c				4,000
	To Sales Return A/c				4,000
	(Being the goods returned to Rakesh, wrongly recorded in sales return book, now rectified)				
(iii)	Sales Return A/c	Dr		1,000	
	Purchases Return A/c	Dr		1,000	
	To Mahesh				2,000
	(Being the goods returned by Mahesh were recorded in purchases return book, now rectified)				
(iv)	Sales Return A/c	Dr		2,000	
	To Purchases A/c				2,000
	(Being the goods returned from Mahesh, recorded in purchases book, now rectified)				

10. Rectify the following errors.

(i) Depreciation provided on machinery ₹ 4,000 was not recorded.

(ii) Bad debts written-off ₹ 5,000 were not recorded.

(iii) Discount allowed to a debtor ₹ 100 on receiving cash from him was not recorded.

(iv) Bills receivable for ₹ 2,000 received from a debtor was not recorded.

Ans.

Rectification Entries in Journal

Date	Particulars		LF	Amt (Dr)	Amt (Cr)
(i)	Depreciation A/c	Dr		4,000	
	To Machinery A/c				4,000
	(Being the depreciation charged on machinery not recorded, now rectified)				
(ii)	Bad Debts A/c	Dr		5,000	
	To Debtor's A/c				5,000
	(Being the bad debts written-off on debtors were not recorded, now rectified)				
(iii)	Discount Allowed A/c	Dr		100	
	To Debtor's A/c				100
	(Being the discount allowed to debtor was not recorded, now rectified)				
(iv)	Bills Receivable A/c	Dr		2,000	
	To Debtor's A/c				2,000
	(Being the bills receivable from debtors not recorded, now rectified)				

11. Rectify the following errors.

(i) Sales return from Megha ₹ 1,600 was posted to her account as ₹ 1,000.

(ii) Cash paid to Neha ₹ 2,000 was not posted to her account.

(iii) Depreciation written-off on furniture ₹ 1,500 was not posted to depreciation account.

(iv) Credit sales to Mohan ₹ 10,000 were posted to his account as ₹ 12,000.

Ans.

Rectification Entries in Journal

Date	Particulars	LF	Amt (Dr)	Amt (Cr)
(i)	Suspense A/c Dr		600	
	To Megha			600
	(Being the short credit in Megha's account, now rectified)			
(ii)	Neha Dr		2,000	
	To Suspense A/c			2,000
	(Being the omission of entry in the debit of Neha's account, now rectified)			
(iii)	Depreciation A/c Dr		1,500	
	To Suspense A/c			1,500
	(Being the omission of posting of amount to the depreciation account, now rectified)			
(iv)	Suspense A/c Dr		2,000	
	To Mohan			2,000
	(Being the excess debit in Mohan's account, now rectified)			

12. Rectify the following errors.

(i) Credit sales to Mohan ₹ 7,000 were recorded as ₹ 7,200.

(ii) Credit purchase from Rohan ₹ 9,000 were recorded as ₹ 9,900.

(iii) Goods returned to Rakesh ₹ 4,000 were recorded as ₹ 4,040.

(iv) Goods returned from Mahesh ₹ 1,000 were recorded as ₹ 1,600.

Ans.

Rectification Entries in Journal

Date	Particulars	LF	Amt (Dr)	Amt (Cr)
(i)	Sales A/c Dr		200	
	To Mohan			200
	(Being the goods sold to Mohan for ₹ 7,000 were recorded as ₹ 7,200, now rectified)			
(ii)	Rohan Dr		900	
	To Purchases A/c			900
	(Being the goods purchased from Rohan for ₹ 9,000 recorded as ₹ 9,900, now rectified)			
(iii)	Purchases Return A/c Dr		40	
	To Rakesh			40
	(Being the goods returned to Rakesh ₹ 4,000 recorded as ₹ 4,040, now rectified)			
(iv)	Mahesh Dr		600	
	To Sales Return A/c			600
	(Being the goods returned by Mahesh for ₹ 1,000 recorded as ₹ 1,600, now rectified)			

13. Rectify the following errors.

(i) Salary paid ₹ 5,000 was debited to employee's personal account.

(ii) Rent paid ₹ 4,000 was posted to landlord's personal account.

(iii) Goods withdrawn by proprietor for personal use ₹ 1,000 were debited to sundry expenses account.

(iv) Cash received from Kohli ₹ 2,000 was posted to Kapur's account.

Ans.

Rectification Entries in Journal

Date	Particulars	LF	Amt (Dr)	Amt (Cr)
(i)	Salaries A/c Dr		5,000	
	To Employee A/c			5,000
	(Being the salary paid to employee ₹ 5,000, wrongly debited to employee's personal account, now rectified)			
(ii)	Rent A/c Dr		4,000	
	To Landlord A/c			4,000
	(Being the rent paid to landlord ₹ 4,000 wrongly posted to landlord's personal account, now rectified)			

Date	Particulars		LF	Amt (Dr)	Amt (Cr)
(iii)	Drawings A/c	Dr		1,000	
	To Sundry Expenses A/c				1,000
	(Being the goods withdrawn by proprietor for his personal use ₹ 1,000 were wrongly recorded as sundry expenses, now rectified)				
(iv)	Kapur	Dr		2,000	
	To Kohli				2,000
	(Being the cash received from Kohli, recorded in Kapur's account, now rectified)				

14. Give journal entries to rectify the following.

   (i) A purchase of goods from Varun amounting to ₹ 300 has been wrongly entered through the sales book.

   (ii) On 31st December, goods of the value of ₹ 600 were returned by X and were taken into stock on the same date but no entry was passed in the books.

   (iii) An amount of ₹ 400 due from Y which had been written-off as a bad debt in a previous year, was unexpectedly recovered and had been posted to the personal account of Y.

   (iv) A cheque for ₹ 200 received from Z was dishonoured and had been posted to the debit of sales return account.

Ans.

Rectification Entries in Journal

Date	Particulars		LF	Amt (Dr)	Amt (Cr)
(i)	Purchases A/c	Dr		300	
	Sales A/c	Dr		300	
	To Varun				600
	(Being the correction of wrong entry in the sales book for a purchases of goods from Varun)				
(ii)	Returns Inwards A/c	Dr		600	
	To X				600
	(Being the entry of goods returned by him and taken in stock omitted from records)				
(iii)	Y	Dr		400	
	To Bad Debts Recovered A/c				400
	(Being the correction of wrong credit to personal account in respect of recovery of previously written-off bad debts)				
(iv)	Z	Dr		200	
	To Sales Return A/c				200
	(Being the correction of wrong debit to sales return account for dishonour of cheque received from Z).				

15. The following errors were found in the books of Rajan & Sons. Give the necessary entries to correct them.

   (i) Repairs made were debited to building account ₹ 100.

   (ii) ₹ 200 paid for rent, debited to landlord's account.

   (iii) Salary ₹ 250 paid to a clerk due to him has been debited to his personal account.

   (iv) ₹ 200 received from Rina & Co. has been wrongly entered as from Reena & Co.

Ans.

Rectification Entries in Journal

Date	Particulars		LF	Amt (Dr)	Amt (Cr)
(i)	Repairs A/c	Dr		100	
	To Building A/c				100
	(Being the correction of wrong debit to building account for repairs made)				
(ii)	Rent A/c	Dr		200	
	To Landlord's (Personal) A/c				200
	(Being the correction of wrong debit to landlord's account for rent paid)				
(iii)	Salaries A/c	Dr		250	
	To Clerk's (Personal) A/c				250
	(Being the correction of wrong debit to clerk's personal account for salaries paid)				
(iv)	Reena & Co.	Dr		200	
	To Rina & Co.				200
	(Being the correction of wrong credit to Reena & Co. instead of Rina & Co.)				

16. Pass journal entries to rectify the following errors.

(i) Credit purchase of goods of ₹ 3,000 from Viraj & Co. was not recorded in the books although the goods were taken into stock.

(ii) Credit sale of goods to Harish amounting to ₹ 10,000 was posted to the account of Haneef.

(iii) Acquisition charges on the purchase of a new building amounting to ₹ 10,000 were debited to the sundry expenses account.

(iv) Outstanding telephone charges of ₹ 6,000 had been completely omitted.

Ans.

Rectification Entries in Journal

Date	Particulars		LF	Amt (Dr)	Amt (Cr)
(i)	Purchases A/c	Dr		3,000	
	To Viraj & Co.				3,000
	(Being the rectification of purchase of goods from Viraj & Co omitted from books)				
(ii)	Harish	Dr		10,000	
	To Haneef				10,000
	(Being the sale made on credit to Harish posted wrongly to the debit of Haneef, now rectified)				
(iii)	Building A/c	Dr		10,000	
	To Sundry Expenses A/c				10,000
	(Being the rectification of wrong debit to sundry expenses account for acquisition charges on purchases of new building)				
(iv)	Telephone Charges A/c	Dr		6,000	
	To Outstanding Telephone Charges A/c				6,000
	(Being the outstanding telephone charges omitted to be recorded, now recorded)				

17. Rectify the following errors and use suspense account where necessary.

  (i) ₹ 2,500 paid for office furniture was debited to office expenses account.

  (ii) A cash sale of ₹ 7,500 to Saksham was correctly entered in the cash book but was posted to the credit of Saksham's account.

  (iii) Goods amounting to ₹ 1,800, returned by Aryan, were entered in the sales book and posted therefrom to the credit of Aryan's account.

  (iv) Bills receivable received from Sangeet for ₹ 5,000 was posted to the credit of bills payable account and credited to Sangeet's account.

Ans.

JOURNAL

Date	Particulars	LF	Amt (Dr)	Amt (Cr)
(i)	Office Furniture A/c Dr		2,500	
	To Office Expenses A/c			2,500
	(Being the capital expenditure treated as revenue, now rectified)			
(ii)	Saksham Dr		7,500	
	To Sales A/c			7,500
	(Being the cash sale credited to Saksham's account, now rectified)			
(iii)	Sales A/c Dr		1,800	
	Returns Inwards A/c		1,800	
	To Suspense A/c			3,600
	(Being the sales return wrongly credited to sales account, now rectified)			
(iv)	Bills Receivable A/c Dr		5,000	
	Bills Payable A/c		5,000	
	To Suspense A/c			10,000
	(Being the bills receivable wrongly recorded as bills payable, now rectified)			

• Long Answer (LA) Type Questions

1. What kinds of errors would cause difference in the trial balance? Also give an example that would not be revealed by a trial balance.   **(NCERT)**

Ans. The errors that lead to the differences in the trial balance are termed as one sided errors. These are those errors that affect only one account. Below are given the errors that cause differences in the trial balance

  (i) Wrong casting of any account, this is termed as the error of casting.

  (ii) Wrong carrying forward of the balances from previous year's books or from one end of page to another. These types of errors are termed as the errors in carrying forward.

  (iii) If entries are posted in the wrong side of accounts.

  (iv) Posting of a wrong amount in account, this is termed as the error of posting.

  (v) If entries are recorded partially, i.e., the entries are not recorded completely, then due to the error of partial omission, trial balance does not agree.

Example of error that would not be revealed in a trial balance

Sales to Mr X, omitted to be recorded in the sales day book.

2. You are presented with a trial balance showing a difference which has been carried to suspense account and the following errors are revealed.

  (i) ₹ 17,000 paid in cash for a typewriter was charged to office expenses account.

  (ii) A cash sale of ₹ 50,000 to Pluto, correctly entered in the cash book, was posted to the credit of Pluto's account in the sales ledger.

  (iii) Goods amounting to ₹ 8,000, returned by Sky, were entered in the sales book and posted therefrom to the credit of Sky's account.

  (iv) Bills receivable from Star for ₹ 30,000 posted to the credit of bills payable account and credited to Star's account.

  (v) Goods amounting to ₹ 1,00,000 sold to Sun were correctly entered in sales book but posted to Sun's account for ₹ 1,80,000.

  (vi) Sales returns book was overcast by ₹ 1,000.

Journalise the necessary corrections.

Ans.

JOURNAL

Date	Particulars		LF	Amt (Dr)	Amt (Cr)
(i)	Office Equipment A/c (Typewriter)	Dr		17,000	
	To Office Expenses A/c				17,000
	(Being the expenditure that should have been capitalised wrongly shown as revenue expenditure, now rectified)				
(ii)	Pluto	Dr		50,000	
	To Sales A/c				50,000
	(Being the cash sales wrongly posted to customer's account, now rectified)				
(iii)	Sales A/c	Dr		8,000	
	Returns Inward A/c	Dr		8,000	
	To Suspense A/c				16,000
	(Being the returns inward wrongly credited to sales, now rectified)				
(iv)	Bills Payable A/c	Dr		30,000	
	Bills Receivable A/c	Dr		30,000	
	To Suspense A/c				60,000
	(Being the bills receivable wrongly recorded as bills payable, now rectified)				
(v)	Suspense A/c	Dr		80,000	
	To Sun				80,000
	(Being the wrong amount posted to his account, now rectified)				
(vi)	Suspense A/c	Dr		1,000	
	To Returns Inward A/c				1,000
	(Being the overcasting of sales returns book rectified)				

3. From the following information, complete the missing rectification entries.

JOURNAL

Date	Particulars		LF	Amt (Dr)	Amt (Cr)
(i)	………	Dr		20,000	
	………				20,000
	(Being sale of old furniture ₹ 20,000 treated as sales of goods, now rectified)				
(ii)	………	Dr		10,00,000	
	To ………				10,00,000
	(Being jewellery purchased worth ₹ 10,00,000 from Manmohan have remained unrecorded so far, now recorded)				
(iii)	Sohanlal & Sons Co.	Dr		…	
	To Suspense A/c				…
	(Being purchase return of ₹ 2,50,000 to Sohanlal & Sons Co's, was posted to their credit now rectified)				
(iv)	………	Dr		1,200	
	………				1,200
	(Being typewriter worth ₹ 1,200 purchased debited to repair account, now rectified)				
(v)	Sanjeev & Co.	Dr		…	
	To Suspense A/c				…
	(Being cash ₹ 25,000 paid to Sanjeev & Co. wrongly credited to their account, now rectified)				
(vi)	………	Dr		50,000	
	To ………				50,000
	(Being no adjustment entry passed for goods worth ₹ 50,000 used for construction of equipments for business use, now rectified)				

Ans.

JOURNAL

Date	Particulars		LF	Amt (Dr)	Amt (Cr)
(i)	Sales A/c	Dr		20,000	
	To Furniture A/c				20,000
	(Being sale of old furniture ₹ 20,000 treated as sales of goods, now rectified)				
(ii)	Purchases A/c	Dr		10,00,000	
	To Manmohan				10,00,000
	(Being jewellery purchased worth ₹ 10,00,000 from Manmohan have remained unrecorded so far, now recorded)				
(iii)	Sohanlal & Sons Co.	Dr		5,00,000	
	To Suspense A/c				5,00,000
	(Being purchase return of ₹ 2,50,000 to Sohanlal & Sons Co's, was posted to their credit, now rectified)				
(iv)	Typewriter A/c	Dr		1,200	
	To Repair A/c				1,200
	(Being typewriter worth ₹ 1,200 purchased debited to repair account, now rectified)				
(v)	Sanjeev & Co.	Dr		50,000	
	To Suspense A/c				50,000
	(Being cash ₹ 25,000 paid to Sanjeev & Co wrongly credited to their account, now rectified)				
(vi)	Equipment A/c	Dr		50,000	
	To Purchase A/c				50,000
	(Being no adjustment entry passed for goods worth ₹ 50,000 used for construction of equipments for business use, now rectified)				

4. In taking out a trial balance, a book-keeper finds that debit total exceeds the credit total by ₹ 7,040. The amount is placed to the credit of a newly opened suspense account. Subsequently, the following mistakes were discovered. You are required to pass the necessary entries for rectifying the mistakes and show the suspense account.

(i) Sales day book was overcast by ₹ 2,000.

(ii) A sale of ₹ 1,000 to Gokul Prasad was wrongly debited to Kanti Prasad.

(iii) General expenses ₹ 360 was posted as ₹ 1,600.

(iv) Cash received from Shanti Prasad was debited to his account ₹ 3,000.

(v) While carrying forward the total of one page of the purchase book to the next, the amount of ₹ 24,700 was entered as ₹ 26,500.

Ans.

Rectification Entries in Journal

Date	Particulars		LF	Amt (Dr)	Amt (Cr)
(i)	Sales A/c	Dr		2,000	
	To Suspense A/c				2,000
	(Being the sales book overcast, now rectified)				
(ii)	Gokul Prasad	Dr		1,000	
	To Kanti Prasad				1,000
	(Being the sales debited to Kanti Prasad, now rectified)				
(iii)	Suspense A/c	Dr		1,240	
	To General Expenses A/c				1,240
	(Being the general expenses overcasted, now rectified)				

Date	Particulars		LF	Amt (Dr)	Amt (Cr)
(iv)	Suspense A/c	Dr		6,000	
	To Shanti Prasad				6,000
	(Being the cash received ₹ 3,000 debited to Shanti Prasad, now rectified)				
(v)	Suspense A/c	Dr		1,800	
	To Purchase A/c				1,800
	(Being the purchases book overcasted, now rectified)				

Dr		Suspense Account			Cr
Particulars	**Amt (₹)**		**Particulars**	**Amt (₹)**	
To General Expenses A/c	1,240		By Difference in Trial Balance	7,040	
To Shanti Prasad	6,000		By Sales A/c	2,000	
To Purchase A/c	1,800				
	9,040			9,040	

5. Rectify the following errors assuming that suspense account was opened.

(i) Purchase of ₹ 4,000 from Bheem was entered in sales book. Although Bheem's personal account was rightly credited.

(ii) Sales to Nakul of ₹ 4,300 credited to his account as ₹ 3,400.

(iii) Sale of old furniture of ₹ 5,400 was credited to sales account as ₹ 4,500.

(iv) Goods worth ₹ 1,000 taken by proprietor for personal use was omitted from being recorded.

(v) Sale to Arjun worth ₹ 2,960 was entered in sales book as ₹ 2,690.

(vi) Sales return book balance of ₹ 2,100 was not included in books.

Ans.

JOURNAL

Date	Particulars		LF	Amt (Dr)	Amt (Cr)
(i)	Purchases A/c	Dr		4,000	
	Sales A/c	Dr		4,000	
	To Suspense A/c				8,000
	(Being the purchase of ₹ 4,000 from Bheem was entered in sales book, but Bheem's personal account was rightly credited, now rectified)				
(ii)	Nakul	Dr		7,700	
	To Suspense A/c				7,700
	(Being the sales to Nakul of ₹ 4,300 credited to his account as ₹ 3,400, now rectified)				
(iii)	Sales A/c	Dr		4,500	
	Suspense A/c	Dr		900	
	To Furniture A/c				5,400
	(Being the sale of old furniture of ₹ 5,400 was credited to sales account as ₹ 4,500, now rectified)				
(iv)	Drawings A/c	Dr		1,000	
	To Purchases A/c				1,000
	(Being the goods worth ₹ 1,000 taken by proprietor for personal use was not recorded)				
(v)	Suspense A/c	Dr		270	
	To Sales A/c				270
	(Being the sale of ₹ 2,960 to Arjun was entered in sales book as ₹ 2,690, now rectified)				
(vi)	Sales Return A/c	Dr		2,100	
	To Suspense A/c				2,100
	(Being the sales return book balance of ₹ 2,100 not included in books, now included)				

6. Rectify the following errors assuming that suspense account was opened to ascertain the difference in trial balance.

(i) Depreciation provided on machinery ₹ 6,250 was not posted to depreciation account.

(ii) Bad debts written-off ₹ 5,890 were not posted to debtor's account.

(iii) Discount allowed to a debtor ₹ 175 on receiving cash from him was not posted to discount allowed account.

(iv) Goods withdrawn by proprietor for personal use ₹ 2,520 were not posted to drawings account.

(v) Bills receivable for ₹ 10,000 received from a debtor was not posted to bills receivable account.

Ans.

JOURNAL

Date	Particulars	LF	Amt (Dr)	Amt (Cr)
(i)	Depreciation A/c Dr		6,250	
	To Suspense A/c			6,250
	(Being the depreciation on machinery was not posted to depreciation account, now rectified)			
(ii)	Suspense A/c Dr		5,890	
	To Debtor's A/c			5,890
	(Being the bad debts written-off were not posted to debtor's account, now rectified)			
(iii)	Discount Allowed A/c Dr		175	
	To Suspense A/c			175
	(Being the discount allowed to customer, not posted to discount account, now rectified)			
(iv)	Drawings A/c Dr		2,520	
	To Suspense A/c			2,520
	(Being the goods withdrawn for personal use, not recorded in drawings account, now rectified)			
(v)	Bills Receivable A/c Dr		10,000	
	To Suspense A/c			10,000
	(Being the bills receivable received from debtors was not recorded in bills receivable account, now rectified)			

Dr   **Suspense Account**   **Cr**

Date	Particulars	JF	Amt (₹)	Date	Particulars	JF	Amt (₹)
	To Debtor's A/c		5,890		By Depreciation A/c		6,250
	To Difference as per Trial Balance (Balancing Figure)		13,055		By Discount Allowed A/c		175
					By Drawings A/c		2,520
					By Bills Receivable A/c		10,000
			18,945				18,945

7. Correct the following errors found in the books of Siddharth. The trial balance was out by ₹ 493 excess credit. The difference thus, has been posted to a suspense account.

(i) An amount of ₹ 100 was received from Parth on 31st December, 2020 but has been omitted to enter in the cash book.

(ii) The total of returns inward book for December has been cast ₹ 100 short.

(iii) The purchase of an office table costing ₹ 300 has been passed through the purchases day book.

(iv) ₹ 375 paid for wages to workmen for making show-cases had been charged to wages account.

(v) A purchase of ₹ 67 had been posted to the creditors account as ₹ 60.

(vi) A cheque for ₹ 200 received from Kanav had been dishonoured and was passed to the debit of 'allowances account'.

(vii) ₹ 1,000 paid for the purchase of a motor cycle for Siddharth had been charged to 'miscellaneous expenses account'.

(viii) Goods amounting to ₹ 100 had been returned by customer and were taken into stock, but no entry in respect there of, was made into the books.

(ix) A sale of ₹ 200 to Rahul & Co. was wrongly credited to their account.

Ans.

Rectification Entries in Journal

Date	Particulars		LF	Amt (Dr)	Amt (Cr)
(i)	Cash A/c	Dr		100	
	To Parth				100
	(Being the amount received)				
(ii)	Returns Inward A/c	Dr		100	
	To Suspense A/c				100
	(Being the mistake in totalling the returns inward book, now rectified)				
(iii)	Furniture A/c	Dr		300	
	To Purchases A/c				300
	(Being the rectification of mistake by which purchase of furniture was entered in purchases book and hence, debited to purchases account)				
(iv)	Furniture A/c	Dr		375	
	To Wages A/c				375
	(Being the wages paid to workmen for making showcases which should be capitalised and not to be charged to wages account)				
(v)	Suspense A/c	Dr		7	
	To Creditor's (Personal) A/c				7
	(Being the mistake in crediting the creditor's account less by ₹ 7, now rectified)				
(vi)	Kanav	Dr		200	
	To Allowances A/c				200
	(Being the cheque of Kanav dishonoured, previously debited to allowance account)				
(vii)	Drawings A/c	Dr		1,000	
	To Miscellaneous Expenses				1,000
	(Being the motor cycle purchased for Siddharth debited to his drawings account instead of miscellaneous expenses account as previously done by mistake)				
(viii)	Returns Inward A/c	Dr		100	
	To Customer's (Personal) A/c				100
	(Being correction of the omission to record return of goods by customers)				
(ix)	Rahul & Co.	Dr		400	
	To Suspense A/c				400
	(Being the correction of mistake by which the account of Rahul & Co was credited by ₹ 200 instead of being debited)				

Dr			Suspense Account			Cr
Date	Particulars	JF	Amt (₹)	Date	Particulars	JF	Amt (₹)
2021				2020			
Dec 31	To Differene in Trial Balance		493	Dec 31	By Returns Inward A/c		100
Dec 31	To Creditor's A/c		7		By Rahul & Co.		400
			500				500

Chapter Test

Multiple Choice Questions

1. If the amount is posted in the wrong account or it is written on the wrong side of an account, what type of error is it?
(a) Error of principle (b) Error of commission (c) Error of omission (d) Compensating errors

2. Which of the following are two sided errors?
(a) Machinery purchased recorded in purchase book (b) Old furniture sold recorded as sale of goods
(c) Both (a) and (b) (d) None of these

3. What will be the rectifying entry, if a credit purchase of ₹ 460 from Sudhakar was recorded as ₹ 640?

(a)	Sudhakar	Dr	180	
	To Purchases A/c			180
(b)	Sudhakar	Dr	460	
	To Purchases A/c			460
(c)	Sudhakar	Dr	640	
	To Purchases A/c			640
(d)	Purchases A/c	Dr	460	
	To Sudhakar			460

4 If suspense account shows a credit balance, it will be taken to
(a) liability side of balance sheet (b) asset side of balance sheet
(c) capital side of balance sheet (d) credit side of profit and loss account

5 If suspense account does not balance off even after rectification of errors, it implies that
(a) there are some one sided errors only in the books yet to be located
(b) there are no more errors yet to be located
(c) there are some two sided errors only yet to be located
(d) there may be both one sided errors and two sided errors yet to be located

6 Which of these errors will be rectified through suspense account?
(a) Sales return book undercast by ₹ 1,000.
(b) Sales return by Madhu ₹ 1,000.
(c) Sales return by Madhu ₹ 1,000 recorded as ₹ 100.
(d) Sales return by Madhu ₹ 1,000 recorded through purchase return account.

7. Rectifying entry for a computer purchased wrongly debited to the purchase account of ₹ 1,00,000 will be

(a)	Cash A/c	Dr	1,00,000	
	To Computer A/c			1,00,000
(b)	Computer A/c	Dr	1,00,000	
	To Purchases A/c			1,00,000
(c)	Purchases A/c	Dr	1,00,000	
	To Computer A/c			1, 00,000
(d)	Computer A/c	Dr	1,00,000	
	To Suspense A/c			1,00,000

8. Material ₹ 10,000 and wages ₹ 3,000 were used for construction of building. No adjustment entry was made in the books. Rectifying entry will be

(a)	Wages A/c	Dr	10,000	
	To Building A/c			10,000
(b)	Material A/c	Dr	10,000	
	Building A/c	Dr	3,000	
	To Cash A/c			13,000
(c)	Building A/c	Dr	13,000	
	To Purchases A/c			10,000
	To Wages A/c			3,000
(d)	None of the above			

Short Answer (SA) Type Questions

1. Rectify the following errors.
   (i) Credit sales to Rajiv for ₹ 6,66,500 recorded in purchases book.
   (ii) Furniture purchased on credit from Aryan for ₹ 70,000 posted to Ayan's account.
   (iii) Credit Purchase from Priya for ₹ 10,000 was not recorded.

2. Explain compensating errors and give atleast one example of such errors.

3. Name the errors, which do not affect the trial balance.

4. Rectify the following errors
   (i) Credit sales to Manas ₹ 16,000 were recorded in the purchases book as ₹ 10,000 and posted to the debit of Manas as ₹ 1,000.
   (ii) Repair on overhauling of second hand machinery purchased ₹ 2,000 was debited to repair account as ₹ 200.
   (iii) Old machinery sold for ₹ 2,000 to Manish recorded through sales book as ₹ 1,800 and posted to the credit of Manish as ₹ 1,200.
   (iv) Furniture purchased from Noor ₹ 6,000 was recorded through purchases book as ₹ 5,000 and posted to the debit of Noor ₹ 2,000.

5. An accountant, while balancing his books found that there was a difference of ₹ 85.95 in the trial balance. Being required to prepare the final accounts, he placed this difference to a newly opened suspense account which was carried forward to the next year, when the following errors were discovered.
   (i) Goods bought from a merchant for ₹ 5.50 had been posted to the credit of his account as ₹ 55.
   (ii) An item of ₹ 10.62 entered in the sales return book had been posted to the debit of the customer who returned the goods.
   (iii) ₹ 60 owing by a customer had been omitted from the schedule of sundry debtors.
   (iv) ₹ 2.31 discount received from a creditor had been duly entered in his account but not posted to discount received account.
   Give journal entries necessary to correct these errors.

Long Answer (LA) Type Questions

1. Rectify the following errors.
   (i) Goods worth ₹ 4,000 returned by X entered in sales book and therefrom posted to the credit of his account.
   (ii) Goods worth ₹ 3,000 bought by owner for personal use, debited to purchases account.
   (iii) Cheque of ₹ 1,000 from Pankaj Kapoor dishonoured has been debited to sales return account.
   (iv) Total of sales book ₹ 52,600 wrongly carried forward to next page as ₹ 25,600.
   (v) Prepaid insurance ₹ 1,000 omitted to be bought forward from previous years' books.
   (vi) Goods worth ₹ 12,000 returned by Ankit taken into stock on same date but omitted to be recorded.

2. Correct the following errors by opening a suspense account.
   (i) The sales book has been totalled ₹ 100 short.
   (ii) Goods worth ₹ 150 returned by Vishal & Co. have not been recorded anywhere.
   (iii) Goods purchased ₹ 250 have been posted to the debit of the supplier Raja & Co.
   (iv) Furniture purchased from Narayan & Brothers ₹ 1,000 has been entered in purchases day book.
   (v) Discount received from Monu & Sonu ₹ 15 has not been entered in the discount column of the cash book.
   (vi) Discount allowed to Naveen & Co. ₹ 18 has not been entered in the discount column of the cash book. The account of Naveen & Co. has, however, been correctly posted.

Answers

Multiple Choice Questions

1. (b)   2. (c)   3. (a)   4. (a)   5. (a)   6. (a)   7. (b)   8. (c)

For Detailed Solutions

Scan the code

PART B

Financial Accounting-II

CHAPTER 04

Financial Statements I
(Without Adjustments)

In this Chapter...

- Meaning of Financial Statements
- Trading Account
- Profit and Loss Account
- Balance Sheet

Meaning of Financial Statements

Financial statements are the final products of an accounting process which begins with the identification of accounting information and recording it in the books of primary entry.

Financial statements are prepared by following the accounting concepts and conventions. These are the statements prepared at the end of accounting period and give information about the financial position and performance of an enterprise.

A complete set of financial statements include

- Balance sheet (or position statement) which shows the financial position of an enterprise at a particular point of time.
- Trading and profit and loss account (or income statement) which shows the financial performance of business operations during an accounting period.
- Schedules and notes to accounts forming a part of balance sheet and profit and loss account.

Objectives of Financial Statements

- To present a true and fair view of the working of the business.
- To help to judge the effectiveness of the management.
- To provide sufficient and reliable information to various users interested in financial statements.
- To facilitate efficient allocation of resources.
- To disclose various accounting policies.
- To provide information about the cash flows.
- To provide information about the earning capacity.
- To provide financial data on assets and liabilities of an enterprise.

Importance of Financial Statements

- Trading account helps in knowing the gross profit earned or gross loss incurred by the business during the accounting period.
- The net profit earned or net loss incurred by the business during the accounting period can be known by preparing profit and loss account.
- Balance sheet provides complete information related to the assets, liabilities and capital of the business at a particular date.
- The profit calculated and various items of balance sheet can be compared with that of previous years.
- The profit and loss account and balance sheet enables the calculation of various ratios.
- It helps in the creation of various provisions and reserves to meet future uncertainties and to strengthen the financial position of the firm.

Users of Financial Statements

There are two users of financial statement which are as follows

1. **Internal Users**
   - (i) Owners
   - (iii) Employees and workers
   - (ii) Management

2. **External Users**
   - (i) Creditors
   - (iii) Banks and financial institutions
   - (v) Other parties
   - (ii) Investors
   - (iv) Government and its authorities
   - (vi) Researchers

Capital and Revenue Items

It is important to make a clear distinction between items of capital nature and revenue nature for the preparation of trading and profit and loss account and balance sheet.

The various capital and revenue items are explained below

1. **Capital Expenditure** It is an expenditure incurred to acquire or increase the value of fixed assets or repayment of long-term liability and its benefits extend to more than one accounting period. The effect of capital expenditure is shown in balance sheet. e.g., installation charges of plant.

2. **Revenue Expenditure** These are incurred for day-to-day conduct of the business. Thus, they are of recurring nature. Their benefit extend upto one accounting period. These are shown in trading and profit and loss account. e.g., whitewash of building.

3. **Deferred Revenue Expenditure** It is a revenue expenditure that is incurred during an accounting period but its benefits extend beyond that accounting period. The part of deferred revenue expenditure written-off is shown in profit and loss account and the balance part is shown in balance sheet as fictitious asset.

4. **Capital Receipts** These are those receipts which are received once in a while. It is the amount received by the business on account of capital, loans or sale proceeds of fixed assets. These are shown in balance sheet. e.g., loan taken from a bank.

5. **Revenue Receipts** These are those receipts which arise in the normal course of business. These are shown in trading account and profit and loss account. e.g., sales made by the firm.

Trading Account

Trading account is the first stage in the preparation of the final accounts. The trading account ascertains the result from basic operational activities of the business. Trading account is prepared to know the gross profit earned or gross loss incurred during the accounting period.

Entries or items of debit side are opening stock, purchases and other direct expenses and on credit side, sales and closing stock are recorded. It discloses gross profit or gross loss.

Gross Profit/Gross Loss The excess of sales over purchases and direct expenses is called gross profit. If the amount of purchases including direct expenses is more than the sales revenue, the resultant figure is gross loss.

The computation of gross profit can be shown in the form of equation as

$$\text{Gross Profit} = \text{Net Sales} - \text{Cost of Goods Sold}$$

where,

$$\text{Net Sales} = \text{Total Sales} - \text{Sales Return}$$

$$\text{Cost of Goods Sold} = \text{Opening Stock} + \text{Net Purchases} + \text{Direct Expenses} - \text{Closing Stock}$$

$$\text{Net Purchases} = \text{Total Purchases} - \text{Purchase Return}$$

In case, we want to determine operating profit from gross profit

Then, Operating Profit = Gross Profit – Operating Expenses + Operating Income

Where,

$$\text{Operating Expenses} = \text{Administration Expenses} + \text{Selling and Distribution Expenses}$$

Need and Importance of Trading Account

- The main objective of preparing trading account is to know the gross profit or gross loss.
- Trading account provides information about those expenses which are directly related with purchasing goods. This enables the management to control such expenses.
- Trading account helps to compare closing stock of current year with that of previous years. In case closing stock shows an increasing trend, reasons must be found out, as more the stock, lesser the selling efficiency of the firm.
- The gross profit ratio is compared with the desired ratios or with the ratio of previous years to evaluate the performance. It enables the businessman to take effective measures to safeguard himself against future losses.

Format of Trading Account

Trading Account
for the year ending on...

Dr | | | | | Cr

Particulars	Amt (₹)		Particulars		Amt (₹)
To Opening Stock	...		By Sales	...	
To Purchases	...		(–) Return Inwards	(...)	...
(–) Return Outwards	(...)	...	By Closing Stock		...
To Direct Expenses	...		By Abnormal Loss of Stock		...
To Wages and Salaries	...		By *Gross Loss (Transferred to profit and loss account)		...
To Freight Inward	...				
To Carriage Inward	...				
To *Gross Profit (Transferred to profit and loss account)	...				
	...				...

*Either gross profit or gross loss shall appear.

Profit and Loss Account

Profit and loss account is prepared after the preparation of trading account. Balance of trading account (gross profit or gross loss) is transferred to profit and loss account. The indirect expenses are transferred to the debit side of the profit and loss account. All revenues/gains other than sales are transferred to the credit side of the profit and loss account.

It shows the financial performance of a business during an accounting period. It is prepared to ascertain the net profit earned or net loss incurred by the business entity during an accounting period.

Net Profit/Net Loss If the total of the credit side of the profit and loss account is more than the total of the debit side, the difference is the net profit for the period, of which it is being prepared.

On the other hand, if the total of the debit side is more than the total of the credit side, the difference is the net loss incurred by the business firm.

In an equation form, it is shown as follows

$$\text{Net Profit} = \text{Gross Profit} + \text{Non-operating Income} - \text{Other Operating Indirect Expenses} - \text{Non-operating Expenses}$$

Need and Importance of Profit and Loss Account

- Profit and loss account discloses the net profit earned or net loss suffered by an enterprise during an accounting period.
- The net profit of the current year can be compared with that of the previous years, to know whether the business is making progress or not.
- It helps in comparing various expenses with the expenses of the previous year which inturn enables to take steps for controlling the unnecessary expenses.
- A balance sheet can only be prepared after ascertaining the net profit through the preparation of profit and loss account.

Difference between Operating Profit and Net Profit

1. **Operating Profit** It is the profit earned through normal operations and activities of the business. Operating profit arises as a result of carrying out operating activities. Operating activities are the principal revenue producing activities of the enterprise and are those activities that are not investing or financing activities.

   It means the excess of operating revenue over operating expenses or it is the excess of gross profit over operating expenses. It is also known as Earning Before Interest and Tax (EBIT).

   It is calculated as

   $$\text{Operating Profit} = \text{Net Sales} - \text{Operating Cost}$$

   $$Or$$

   $$= \text{Net Sales} - (\text{Cost of Goods Sold} + \text{Administration and Office Expenses}$$
   $$+ \text{Selling and Distribution Expenses})$$

   $$Or$$

   $$= \text{Net Profit} + \text{Non-operating Expenses} - \text{Non-operating Incomes}$$

   Note *Operating expenses include office and administrative expenses, selling and distribution expenses, cash discount allowed, interest on bills payable and other short-term debts, bad debts and so on.*

2. **Net Profit** It means the excess of revenue (operating or non-operating) over expenses and losses (operating or non-operating). In other words, net profit is arrived at by deducting non-operating expenses and adding non-operating incomes from and in operating profit.

   Note *Non-operating expenses are expenses which are incidental or indirect to the main operations of the business, they include interest on loan, charities and donations, loss on sale of fixed assets, extraordinary losses due to theft, loss by fire and so on.*

   Non-operating incomes include receipt of interest, rent, dividend, profit on sale of fixed assets, etc.

Format of Profit and Loss Account

Profit and Loss Account
for the year ending…

Dr   Cr

Particulars	Amt (₹)	Particulars	Amt (₹)
To Gross Loss (transferred from trading account)*	…	By Gross Profit (transferred from trading account)*	…
To Salaries	…	By Rent Received	…
To Rent, Rates and Taxes	…	By Discount Received	…
To Stationery and Printing	…	By Commission Earned	…
To Postage and Telegrams	…	By Interest	…
To Audit Fees	…	By Bad Debts Recovered	…
To Legal Charges	…	By Income from Investment	…
To Telephone Expenses	…	By Dividends on Shares	…
To Insurance Premium	…	By Miscellaneous Revenue Gains	…
To Business Promotion Expenses	…	By Income from Any Other Sources	…
To Repairs and Renewals	…	By Net Loss (transferred to capital account)**	…
To Depreciation	…		
To Interest	…		
To Sundry Expenses	…		
To Conveyance	…		
To Bank Charges	…		

Particulars	Amt (₹)	Particulars	Amt (₹)
To Establishment Expenses	...		
To General Expenses	...		
To Car Running and Maintenance	...		
To Electricity Expenses	...		
To Loss by Fire or Theft	...		
To Commission	...		
To Advertisement	...		
To Freight and Carriage Outwards	...		
To Discount Allowed	...		
To Travelling Expenses	...		
To Bad Debts	...		
To Net Profit (transferred to capital account)**	...		
	...		...

*Either of the two will appear.   **Either of the two will appear.

Balance Sheet

The balance sheet is a statement prepared for showing the financial position of the business summarising its assets and liabilities at a given date. It is prepared at the end of the accounting period after the trading and profit and loss account have been prepared.

The assets reflect debit balances and liabilities (including capital) reflect credit balances.

It is called a balance sheet because it is a statement of balances of ledger accounts which have not been closed till the preparation of the trading and profit and loss account.

Format of Balance Sheet

Balance Sheet
as at ...

Liabilities	Amt (₹)		Assets	Amt (₹)
Sundry or Trade Creditors		...	Cash in Hand Including Petty Cash	...
Bills Payable		...	Cash at Bank	...
Bank Overdraft		...	Bills Receivable	...
Employees Provident Fund		...	Sundry Debtors/Book Debts	...
Loans (Credit)		...	Loans (Debit)	...
Mortgage		...	Closing Stock	...
Reserves or Reserve Fund		...	Loose Tools	...
Capital	...		Investments	...
(+) Interest on Capital	...		Furniture and Fittings	...
Net Profit	...		Plant and Machinery	...
(−) Drawings	(...)		Land and Building	...
Income Tax	(...)		Freehold/Leasehold Land	...
Interest on Drawings	(...)		Business Premises	...
Net Loss	(...)	...	Patents and Trademarks, etc.	...
			Goodwill	...
		...		...

Need and Importance of Preparation of Balance Sheet

- It helps to ascertain the true financial position of the business at a particular point of time.
- It helps in ascertaining the nature and cost of various assets of the business such as the amount of closing stock, amount owing from debtors, amount of fictitious assets, etc.
- It helps in determining the nature and amount of various liabilities of the business.
- It gives information about the exact amount of capital at the end of the year and the addition or deduction made from it during the course of the current year.
- It helps in finding out whether the firm is solvent or not.
- It helps in preparing the opening entries in the beginning of the next year.

Grouping and Marshalling of Assets and Liabilities

1. **Grouping of Assets and Liabilities** The term grouping means putting together items of similar nature under a common heading. The various items appearing in the balance sheet can also be properly grouped, For example, the balance of accounts of cash, bank, debtors, etc., can be grouped and shown under the heading of 'current assets'.

2. **Marshalling of Assets and Liabilities** Marshalling refers to the arrangement of assets and liabilities in a particular order. In a balance sheet, the assets and liabilities are arranged either in the order of liquidity or permanence. These are

   (i) **Order of Permanence** In case of permanence, the most permanent assets or liabilities are put on the top in a balance sheet and thereafter they are arranged in their reducing level of permanence.

   In other words, in case of assets, the ones which are to be used permanently in the business and are not meant to be sold are written first, for example, goodwill and the ones which are most liquid are written last, e.g. cash-in-hand.

   In case of liabilities, the payments to be made which are least urgent are written first, for example, capital and the payments to be made which are most urgent are written last, for example, short-term liabilities say short-term creditors (i.e., firstly capital, then long-term liabilities and at last short-term liabilities).

   (ii) **Order of Liquidity** Liquidity means the facility with which the assets may be converted into cash. In case of liquidity, the order is reversed. In case of assets, the most liquid assets are written first, for example, cash in hand and the least liquid assets are written last, for example, goodwill.

   In case of liabilities, the most urgent payments to be made are written first, for example, short-term creditors and the least urgent payments to be made are written last, for example, capital (i.e., firstly short-term liabilities, then long-term liabilities and in last capital).

   It can be better understood with the general format of balance sheet in order of liquidity given on the previous page.

Methods of Preparation of Financial Statements

The financial statements, i.e., trading and profit and loss account and balance sheet can be presented in two ways

1. **Horizontal Form** Under this form of presentation, the items are presented in 'T' shape, i.e., the items are shown side by side in trading and profit and loss account and also in the balance sheet. This form of preparing financial statements has been already discussed in the chapter.

2. **Vertical Form** Under vertical presentation, the final accounts are prepared in a form of statement, i.e., the items are presented in a single column with different items being shown one below the other in a purposeful sequence. This form is outside the scope of syllabus.

Solved Examples

Example 1. State with reasons whether following are capital or revenue expenditures.

    (i) Custom duty paid on import of a machinery.

    (ii) Wages paid in connection with the erection of a new machinery.

    (iii) ₹ 5,000 spent on repainting the factory.

    (iv) Repairs for ₹ 2,000 necessiated by negligence of an operator of an machine.

    (v) ₹ 10,000 paid for electricity bill.

Ans. (i) Custom duty paid is capital expenditure becauses it relates to acquisition of an asset.

    (ii) Wages paid for erection of a new machinery is also capital expenditure because it is related to a new asset.

    (iii) ₹ 5,000 spent on repainting is revenue expenditure as it is related to maintenance cost of factory.

    (iv) It is a revenue expenditure because repair charges will not improve the working of the machine.

    (v) It is also a revenue expenditure because it is a part of operating cost.

Example 2. Calculate net sales and gross profit from the following information. Cost of goods sold ₹ 2,00,000 gross profit 20% on sales.

Ans. If sales is ₹ 100, gross profit will be ₹ 20 and cost $= 100 - 20 = ₹ 80$

Hence, if cost of goods sold is ₹ 80, sales will be ₹ 100

If cost of goods sold is ₹ 2,00,000, sales will be $\dfrac{100}{80} \times 2,00,000 = ₹ 2,50,000$

Gross Profit = Sales – Cost of Goods Sold = 2,50,000 – 2,00,000 = ₹ 50,000

Example 3. Calculate gross profit when total purchases during the year are ₹ 8,00,000; return outwards ₹ 20,000; direct expenses ₹ 60,000 and 2/3rd of the goods are sold for ₹ 6,10,000.

Ans. Cost of Goods Sold = Total Purchases – Return Outwards + Direct Expenses

$$= 8,00,000 - 20,000 + 60,000 = ₹ 8,40,000$$

2/3rd goods sold for ₹ 6,10,000

Cost of 2/3rd goods = 8,40,000 × 2/3 = ₹ 5,60,000, Gross profit = 6,10,000 – 5,60,000 = ₹ 50,000

Example 4. From the following information, prepare trading account for the year ended 31st March, 2020, cash purchases ₹ 4,50,000; credit purchases ₹ 27,00,000; return inwards ₹ 60,000; cash sales ₹ 4,80,000; credit sales ₹ 33,00,000; return outwards ₹ 30,000; freight inwards ₹ 9,000; carriage inwards ₹ 9,000; wages and salaries ₹ 12,000; opening stock ₹ 4,50,000; closing stock ₹ 2,64,000 but its market value is ₹ 2,52,000.

Ans.

Trading Account
for the year ended 31st March, 2020

Dr   Cr

Particulars	Amt (₹)		Particulars	Amt (₹)	
To Opening Stock		4,50,000	By Sales		
To Purchases			Cash Sales	4,80,000	
Cash Purchases	4,50,000		Credit Sales	33,00,000	
Credit Purchases	27,00,000			37,80,000	
	31,50,000		(–) Return Inwards	(60,000)	37,20,000
(–) Return Outwards	(30,000)	31,20,000			

Particulars	Amt (₹)	Particulars	Amt (₹)
To Freight Inwards	9,000	By Closing Stock	2,52,000
To Carriage Inwards	9,000	(Valued at cost or market value whichever is less)	
To Wages and Salaries	12,000		
To Gross Profit transferred to Profit and Loss A/c	3,72,000		
	39,72,000		39,72,000

Example 5. Ascertain cost of goods sold and gross profit from the following.

Particulars	Amt (₹)
Opening Stock	64,000
Purchases	5,60,000
Direct Expenses	40,000
Indirect Expenses	90,000
Closing Stock	1,00,000
Sales	8,00,000
Sales Return	16,000

Ans. Cost of Goods Sold = Opening Stock + Purchases + Direct Expenses − Closing Stock

$$= 64,000 + 5,60,000 + 40,000 - 1,00,000$$

Cost of Goods Sold = ₹ 5,64,000

Gross Profit = Net Sales − Cost of Goods Sold

$$= (\text{Sales} - \text{Sales Return}) - (\text{Cost of Goods Sold})$$
$$= (8,00,000 - 16,000) - (5,64,000) = 7,84,000 - 5,64,000$$

Gross Profit = ₹ 2,20,000

Thus, Cost of Goods Sold = ₹ 5,64,000 and Gross Profit = ₹ 2,20,000

Example 6. From the following information, prepare the trading account for the year ended 31st March, 2020. Adjusted purchases ₹ 48,00,000; freight and carriage inwards ₹ 40,000; freight and carriage outwards ₹ 30,000; wages ₹ 3,36,000; octroi charges ₹ 4,000; fuel and power ₹ 60,000; office rent ₹ 36,000; trade expenses ₹ 20,000; sales ₹ 60,00,000; closing stock ₹ 3,00,000.

Ans.

Trading Account
for the year ended 31st March, 2020

Dr   Cr

Particulars	Amt (₹)	Particulars	Amt (₹)
To Adjusted Purchases	48,00,000	By Sales	60,00,000
To Freight and Carriage Inwards	40,000		
To Wages	3,36,000		
To Octroi Charges	4,000		
To Fuel and Power	60,000		
To Gross Profit transferred to Profit and Loss A/c	7,60,000		
	60,00,000		60,00,000

Note (i) Adjusted Purchases = Net Purchases + Opening Stock − Closing Stock

(ii) Closing stock has not been shown on the credit side of trading account since it has already been adjusted while computing the adjusted purchases.

(iii) Following items are not entered in the trading account because they are indirect expenses and will appear in the profit and loss account.

(a) Freight and carriage outwards   (b) Office rent   (c) Trade expenses

Example 7. Following is the trial balance of J Subramanium on 31st March, 2020. Pass the closing entries and prepare the trading and profit and loss account for the year ended 31st March, 2020 and the balance sheet as at the date.

Trial Balance
as on 31st March, 2020

Name of Account	Debit Balance (₹)	Credit Balance (₹)
Capital A/c	—	30,000
Stock A/c (1st April, 2019)	6,000	—
Cash at Bank	3,000	—
Cash in Hand	1,320	—
Machinery A/c	18,000	—
Furniture and Fittings A/c	4,080	—
Purchases A/c	45,000	—
Wages A/c	30,000	—
Fuel and Power A/c	9,000	—
Factory Lighting A/c	600	—
Salaries A/c	21,000	—
Discount Allowed A/c	1,500	—
Discount Received A/c	—	900
Advertising A/c	15,000	—
Sundry Office Expenses A/c	12,000	—
Sales A/c	—	1,50,000
Sundry Debtors	25,500	—
Sundry Creditors	—	11,100
Total	**1,92,000**	**1,92,000**

Value of closing stock as on 31st March, 2020 was ₹ 8,100.

Ans.

JOURNAL

Date	Particulars	LF	Amt (Dr)	Amt (Cr)
2020 Mar 31	Trading A/c Dr		90,600	
	To Stock A/c			6,000
	To Purchases A/c			45,000
	To Wages A/c			30,000
	To Fuel and Power A/c			9,000
	To Factory Lighting A/c			600
	(Being the accounts in the trial balance which have to be transferred to the trading account, debit side are transferred)			
Mar 31	Sales A/c Dr		1,50,000	
	To Trading A/c			1,50,000
	(Being the amount of sales transferred to the credit of the trading account)			
Mar 31	Closing Stock A/c Dr		8,100	
	To Trading A/c			8,100
	(Being the value of stock on hand on 31st March, 2020)			
Mar 31	Trading A/c Dr		67,500	
	To Profit and Loss A/c			67,500
	(Being the transfer of gross profit)			

Date	Particulars		LF	Amt (Dr)	Amt (Cr)
Mar 31	Profit and Loss A/c	Dr		49,500	
	To Discount Allowed A/c				1,500
	To Salaries A/c				21,000
	To Advertising A/c				15,000
	To Sundry Office Expenses A/c				12,000
	(Being the various expenses accounts transferred to the debit of the profit and loss account)				
Mar 31	Discount Received A/c	Dr		900	
	To Profit and Loss A/c				900
	(Being the credit balance of discount received transferred to the profit and loss account)				
Mar 31	Profit and Loss A/c	Dr		18,900	
	To Capital A/c				18,900
	(Being the net profit transferred to the capital account)				

Trading and Profit and Loss Account

Dr   for the year ended 31st March, 2020   Cr

Particulars	Amt (₹)	Particulars	Amt (₹)
To Stock	6,000	By Sales	1,50,000
To Purchases	45,000	By Closing Stock	8,100
To Wages	30,000		
To Fuel and Power	9,000		
To Factory Lighting	600		
To Gross Profit transferred to Profit and Loss A/c	67,500		
	1,58,100		1,58,100
To Salaries	21,000	By Gross Profit transferred from Trading A/c	67,500
To Discount Allowed	1,500	By Discount Received	900
To Advertising	15,000		
To Sundry Office Expenses	12,000		
To Net Profit transferred to Capital A/c	18,900		
	68,400		68,400

Balance Sheet
as on 31st March, 2020

Liabilities		Amt (₹)	Assets	Amt (₹)
Capital	30,000		Closing Stock	8,100
(+) Net Profit	18,900	48,900	Cash at Bank	3,000
Sundry Creditors		11,100	Cash in Hand	1,320
			Machinery A/c	18,000
			Furniture and Fittings A/c	4,080
			Sundry Debtors	25,500
		60,000		60,000

Chapter Practice

Objective Questions

• Multiple Choice Questions

1. The financial statements consist of
(a) trial balance   (b) profit and loss account   (c) balance sheet   (d) Both (b) and (c)

Ans. (d) Both (b) and (c)

2. Match the following.

Column I	Column II
A. Loss by Theft	(i) Net Sales – Cost of Goods Sold
B. Dock Charges	(ii) Indirect Expenses shown to Debit of Proft and Loss Account
C. Oprating Profit	(iii) Direct Expense shown to Debit of Trading Account
D. Gross Profit	(iv) Net Sales – Operating Cost

Codes

	A	B	C	D			A	B	C	D
(a)	(iii)	(ii)	(iv)	(i)		(b)	(ii)	(iii)	(iv)	(i)
(c)	(ii)	(iii)	(i)	(iv)		(d)	(iii)	(ii)	(i)	(iv)

Ans. (b) (ii) (iii) (iv) (i)

3. Profit and loss account is prepared ………. .
(a) for the whole year   (b) for a particular period   (c) on a particular date   (d) None of these

Ans. (b) Profit and loss account relates to a particular period and is prepared at the end of that period. It shows the performance of the business during an accounting period.

4. Ram is the owner of a firm. He brought additional capital of ₹ 1,00,000 to the firm. The receipt of money in business is ………. .
(a) revenue receipt   (b) capital receipt   (c) revenue expenditure   (d) capital expenditure

Ans. (b) If the receipts imply an obligation to return the money, these are capital receipt.

5. Choose the correct chronological order of ascertainment of the following profits from the profit and loss.
(a) Operating Profit, Net Profit, Gross Profit   (b) Operating Profit, Gross Profit, Net Profit
(c) Gross Profit, Operating Profit, Net Profit   (d) Gross Profit, Net Profit, Operating Profit

Ans. (c) Following is the sequence of knowing the profitability
- Gross profit by preparing trading account.
- Operating profit by deducting operating expenses from gross profit.
- Net profit after deducting non-operating expenses from operating profit and adding non-operating income.

6. Liability which is payable on the happening of an event is

(a) contingent liability   (b) fluctuating liability   (c) current liability   (d) None of these

Ans. (a) Liabilities in respect of bill discounted, guarantee for a loan or disputed claims are the examples of contingent liabilities. These liabilities are payable on the happening of an event or contingency in future.

7. Capital expenditure .... the earning capacity or .... the operating expenses of a business.

(a) increases, reduces   (b) reduces, increases   (c) maintain, reduces   (d) reduces, maintain

Ans. (a) increases, reduces

8. Depreciation or the expired cost of fixed assets will be

(a) revenue expenditure   (b) capital expenditure
(c) deferred revenue expenditure   (d) None of these

Ans. (a) Revenue expenditure is an expenditure, the benefit of which is consumed within the accounting period. It is treated as an expense of the current year.

9. On which assumption the expenditure is classified as capital and revenue expenditure?

(a) Going concern assumption   (b) Accrual assumption
(c) Money measurement assumption   (d) Consistency assumption

Ans. (a) Going concern assumption

10. While calculating operating profit, the following are not taken into account   **(NCERT)**

(a) normal transactions   (b) abnormal items
(c) expenses of a purely financial nature   (d) Both (b) and (c)

Ans. (d) Operating profit means profit from operating activities of the business. Operating activities are the principal revenue producing activities of the enterprise and are those activities that are not investing or financing activities. That's why we will ignore abnormal items and expenses of a purely financial nature.
Operating Profit = Gross Profit – Operating Expenses

11. Which of the following is correct?

(a) Net Sales = Cash Sales + Credit Sales – Sales Return
(b) Net Sales = Cash Sales + Credit Sales + Sales Return
(c) Net Sales = Total Sales – Credit Sales
(d) Net Sales = Sales + Credit Sales

Ans. (a) Net Sales = Cash Sales + Credit Sales – Sales Return

12. Consider the following statement.

(i) Balance sheet contains only the balances of personal and real accounts.

(ii) Assets side of balance sheet is always equal to capital side.

(iii) Drawings are not shown in the balance sheet as it is a personal expense of the owner.

Alternatives

(a) Only (i) is correct   (b) Only (ii) and (iii) is correct
(c) All are correct   (d) All are incorrect

Ans. (a) Asset side of balance sheet is always equal to liabilities side of balance sheet.

Drawings are deducted from capital after adding net profit in balance sheet.

13. Which of the following statement(s) is/are true?

(i) Revenue expenditure gives benefit within the accounting period.

(ii) Revenue expenditures are non-recurring in nature.

Alternatives

(a) Both (i) and (ii)   (b) Only (i)   (c) Only (ii)   (d) Neither (i) nor (ii)

Ans. (b) Revenue expenditures are recurring in nature. The benefit of revenue expenditures expire within a financial year.

14. Operating profit earned by Harshad Mehta in 2020-21 was ₹ 8,50,000. His non-operating incomes were ₹ 75,000 and non-operating expenses were ₹ 1,87,500. Calculate the profit earned during the year.

(a) ₹ 7,37,500 (b) ₹ 9,62,500 (c) ₹ 5,87,500 (d) ₹ 11,12,500

Ans. (a) Net Profit = Operating Profit − Non-operating Expenses + Non-Operating Income

$$= 8,50,000 - 1,87,500 + 75,000 = ₹\ 7,37,500$$

15. Opening Stock = ₹ 9,60,000

Purchases = ₹ 27,20,000

Sales = ₹ 39,00,000

Gross Profit is 30% on cost

Which of the following will be the amount of closing stock?

(a) ₹ 7,80,000 (b) ₹ 6,80,000 (c) ₹ 47,60,000 (d) ₹ 12,40,000

Ans. (b) Let CoGS be x

$$\text{Sales} = \text{CoGS} + \text{Gross Profit}$$

$$39,00,000 = x + \frac{30}{100} \times x$$

$$39,00,000 = x + 0.3x$$

$$\Rightarrow \qquad x = ₹\ 30,00,000$$

Thus, CoGS is ₹ 30,00,000

$$\text{CoGS} = \text{Opening Stock} + \text{Purchases} + \text{Direct Expenses} - \text{Closing Stock}$$

$$30,00,000 = 9,60,000 + 27,20,000 - \text{Closing stock}$$

$$\Rightarrow \qquad \text{Closing Stock} = ₹\ 6,80,000$$

• Assertion-Reasoning MCQs

Directions *(Q. Nos 1 to 6) There are the two statements marked as Assertion (A) and Reason (R). Read the statements and choose the appropriate option from the options given below.*

(a) Assertion (A) is correct, but Reason (R) is wrong (b) Both Assertion (A) and Reason (R) are correct

(c) Assertion (A) is wrong, but Reason (R) is correct (d) Both Assertion (A) and Reason (R) are wrong

1. **Assertion** (A) Warehousing expenses, export duties, royalty, etc are shown to debit side of trading account.

Reason (R) Direct expenses are shown to debit side of trading account.

Ans. (c) Warehousing expenses, export duties are indirect expenses and are shown in profit and loss account.

2. **Assertion** (A) ₹ 10,000 spent on installing the machine is capital expenditure.

Reason (R) Capital expenditure increase the value of fixed assets and its benefits extend upto one accounting period.

Ans. (a) ₹ 10,000 is capital expenditure asset as it is related to making the machine ready to use. Capital expenditure give benefits which extend to more than one accounting period.

3. **Assertion** (A) Advertising, packing expenses, interest paid on loan, legal expenses are shown to debit side of profit and loss account.

Reason (R) All indirect expenses are shown to debit side of profit and loss account.

Ans. (b) Indirect expenses are transferred to debit side of the profit and loss account while all the gains are transferred to credit side of profit and loss account.

4. Assertion (A) Loan taken by Anuj Enterprises from SBI is revenue receipt.

Reason (R) Revenue receipts are those receipts which arise in normal course of business.

Ans. (c) Revenue receipts are of recurring nature. Thus, loan taken by Anuj Enterprises is capital receipt.

5. Assertion (A) Heavy advertising to launch a new product is deferred revenue expenditure.

Reason (R) Deferred revenue expenditure is a revenue expenditure that is incurred during an accounting period but its benefit extends beyond that accounting period.

Ans. (b) Amount spent on advertising will give benefits beyond the accounting period in which it is incurred.

6. Assertion (A) Closing stock is valued at cost or net realisable value whichever is higher.

Reason (R) According to conservatism principle, all prospective losses are taken into consideration but not the prospective profits.

Ans. (c) According to prudence or conservatism, closing stock is valued at cost or net realisable value whichever is lower.

• Case Based MCQs

1. Direction *Read the following case study and answer the question no. (i) to (iv) on the basis of the same.*

Shamita studies in class 11th in Happy Public School. She comes from a CA family. She has two CA sisters and her father CA Arjun owns his firm at Darya Ganj.

She spent most of her day reading novels and devote very less hours for study. As a result, she scored very less marks in Ist term exam in accountancy. Ms Ritika Sachdeva, her accountancy teacher has now decided to give remedial classes to all weak students. Her father is also giving his time to teach her. One day, her teacher introduced the chapter financial statements in class but Shamita found it very hard. She asked her sister CA Isha to teach her financial statements. Isha showed financial statements of their father's firm which aroused her curiosity. She even grasped the concept quickly of trading account, profit and loss account and balance sheet.

Isha realised that Shamita can only progress if she is shown visual aids, real objects, things, etc. She teaches her with this method and is successful as Shamita got good marks.

(i) What is prepared in sole proprietorship business with the objective of calculating gross profit or gross loss of the business?

   (a) Trading account   (b) Profit and loss account   (c) Balance sheet   (d) None of these

Ans. (a) Trading account

(ii) Freight inward of ₹ 5,600 is outstanding at the end of year. Where it is recorded in final accounts?

   (a) Trading account and balance sheet   (b) Profit and loss account and balance sheet

   (c) Trading account and profit and loss account   (d) Trading account (debit) and balance sheet (assets)

Ans. (a) It is a direct expense and liability for business

(iii) Trading account is a

   (a) personal account   (b) real account   (c) nominal account   (d) asset account

Ans. (c) Trading account is a nominal account which is prepared at the end of accounting year. It helps to find out gross profit or gross loss during the accounting period.

All direct expenses are debited and all direct incomes are credited in trading account.

(iv) Closing stock is given outside of the trial balance with book value ₹ 60,000 and market value of ₹ 80,000 as on 31st March, 2020. It will be recorded in balance sheet at which amount?

   (a) ₹ 60,000   (b) ₹ 80,000   (c) ₹ 20,000   (d) ₹ 1,40,000

Ans. (a) Closing stock is shown at market value or net realisable value whichever is lower.

2. Direction *Read the following case study and answer the question no. (i) to (iv) on the basis of the same.*

Aditi is an engineer, who is working as a content developer and educator at ABC Limited. Along with her job, she is also preparing for various competitive exams.

During weekend, Aditi was studying about financial statements. After doing all the theory, she tried to attempt a question but she got struck as her balance sheet total didn't agree. Immediately, she called her friend Shweta and asked her to find her mistakes.

Shweta found her conceptual errors and also sent her correct solution for the same.

Following trading account and profit and loss account as on 31st March, 2020 and balance sheet as at that date were prepared by Aditi from the balances as on 31st March, 2020 given in her book.

Question given in Aditi's book

From the following balances, as on 31st March, 2020, prepare trading and profit and loss account and the balance sheet.

Particulars	Amt (₹)	Particulars	Amt (₹)
Capital Account	50,000	Return Outwards	2,500
Plant and Machinery	20,000	Rent	2,000
Sundry Debtors	12,000	Sales	82,000
Sundry Creditors	6,000	Manufacturing Expenses	4,000
Drawings	6,000	Trade Expenses	3,500
Purchases	52,500	Bad Debts	1,000
Wages	25,000	Carriage	750
Bank	5,000	Bills Payable	3,500
Repairs	250	Return Inwards	2,000
Stock (1st April, 2019)	10,000		

Closing stock (31st March, 2020) was valued at ₹ 7,250.

Trading Account

Dr
for the year ended 31st March, 2020
Cr

Particulars	Amt (₹)	Particulars	Amt (₹)
To Opening Stock	10,000	By Sales (82,000 − 2,000)	80,000
To Net Purchases (52,500 − 2,500)	50,000	By Closing Stock	7,250
To Wages	25,000	By Gross Loss	5,250
To Manufacturing Expenses	4,000		
To Trade Expenses	3,500		
	92,500		92,500

Profit and Loss Account

Dr
for the year ended 31st March, 2020
Cr

Particulars	Amt (₹)	Particulars	Amt (₹)
To Gross Loss	5,250	By Net Loss	9,250
To Repairs	250		
To Rent	2,000		
To Bad Debts	1,000		
To Carriage	750		
	9,250		9,250

Balance Sheet
as on 31st March, 2020

Liabilities		Amt (₹)	Assets	Amt (₹)
Capital	50,000		Plant and Machinery	20,000
(−) Net Loss	(9,250)		Sundry Debtors	12,000
Drawing	(6,000)	34,750		
Sundry Creditors		6,000		
Bills Payable		3,500		
		44,250		32,000

(i) Which of the following is correct amount of gross profit/gross loss?

    (a) Gross profit ₹ 2,500   (b) Gross loss ₹ 2,500   (c) Gross profit ₹ 5,000   (d) Gross loss ₹ 5,000

Ans. (b)

Trading Account

Dr   for the year ended 31st March, 2020   Cr

Particulars	Amt (₹)	Particulars	Amt (₹)
To Opening Stock	10,000	By Net Sales	80,000
To Net Purchases	50,000	By Closing Stock	7,250
To Wages	25,000	By Gross Loss	2,500
To Manufacturing Expenses	4,000		
To Carriage	750		
	89,750		89,750

(ii) Which of the undermentioned net profit/net loss is correct?

    (a) Net loss ₹ 9,250   (b) Net profit ₹ 9,250   (c) Net profit ₹ 10,000   (d) Net loss ₹ 10,000

Ans. (a)

Profit and Loss Account

Dr   for the year ended 31st March, 2020   Cr

Particulars	Amt (₹)	Particulars	Amt (₹)
To Gross Loss	2,500	By Net Loss	9,250
To Repairs	250		
To Trade Expenses	3,500		
To Bad Debts	1,000		
To Rent	2,000		
	9,250		9,250

(iii) Total of balance sheet is ....

    (a) ₹ 94,250   (b) ₹ 44,250   (c) ₹ 84,250   (d) ₹ 74,250

Ans. (b)

Balance Sheet
as on 31st March, 2020

Liabilities		Amt (₹)	Liabilities	Amt (₹)
Capital	50,000		Closing stock	7,250
(−) Net Loss	(9,250)		Sundry Debtors	12,000
Drawings	(6,000)	34,750	Plant and Machinery	20,000
Sundry Creditors		6,000	Bank	5,000
Bills Payable		3,500		
		44,250		44,250

(iv) Opening Stock + Purchases – Purchases Return + Direct Expenses – Closing Stock = ...

    (a) Cost of Raw Material   (b) Gross Profit   (c) Closing Capital   (d) Cost of Goods Sold

Ans. (d) Cost of Goods Sold

PART 2
Subjective Questions

• Short Answer (SA) Type Questions

1. What are financial statements and what information is provided by them?   **(NCERT)**

Ans. Financial statements are the final/end products of an accounting process, which begins with the identification of accounting information and recording it in the books of primary entry.

Financial statements are prepared following the accounting concepts and conventions. These statements are prepared at the end of accounting period and give information about the financial position and performance of an enterprise.

Trading and profit and loss account present a true and fair view of the financial performance of the business in the form of profit and loss during the year. Balance sheet presents a true and fair view of the financial position of the business.

2. What are the objectives of preparing financial statements?   **(NCERT)**

Ans. The basic objectives of preparing financial statements are

    (i) To present a true and fair view of the working of the business.

    (ii) To help to judge the effectiveness of the management.

    (iii) To provide sufficient and reliable information to various users interested in financial statements.

    (iv) To facilitate efficient allocation of resources.

    (v) To disclose various accounting policies.

    (vi) To provide information about the cash flows.

    (vii) To provide information about the earning capacity.

    (viii) To provide financial data on assets (economic resources) and liabilities (obligations) of an enterprise.

3. What are the features of a trading account?

Ans. Features of trading account are

    (i) Trading account is the first stage in the preparation of final accounts.

    (ii) It provides information about gross profit and gross loss.

    (iii) Balance of trading account is transferred to profit and loss account.

    (iv) Trading account is a nominal account.

    (v) Trading account relates to a particular accounting period and is prepared at the end of that period.

    (vi) Trading account records only revenue items and not capital items.

4. Discuss the need of preparing a balance sheet.   **(NCERT)**

Ans. The need and importance of preparing a balance sheet is stated in the following points

    (i) It helps to ascertain the true financial position of the business at a particular point of time.

    (ii) It helps in ascertaining the nature and cost of various assets of the business such as the amount of closing stock, amount owing from debtors, amount of fictitious assets, etc.

    (iii) It helps in determining the nature and amount of various liabilities of the business.

    (iv) It gives information about the exact amount of capital at the end of the year and the addition or deduction made into it in the current year.

    (v) It helps in finding out whether the firm is solvent or not. The firm is solvent if the assets exceed the external liabilities. It would be insolvent if opposite is the case.

    (vi) It helps in preparing the opening entries at the beginning of the next year.

5. Distinguish between capital receipts and revenue receipts.

Ans. The differences between capital receipts and revenue receipts are

Basis	Capital Receipts	Revenue Receipts
Meaning	The amount received in form of capital introduced, loans taken and sale proceeds of the fixed assets is known as capital receipts.	The amount received mainly by selling of goods and services is known as revenue receipts.
Nature	Capital receipts are capital in nature.	Revenue receipts are revenue (i.e., day-to-day activities) in nature.
Shown	Capital receipts are shown on the liabilities side of balance sheet.	Revenue receipts are shown on the credit of either trading account or profit and loss account.
Examples	Sale of fixed assets, capital contribution and loans taken, etc., are some examples of capital receipts.	Profit on sale of assets, sale of goods, interest received on loans (advanced), royalty, etc., are some examples of revenue receipts.

6. State whether the following statements are items of capital or revenue expenditure, with reason.
   (i) Expenditure incurred on repairs and white washing at the time of purchase of an old building in order to make it usable.
   (ii) Registration fees paid at the time of purchase of a building.
   (iii) Depreciation on plant and machinery.

Ans. (i) **Capital Expenditure** Any expenditure on purchase of an asset to make it usable is capital expenditure.
   (ii) **Capital Expenditure** Registration fee is part of cost of an asset.
   (iii) **Revenue Expenditure** Depreciation is charged on yearly basis throughout the life of an asset.

7. Calculate gross profit from the following.

Opening Stock	₹ 20,000	Purchases	₹ 3,50,000
Carriage on Purchases	₹ 3,000	Closing Stock	₹ 90,000
Sales	₹ 6,50,000	Office Rent	₹ 15,000
Carriage on Sales	₹ 6,000	Return Inward	₹ 10,000

Ans. Cost of Goods Sold (CoGS) = Opening Stock + Purchases − Purchase Return + Direct Expenses − Closing Stock

$$= 20,000 + 3,50,000 + 3,000 - 90,000 = 3,73,000 - 90,000 = ₹\,2,83,000$$

Where, carriage on purchases is direct expense.

$$\text{Gross Profit} = \text{Net Sales} - \text{CoGS} = \text{Sales} - \text{Sales Return} - \text{CoGS}$$
$$= 6,50,000 - 10,000 - 2,83,000 = ₹\,3,57,000$$

8. Calculate the amount of gross profit and operating profit on the basis of the following balances extracted from the books of M/s Rajiv and Sons for the year ended 31st March, 2020.

Particulars	Amt (₹)
Opening Stock	1,50,000
Net Sales	33,00,000
Net Purchases	18,00,000
Direct Expenses	1,80,000
Administration Expenses	1,35,000
Selling and Distribution Expenses	1,95,000
Loss due to Fire	60,000
Closing Stock	2,10,000

Ans.

Trading Account

Dr   for the year ending 31st March, 2020   Cr

Particulars	Amt (₹)	Particulars	Amt (₹)
To Opening Stock A/c	1,50,000	By Sales A/c	33,00,000
To Purchases A/c	18,00,000	By Closing Stock A/c	2,10,000
To Direct Expenses A/c	1,80,000		
To Gross Profit (Balancing figure)	13,80,000		
	35,10,000		35,10,000

$$\text{Operating Profit} = \text{Gross Profit} - (\text{Operating Expenses* } + \text{Operating Income})$$
$$= 13,80,000 - (3,30,000 + 0) = ₹\,10,50,000$$

Note *(i) Loss due to fire is a non-operating expense.*

*(ii) *Operating Expenses = Administration Expenses + Selling and Distribution Expenses = 1,35,000 + 1,95,000 = ₹ 3,30,000*

9. Calculate the gross profit from the following for 50% goods sold. Total purchases during the current year are ₹ 9,00,000, Return outward ₹ 50,000, Lighting ₹ 30,000, Wages ₹ 80,000 and Electricity ₹ 8,000 and 1/2nd goods are sold for ₹ 8,00,000.

Ans. Cost of Goods Sold (CoGS) = Opening Stock + Total Purchases − Return Outward + Direct Expenses
$$- \text{Closing Stock}$$
$$= 0 + 9,00,000 - 50,000 + (30,000 + 80,000) - 0$$
$$= 8,50,000 + 1,10,000 = ₹\,9,60,000$$
$$\text{1/2nd value of CoGS} = 9,60,000 \times 1/2 = ₹\,4,80,000$$
Gross Profit (for 1/2nd goods only) = Value of Sales (for half goods) − Half value of CoGS
Gross Profit (for 1/2nd goods only) = 8,00,000 − 4,80,000
$$= ₹\,3,20,000$$

10. Calculate closing stock from the following details.

Particulars	Amt (₹)
Opening Stock	20,000
Cash Sales	60,000
Purchases	70,000
Credit Sales	40,000

Rate of gross profit on cost $33\frac{1}{3}\%$.

Ans. Total Sales = Cash Sales + Credit Sales = 60,000 + 40,000

∴   Total Sales = ₹ 1,00,000

Gross Profit is $\dfrac{100}{3}\%$ on cost.

Let cost be x

∴ $$\text{Gross Profit} = x \times \frac{100}{300} = \frac{x}{3}$$

$$\text{Sales} = \text{Cost} + \text{Gross Profit} \Rightarrow 1,00,000 = x + \frac{x}{3} \Rightarrow \frac{4x}{3} = 1,00,000$$

∴ $$(\text{Cost})\, x = \frac{1,00,000}{4} \times 3 = ₹\,75,000$$

Cost = Opening Stock + Purchases + Direct Expenses − Closing Stock

⇒   Closing Stock = Opening Stock + Purchases + Direct Expenses − Cost
$$= 20,000 + 70,000 + \text{Nil} - 75,000 = ₹\,15,000$$

11. Calculate opening stock from the following details

Particulars	Amt (₹)
Closing Stock	20,000
Cash Sales	60,000
Net Purchases	70,000
Net Credit Sales	40,000
Return Outward	5,000
Return Inward	7,000

Rate of gross profit on cost $33\dfrac{1}{3}\%$.

Ans. Net Sales = Cost of Goods Sold (CoGS) + Gross Profit (GP)

Cash Sales + Net Credit Sales = CoGS + GP

$$60,000 + 40,000 = x + x \times \dfrac{1}{3} \qquad\qquad \left[\because 33\dfrac{1}{3}\% = \dfrac{1}{3}\right]$$

$$1,00,000 = x + \dfrac{x}{3} \quad\Rightarrow\quad 1,00,000 = \dfrac{3x + x}{3} = \dfrac{4x}{3} \quad\Rightarrow\quad x = \dfrac{1,00,000 \times 3}{4} = 75,000$$

$$\text{CoGS} = \text{Opening Stock} + \text{Net Purchases} + \text{Direct Expenses} - \text{Closing Stock}$$

$$75,000 = \text{Opening Stock} + 70,000 + 0 - 20,000$$

$$\therefore \qquad 75,000 - 50,000 = \text{Opening Stock}$$

$$\therefore \qquad \text{Opening Stock} = ₹\,25,000$$

12. From the following information, find cost of goods sold and net sales.

Particulars	Amt (₹)	Particulars	Amt (₹)
Opening Stock	3,00,000	Wages	6,000
Purchases	8,40,000	Freight	10,800
Closing Stock	2,40,000	Carriage Inwards	3,000

The percentage of gross profit on sales is 20%.

Ans.

Calculation of Cost of Goods Sold	Amt (₹)
Opening Stock	3,00,000
(+) Purchases	8,40,000
Wages	6,000
Freight	10,800
Carriage Inwards	3,000
	11,59,800
(–) Closing Stock	(2,40,000)
Cost of Goods Sold	9,19,800

Calculation of Net Sales

Let sales = 100, gross profit will be = ₹ 20.

Therefore, cost of sales will be = 100 – 20 = ₹ 80.

When cost of sales is 80, then sales =100.

When cost of sales is 1, then sales = 100/ 80.

When cost of sales is ₹ 9,19,800, then sales = 100 / 80 × 9,19,800 = ₹ 11,49,750

13. Trading account of M/s Volvoline Technologies is given below

Trading Account

Dr — for the year ended 31st December, 2020 — Cr

Particulars	Amt (₹)	Particulars	Amt (₹)
To Opening Stock	3,37,500	By Net Sales	12,82,500
To Net Purchases	5,12,500	By Closing Stock	2,67,500
To Wages and Salaries	1,57,500		
To Freight Inwards	33,500		
To Other Direct Expenses	60,000		
To Gross Profit c/d	4,49,000		
	15,50,000		15,50,000

Pass closing journal entries on the basis of the above trading account. Also, transfer the gross profit to profit and loss account.

Ans.

JOURNAL

Date	Particulars	LF	Amt (Dr)	Amt (Cr)
	Trading A/c Dr		11,01,000	
	To Opening Stock A/c			3,37,500
	To Net Purchases A/c			5,12,500
	To Wages and Salaries A/c			1,57,500
	To Freight Inwards A/c			33,500
	To Other Direct Expenses A/c			60,000
	(Being the opening stock, net purchases, wages and salaries, freight inwards and other direct expenses transferred to trading account)			
	Net Sales A/c Dr		12,82,500	
	Closing Stock A/c Dr		2,67,500	
	To Trading A/c			15,50,000
	(Being the net sales and closing stock transferred to trading account)			
	Trading A/c Dr		4,49,000	
	To Profit and Loss A/c			4,49,000
	(Being the gross profit transferred to profit and loss account)			

14. From the following information, prepare trading account for the year ended 31st March, 2020.

Particulars	Amt (₹)
Cost of Goods Sold	45,00,000
Sales	72,00,000
Closing Stock	2,40,000
Wages	25,000

Ans.

Trading Account

Dr   for the year ended 31st March, 2020   Cr

Particulars	Amt (₹)	Particulars	Amt (₹)
To Cost of Goods Sold	45,00,000	By Sales	72,00,000
To Gross Profit Transferred to			
Profit and Loss A/c	27,00,000		
	72,00,000		72,00,000

Note *Wages has not been shown on the debit side and closing stock has not been shown on the credit side of the trading account because it has already been adjusted while calculating the cost of goods sold.*

15. From the following details, calculate operating profit.

Particulars	Amt (₹)
Net Profit	2,00,000
Rent Received	20,000
Gain on Sale of Machine	30,000
Interest on Loan	40,000
Donation	4,000

Ans. Net Profit = Operating Profit − Non-operating Expenses + Non-operating Income

Net Profit = Operating Profit − (Interest on Loan + Donation) + (Rent Received + Gain on Sale of Machine)

2,00,000 = Operating Profit − (40,000 + 4,000) + (20,000 + 30,000)

2,00,000 = Operating Profit − 44,000 + 50,000

Operating Profit = 2,00,000 − 6,000

∴ Operating Profit = ₹ 1,94,000

16. Calculate gross profit, operating profit and net profit from the following.

Particulars	Amt (₹)	Particulars	Amt (₹)
Opening Stock	4,00,000	Commission Paid	4,800
Purchases	38,00,000	Commission Received	12,000
Sales	50,00,000	Travelling Expenses	9,600
Purchases Return	1,40,000	Office Expenses	7,000
Sales Return	2,00,000	Interest on Long-term Loans	44,000
Wages	1,60,000	Dividend on Investments	5,600
Advertising	24,000	Printing and Stationery	7,200
Salaries	3,56,000	Loss on Sale of Machinery	70,000
Rent and Taxes	1,24,000	Carriage Outwards	2,800
Lighting	30,000	Loss by Theft	50,200
		Gain on Sale of Building	1,00,000

Closing stock was valued at ₹ 5,00,000.

Ans.

Trading and Profit and Loss Account
Dr   for the year ended ....   Cr

Particulars	Amt (₹)	Particulars		Amt (₹)
To Opening Stock	4,00,000	By Sales	50,00,000	
To Purchases 38,00,000		(−) Sales Return	(2,00,000)	48,00,000
(−) Purchases Return (1,40,000)	36,60,000	By Closing Stock		5,00,000
To Wages	1,60,000			
To Gross Profit Transferred to Profit and Loss A/c	10,80,000			
	53,00,000			53,00,000
To Advertising	24,000	By Gross Profit b/d		10,80,000
To Salaries	3,56,000	By Commission Received		12,000
To Rent and Taxes	1,24,000			
To Lighting	30,000			
To Commission Paid	4,800			
To Travelling Expenses	9,600			
To Office Expenses	7,000			
To Printing and Stationery	7,200			
To Carriage Outwards	2,800			
To Operating Profit c/d	5,26,600			
	10,92,000			10,92,000
To Interest on Long-term Loans	44,000	By Operating Profit b/d		5,26,600
To Loss on Sale of Machinery	70,000	By Dividend on Investments		5,600
To Loss by Theft	50,200	By Gain on Sale of Building		1,00,000
To Net Profit Transferred to Capital A/c	4,68,000			
	6,32,200			6,32,200

17. From the following information, prepare a balance sheet of Mr Raghav as at 31st March, 2021. (i) in order of permanence (ii) in order of liquidity. (either of two methods can come in 4 marks)

Particulars	Amt (₹)	Particulars	Amt (₹)
Plant and Machinery	2,00,000	Furniture and Fixtures	40,000
Prepaid Expenses	2,000	Accrued Income	4,000
Income Received in Advance	4,000	Outstanding Expenses	2,000
Bills Payable	6,000	Bills Receivables	4,000
Sundry Debtors	2,00,000	Sundry Creditors	1,98,000
Bank Overdraft	20,000	Investments in Shares of X Ltd.	20,000
Long-term Loan from Bank	2,00,000	Closing Stock	1,70,000
Capital	4,00,000	Building	2,00,000
Land	20,000	Goodwill	20,000
Drawings	20,000	Net Profit	1,20,000
Cash in Hand	10,000	Cash at Bank	38,000
Income Tax Paid	2,000		

Ans. (i)

Balance Sheet
as at 31st March, 2021

Liabilities	Amt (₹)		Assets	Amt (₹)
Capital			**Fixed Assets**	
Opening Balance	4,00,000		Goodwill	20,000
(+) Net Profit	1,20,000		Land	20,000
	5,20,000		Building	2,00,000
(−) Drawings	(20,000)		Plant and Machinery	2,00,000
(−) Income Tax	(2,000)	4,98,000	Furniture and Fixtures	40,000
Long-term Liabilities			**Investments**	
Long-term Loan		2,00,000	Shares of Raghav Ltd.	20,000
Current Liabilities			**Current Assets**	
Income Received-in-Advance		4,000	Closing Stock	1,70,000
Sundry Creditors		1,98,000	Accrued Income	4,000
Outstanding Expenses		2,000	Prepaid Expenses	2,000
Bills Payable		6,000	Sundry Debtors	2,00,000
Bank Overdraft		20,000	Bills Receivable	4,000
			Cash at Bank	38,000
			Cash in Hand	10,000
		9,28,000		9,28,000

(ii)

Balance Sheet
as at 31st March, 2021

Liabilities	Amt (₹)		Assets	Amt (₹)
Current Liabilities			**Current Assets**	
Bank Overdraft		20,000	Cash in Hand	10,000
Bills Payable		6,000	Cash at Bank	38,000
Outstanding Expenses		2,000	Bills Receivable	4,000
Sundry Creditors		1,98,000	Sundry Debtors	2,00,000
Income Received in Advance		4,000	Prepaid Expenses	2,000
Long-term Liabilities			Accrued Income	4,000
Long-term Loan		2,00,000	Closing Stock	1,70,000
Capital			**Investments**	
Opening Balance	4,00,000		Shares of Raghav Ltd.	20,000
(+) Net Profit	1,20,000		**Fixed Assets**	
	5,20,000		Furniture and Fixtures	40,000
(−) Drawings	(20,000)		Plant and Machinery	2,00,000
(−) Income Tax	(2,000)	4,98,000	Building	2,00,000
			Land	20,000
			Goodwill	20,000
		9,28,000		9,28,000

• Long Answer (LA) Type Questions

1. What is a balance sheet? What are its characteristics?   (NCERT)

Ans. The balance sheet is a statement prepared for showing the financial position of the business summarising its assets and liabilities at a given date. It is prepared at the end of the accounting period after the trading and profit and loss account have been prepared. The assets reflect debit balances and liabilities (including capital) reflect credit balances.

It is called a balance sheet because it is a statement of balances of ledger accounts which have not been closed till the preparation of the trading and profit and loss account.

Features/Characteristics of balance sheet are as follows

   (i) Balance sheet is prepared at a particular point of time and not for a particular period.

  (ii) It is only a statement and not an account.

 (iii) It is prepared after the preparation of trading and profit and loss account.

 (iv) It shows the financial position of the business.

  (v) It is a summary of balances of those ledger accounts which have not been closed by transferring to the trading and profit and loss account.

 (vi) It shows the nature and value of assets.

(vii) It shows the nature and amount of liabilities.

(viii) The total of assets side must be equal to the liabilities side.

2. Distinguish between profit and loss account and balance sheet.

Ans. The differences between profit and loss account and balance sheet are

Basis	Profit and Loss Account	Balance Sheet
Types of Account	Only nominal accounts are entered in profit and loss account.	It records personal and real accounts.
Objective	The objective of preparing profit and loss account is to ascertain the net profit or loss of the business.	The purpose of preparing balance sheet is to understand the financial position of the firm.
Sides	The left hand side of the profit and loss account is the debit and the right hand side is credit.	It has liabilities at its left hand side and assets at right hand side.
Nature	Profit and loss account is an account. We use the word 'To' before accounts at the debit side and 'By' at the credit side.	Balance sheet is not an account, it is a statement. We do not use 'To' or 'By' in it.
Specific Date/Period	Profit and loss account shows the performance of the accounting period, generally a year.	Balance sheet shows the position of assets and liabilities on a particular date.
Types of Expenditure	Revenue expenditure is recorded in the profit and loss account.	Capital expenditure is entered on the assets side of the balance sheet.

3. Distinguish between capital expenditure and revenue expenditure and state whether the following statements are items of capital or revenue expenditure.

   (i) Expenditure incurred on repairs and white washing at the time of purchase of an old building in order to make it usable.

  (ii) Expenditure incurred to provide one more exit in a cinema hall in compliance with a government order.

 (iii) Registration fees paid at the time of purchase of a building.

 (iv) Expenditure incurred in the maintenance of a tea garden which will produce tea after 4 years.

  (v) Depreciation charged on a plant.

 (vi) The expenditure incurred in erecting a platform on which a machine will be fixed.

(vii) Advertising expenditure, the benefits of which will last for 4 years.   (NCERT)

Ans. The differences between capital expenditure and revenue expenditure are

Basis	Capital Expenditure	Revenue Expenditure
Effect on Earning Capacity	Capital expenditure increases the earning capacity of business.	Revenue expenditure is incurred to maintain the earning capacity.
Purpose	It is incurred to acquire fixed assets for operation of business.	It is incurred on day-to-day conduct of business.
Nature	Capital expenditure is non-recurring in nature.	Revenue expenditure is generally recurring in nature.
Period	Its benefit extend to more than one accounting year.	Its benefit normally extend to one accounting year.
Recorded	Capital expenditure (subject to depreciation) is recorded in balance sheet.	Revenue expenditure (subject to adjustment for outstanding and prepaid amount) is transferred to trading and profit and loss account.

(i) Expenditure incurred on repairs and white washing at the time of purchase of an old building in order to make it usable — Capital Expenditure

(ii) Expenditure incurred to provide one more exit in a cinema hall in compliance with a government order — Capital Expenditure

(iii) Registration fees paid at the time of purchase of a building — Capital Expenditure

(iv) Expenditure incurred in the maintenance of a tea garden which will produce tea after 4 years — Revenue Expenditure

(v) Depreciation charged on a plant — Revenue Expenditure

(vi) The expenditure incurred in erecting a platform on which a machine will be fixed — Capital Expenditure

(vii) Advertising expenditure, the benefits of which will last for 4 years—Deferred Revenue Expenditure.

4. The following trial balance is extracted from the books of M/s Ram on 31st March, 2020. You are required to prepare trading and profit and loss account and the balance sheet as on that date. **(NCERT)**

Name of Account	Debit Balance (₹)	Name of Account	Credit Balance (₹)
Debtors	12,000	Apprenticeship Premium	5,000
Purchases	50,000	Loan	10,000
Coal, Gas and Water	6,000	Bank Overdraft	1,000
Factory Wages	11,000	Sales	80,000
Salaries	9,000	Creditors	13,000
Rent	4,000	Capital	20,000
Discount	3,000		
Advertisement	500		
Drawings	1,000		
Loan	6,000		
Petty Cash	500		
Sales Return	1,000		
Machinery	5,000		
Land and Building	10,000		
Income Tax	100		
Furniture	9,900		
Total	1,29,000		1,29,000

Ans.

Trading and Profit and Loss Account
for the year ended 31st March, 2020

Dr   Cr

Particulars	Amt (₹)	Particulars		Amt (₹)
To Purchases	50,000	By Sales	80,000	
To Coal, Gas and Water	6,000	(−) Sales Return	(1,000)	79,000
To Factory Wages	11,000			
To Gross Profit Transferred to Profit and Loss A/c	12,000			
	79,000			79,000
To Salaries	9,000	By Gross Profit b/d		12,000
To Rent	4,000	By Apprenticeship Premium		5,000
To Discount	3,000			
To Advertisement	500			
To Net Profit transferred to Capital A/c	500			
	17,000			17,000

Balance Sheet
as on 31st March, 2020

Liabilities		Amt (₹)	Assets	Amt (₹)
Capital	20,000		Debtors	12,000
(+) Net Profit	500		Loan	6,000
	20,500		Machinery	5,000
(−) Drawings	(1,000)		Land and Building	10,000
Income tax	(100)	19,400	Furniture	9,900
Creditors		13,000	Petty Cash	500
Loan		10,000		
Bank Overdraft		1,000		
		43,400		43,400

5 The following is the trial balance of Manju Chawla on 31st March, 2021. You are required to prepare trading and profit and loss account and a balance sheet as on that date.   **(NCERT)**

Name of Account	Debit Balance (₹)	Credit Balance (₹)
Opening Stock	10,000	—
Purchases and Sales	40,000	80,000
Returns	200	600
Productive Wages	6,000	—
Dock and Clearing Charges	4,000	—
Donation and Charity	600	—
Delivery Van Expenses	6,000	—
Lighting	500	—
Sales Tax Collected	—	1,000
Bad Debts	600	—
Miscellaneous Incomes	—	6,000
Rent from Tenants	—	2,000
Royalty	4,000	—
Capital	—	40,000
Drawings	2,000	—
Debtors and Creditors	6,000	7,000
Cash	3,000	—
Investment	6,000	—
Patents	4,000	—
Land and Machinery	43,000	—

Closing Stock ₹ 2,000

Ans.

Trading and Profit and Loss Account

Dr   for the year ended 31st March, 2021   Cr

Particulars		Amt (₹)	Particulars		Amt (₹)
To Opening Stock		10,000	By Sales	80,000	
To Purchases	40,000		(−) Sales Return	(200)	79,800
(−) Purchases Return	(600)	39,400	By Closing Stock		2,000
To Productive Wages		6,000			
To Dock and Clearing Charges		4,000			
To Royalty		4,000			
To Gross Profit Transferred to Profit and Loss A/c		18,400			
		81,800			81,800
To Donation and Charity		600	By Gross Profit b/d		18,400
To Delivery Van Expenses		6,000	By Rent From Tenants		2,000
To Lighting		500	By Miscellaneous Incomes		6,000
To Bad Debts		600			
To Net Profit transferred to Capital A/c		18,700			
		26,400			26,400

Balance Sheet

as at 31st March, 2021

Liabilities		Amt (₹)	Assets	Amt (₹)
Capital	40,000		Investment	6,000
(+) Net Profit	18,700		Patents	4,000
	58,700		Land and Machinery	43,000
(−) Drawings	(2,000)	56,700	Cash	3,000
Creditors		7,000	Debtors	6,000
Sales Tax Collected		1,000	Suspense Account	700
			Closing Stock	2,000
		64,700		64,700

Note *There is a difference of ₹ 700 in debit side of trial balance, so it will be shown in the assets side of the balance sheet.*

6 From the following balances of M/s Nilu Sarees as on 31st March, 2021. Prepare trading and profit and loss account and balance sheet as on that date.   **(NCERT)**

Particulars	Amt (₹)	Particulars	Amt (₹)
Opening Stock	10,000	Sales	2,28,000
Purchases	78,000	Capital	70,000
Carriage Inwards	2,500	Interest	7,000
Salaries	30,000	Commission	8,000
Commission	10,000	Creditors	28,000
Wages	11,000	Bills Payable	2,370
Rent and Taxes	2,800		
Repair	5,000		
Telephone Expenses	1,400		
Legal Charges	1,500		
Sundry Expenses	2,500		
Cash in Hand	12,000		
Debtors	30,000		
Machinery	60,000		
Investments	90,000		
Drawings	18,000		

Closing stock as on 31st March, 2021 ₹ 22,000.

Ans.

Trading and Profit and Loss Account
for the year ended 31st March, 2021

Dr   Cr

Particulars	Amt (₹)	Particulars	Amt (₹)
To Opening Stock	10,000	By Sales	2,28,000
To Purchases	78,000	By Closing Stock	22,000
To Carriage Inwards	2,500		
To Wages	11,000		
To Gross Profit Transferred to Profit and Loss A/c	1,48,500		
	2,50,000		2,50,000
To Salaries	30,000	By Gross Profit Transferred from Trading A/c	1,48,500
To Commission	10,000	By Interest	7,000
To Rent and Taxes	2,800	By Commission	8,000
To Repair	5,000		
To Telephone Expenses	1,400		
To Legal Charges	1,500		
To Sundry Expenses	2,500		
To Net Profit transferred to Capital A/c	1,10,300		
	1,63,500		1,63,500

Balance Sheet
as at 31st March, 2021

Liabilities		Amt (₹)	Assets	Amt (₹)
Capital	70,000		Machinery	60,000
(+) Net Profit	1,10,300		Investment	90,000
	1,80,300		Debtors	30,000
(−) Drawings	(18,000)	1,62,300	Cash in Hand	12,000
Creditors		28,000	Closing Stock	22,000
Bills Payable		2,370		
Suspense Account		21,330		
		2,14,000		2,14,000

Note

(i) Total of debit side of trial balance is ₹ 3,64,700 and total of credit side of trial balance is ₹ 3,43,370. The difference in credit side is ₹ 21,330.

(ii) Difference in credit side of trial balance ₹ 21,330 will be treated as liabilities and posted in liabilities side of balance sheet.

Multiple Choice Questions

1. The benefit of .... generally lasts between 3 to 7 years.
   (a) revenue expenditure
   (b) capital expenditure
   (c) deferred revenue expenditure
   (d) working capital expenditure

2. Which of the following is correct?
   (a) Gross Profit = Net Profit – Other Income + Indirect Expenses
   (b) Gross Profit = Net Profit – Indirect Expenses + Other Incomes
   (c) Gross Profit = Net Profit + Cost of Goods Sold
   (d) Gross Profit = Net Profit – Cost of Goods Sold

3. Which of the following is the journal entry for unsold stock at the end of the accounting year 31st March, 2021 of ₹ 40,500?

   (a)   Closing Stock A/c   Dr   40,500
   　　　　　To Profit and Loss A/c   40,500
   (b)   Trading A/c   Dr   40,500
   　　　　　To Profit and Loss A/c   40,500
   (c)   Closing Stock A/c   Dr   40,500
   　　　　　To Trading A/c   40,500
   (d)   Trading A/c   Dr   40,500
   　　　　　To Closing Stock A/c   40,500

4. If sales are ₹ 60,000 and the rate of gross profit on cost of goods sold is 25%. Cost of goods sold will be
   (a) ₹ 45,000　　　　(b) ₹ 50,000　　　　(c) ₹ 48,000　　　　(d) None of these

5. Match the following and tick the correct option.

	Column I	Column II
A.	Trading account	(i) Net Purchase + Opening Stock – Closing Stock
B.	Cost of goods sold	(ii) Debit side of trading account
C.	Adjusted purchases	(iii) For the year ended
D.	Wages	(iv) Opening Stock + Purchases + Direct Expenses – Closing Stock

Codes

	A	B	C	D
(a)	(iv)	(ii)	(iii)	(i)
(b)	(i)	(ii)	(iii)	(iv)
(c)	(iii)	(iv)	(i)	(ii)
(d)	(iii)	(iv)	(ii)	(i)

6. Net sales during the year, 2020 is ₹ 2,85,000. Gross profit is 25% on sales. Find out cost of goods sold.
   (a) ₹ 2,85,000　　　　(b) ₹ 2,13,750　　　　(c) ₹ 71,250　　　　(d) Zero

7. Which of the following is correct?
   (a) Operating Profit = Operating Profit – Non-Operating Expenses – Non-Operating Incomes
   (b) Operating Profit = Net Profit + Non-Operating Expenses + Non-Operating Incomes
   (c) Operating Profit = Net Profit + Non-Operating Expenses – Non-Operating Incomes
   (d) Operating Profit = Net Profit – Non-Operating Expenses + Non-Operating Incomes

Short Answer (SA) Type Questions

1. What is the purpose of preparing trading and profit and loss account?

2. What are closing entries? Give examples of closing entries of trading account.

3. Calculate closing stock from the following details.

Opening stock ₹ 80,000; cash sales ₹ 2,40,000; credit sales ₹ 1,60,000; purchases ₹ 2,80,000. Rate of gross profit on cost $33\frac{1}{3}$%.

4. Calculate net purchases from the following details.

Particulars	Amt (₹)
Gross Profit	90,000
Net Profit	48,000
Net Sales	3,00,000
Return Inward	10,000
Return Outward	20,000
Freight Inward	5,000
Wages	10,000
Lighting	15,000
Closing Stock	20,000

Opening stock is one and half times of closing stock.

5. Calculate closing stock and cost of goods sold from the following items.

Opening stock ₹ 30,000, sales ₹ 96,000, carriage inwards ₹ 6,000, sales return ₹ 6,000, gross profit ₹ 36,000, purchases ₹ 60,000 and purchase return ₹ 5,400.

Long Answer (LA) Type Questions

1. Following is the trial balance of PC Mukherjee as on 31st March, 2021.

Debit Balances	Amt (₹)	Credit Balances	Amt (₹)
Stock [1 st April, 2020]	20,000	Discount Received	1,500
Purchases	1,16,000	Return Outwards	5,200
Wages	4,000	Sales	1,97,300
Return Inwards	7,040	Bills Payable	6,000
Carriage on Purchases	4,720	Sundry Creditors	11,200
Carriage on Sales	1,420	Creditors for Rent	1000
Office Salaries	9,600	Capital	80,000
Duty on Imported Goods	5,400	Loan from Damodar	20,000
Rent and Taxes	4,800	Commission	2,400
Cash	2,200		
Bank Balance	15,640		
Bad Debts	1,200		
Discount Allowed	1,280		
Land and Building	40,000		
Scooter	13,200		
Scooter Repairs	1,700		
Bills Receivable	7,000		
Commission	3,600		
Sundry Debtors	50,800		
Interest on Damodar 's Loan	3,000		
Drawings	12,000		
	3,24,600		3,24,600

Prepare a trading and profit and loss account for the year ended 31st March, 2021 and the balance sheet as at that date. The stock on 31st March, 2021 was ₹ 44,000.

2. Following is the trial balance of Vandana Vohra as on 31st March, 2020. Draw the final accounts from the balances therefrom.

Name of Account	Debit Balance (₹)	Credit Balance (₹)
Capital	—	3,00,000
Stock on 1 st April, 2019	60,000	—
Cash at Bank	20,000	—
Cash in Hand	10,000	—
Machinery	2,00,000	—
Furniture	26,000	—
Purchases	4,00,000	—
Wages	1,00,000	—
Carriage Inwards	66,000	—
Salaries	1,40,000	—
Discount Allowed	8,000	—
Discount Received	—	10,000
Advertising	1,00,000	—
Office Expenses	80,000	—
Sales	—	10,00,000
Sundry Debtors	1,80,000	—
Sundry Creditors	—	80,000
	13,90,000	13,90,000

Value of closing stock as on 31st March, 2020 was ₹ 1,00,000.

Answers

Multiple Choice Questions

1. (c)   *2. (a)*   *3. (c)*   *4. (c)*   *5. (c)*   *6. (b)*   *7. (c)*

For Detailed Solutions

Scan the code

CHAPTER 05

Financial Statements-II
(With Adjustments)

In this Chapter...

- Introduction
- Adjustments in Preparation of Financial Statements

Introduction

We have learnt to prepare final accounts in the form of trading and profit and loss account and balance sheet without adjustments. Sometimes it is noticed that after preparation of trial balance, but before final accounts are prepared, some business transactions have been completely or partially omitted or are wrongly recorded.

Besides this, there are some incomes or expenses, which relate to the next year, but have been received or paid in the current year. Therefore, it is necessary to incorporate these adjustments while preparing final accounts.

Need for Adjustments in Preparing the Final Accounts

In order to ascertain true profit or loss of a business for a particular year, it is necessary that all expenses and incomes related to that period should be taken into consideration. The need for making various adjustments are stated below

- To ascertain the true profit or loss of the business.
- To determine the true financial position of the business.
- To make a record of the transactions earlier omitted in the books.
- To rectify the errors committed in the books.
- To complete the incomplete transactions.
- To make a record of accrued income (i.e., income which have been accrued but have not been received).
- To make a record of outstanding expenses (i.e., expenses which are due but have not been paid).
- To make adjustment for prepaid expenses (i.e., expenses which have been paid in advance).
- To make adjustment for unearned income (i.e., income which have been received in advance).
- To provide for other reserves and provisions, depreciation, etc.

Adjustments in Preparation of Financial Statements

All such items which need to be brought into books of accounts at the time of preparing the final accounts are referred to as 'adjustments'.

Journal entries which are recorded to give effect to these adjustments are known as **adjusting entries**. All adjustments are reflected in the final accounts at two places to complete the double entry.

The items which usually need adjustments are as follows

1. **Closing Stock** It implies the value of unsold goods at the end of an accounting period. Closing stock is valued at cost or net realisable value, whichever is lower.

   If Given in Adjustment

Accounting Treatment

Adjusting Entry		Trading Account	Balance Sheet
Closing Stock A/c To Trading A/c (Being the closing stock recorded in the books)	Dr	Shown on the credit side.	Shown on the assets side under current assets.

   If Given in Trial Balance

Accounting Treatment

Trading Account	Balance Sheet
Nil	Shown on the assets side under current assets.

2. **Outstanding Expenses** (Expenses Due but Not Paid or Expenses Unpaid or Due) There are certain business expenses which become due during the current accounting period but are actually paid in the next accounting period. Such expenses are termed as outstanding expenses.

   If Given in Adjustment

Accounting Treatment

Adjusting Entry		Trading Account	Profit and Loss Account	Balance Sheet
Concerned Expenses A/c To Outstanding Expenses A/c (Being the unpaid expenses provided)	Dr	If it is a direct expense For example, wages Added to the related expense on the debit side.	If it is an indirect expense For example, salaries Added to the related expense on the debit side.	Shown on the liabilities side as a current liability.

   If Given in Trial Balance

Accounting Treatment

Trading Account	Profit and Loss Account	Balance Sheet
Nil	Nil	Shown on the liabilities side as a current liability.

3. **Prepaid Expenses** (Expenses Paid in Advance or Unexpired Expenses) There may be certain business expenses, the payment of which might have been made in the current accounting year but which relate to the next accounting year. Such expenses are called prepaid expenses.

If Given in Adjustment

Accounting Treatment

Adjusting Entry		Trading Account	Profits and Loss Account	Balance Sheet
Prepaid Expenses A/c To Concerned Expenses A/c (Being the concerned expenses paid in advance)	Dr	(If it is a direct expense For example, wages) Deducted from the related expense on the debit side.	(If it is an indirect expense For example, insurance premium) Deducted from the related expense, on the debit side.	Shown on the assets side as current assets.

If Given in Trial Balance

Accounting Treatment

Trading Account	Profit and Loss Account	Balance Sheet
Nil	Nil	Shown on the asset side as a current asset.

4. **Accrued Income** (Outstanding Income or Income Receivable) It refers to the income which has been earned but not received during the current accounting period.

If Given in Adjustment

Accounting Treatment

Adjusting Entry		Profit and Loss Account	Balance Sheet
Accrued Income A/c To Concerned Income A/c (Being the concerned income receivable)	Dr	Added to the respective income on the credit side.	Shown on the asset side as a current asset.

If Given in Trial Balance

Accounting Treatment

Profit and Loss Account	Balance Sheet
Nil	Shown on the assets side as a current asset.

5. **Income Received in Advance** (Unearned Income or Unaccrued Income) The income or portion of income which is received during the current accounting year but it has not been earned, is called unearned income.

If Given in Adjustment

Accounting Treatment

Adjusting Entry		Profit and Loss Account	Balance Sheet
Concerned Income A/c To Income Received in Advance A/c (Being the adjustment for unearned income)	Dr	Deducted from the concerned income on the credit side.	Shown on the liabilities side.

If Given in Trial Balance

Accounting Treatment

Profit and Loss Account	Balance Sheet
Nil	Shown on the liabilities side.

6. **Depreciation** It refers to the decrease in the value of assets on account of wear and tear and passage of time.

If Given in Adjustment

Accounting Treatment

Adjusting Entry	Profit and Loss Account	Balance Sheet

Depreciation A/c   Dr
   To Concerned Asset A/c/Provision for
   Depreciation A/c
(Being the depreciation charged)
	Shown on the debit side as a separate item.	Shown on the assets side by way of deduction from the value of concerned fixed assets.
		
		If provision for depreciation account is maintained, amount of depreciation is added to provision for depreciation account and the total accumulated depreciation is shown on the asset side by way of deduction from the original cost of the asset.

If Given in Trial Balance

Accounting Treatment

Profit and Loss Account	Balance Sheet
Shown on the debit side	Nil

7. **Bad Debts** The amount which cannot be recovered from the debtors is known as bad debts.

If Given in Adjustment

Accounting Treatment

Adjusting Entries	Profit and Loss Account	Balance Sheet
Bad Debts A/c Dr To Debtors A/c (Being the bad debts written-off)	Shown on the debit side as a separate item, or as a addition to the bad debts already written off.	Shown on the assets side by way of deduction from the debtors.
Profit and Loss A/c Dr To Bad Debts A/c (Being the bad debts transferred to profit and loss account)		

If Given in Trial Balance

Accounting Treatment

Profit and Loss Account	Balance Sheet
Shown on the debit side	Nil

It is to be noted that both type of bad debts i.e., appearing in trial balance and outside the trial balance are charged to profit and loss account but only those bad debts which are given outside the trial balance are deducted from debtors.

8. **Provision for Doubtful Debts** A provision for bad debts is created in accordance to convention of conservatism to cover any possible loss an account of bad debts likely to occur in future.

If Given in Adjustment

Accounting Treatment

Adjusting Entry	Profit and Loss Account	Balance Sheet
Profit and Loss A/c Dr To Provision for Doubtful Debts A/c (Being the adjustment for provision for doubtful debt)	Shown as a separate item or added to the bad debts on the debit side	Shown on the assets side by way of deduction from the amount of sundry debtors

If Given in Trial Balance

Profit and Loss Account	Balance Sheet
Shown as a deduction from total of bad debts and new provision	Nil

9. **Provision for Discount on Debtors** Generally, business allows cash discount to those debtors from whom the payment is received within a fixed period. Therefore, a provision for such discount is made in the current year, for those debtors who will make early payment in the next accounting period.

If Given in Adjustment

Accounting Treatment

Adjusting Entry	Profit and Loss Account	Balance Sheet
Profit and Loss A/c Dr To Provision for Discount on Debtors A/c (Being the adjustment of discount on debtors adjusted)	Shown on debit side as a separate item.	Shown on the assets side by way of deduction from sundry debtors.

If Given in Trial Balance

Accounting Treatment

Profit and Loss Account	Balance Sheet
Shown as a deduction from total of bad debts and provision for bad debts	Nil

10. **Manager's Commission** Sometimes, the manager is entitled to commission on profits in addition to salary. Such commission is calculated at the end of the accounting period and is always given as an adjustment. It is calculated as a fixed percentage of the profits.

Commission payable can be calculated as follows

(i) **When Commission is paid at a Fixed Percentage of Net Profit before Charging such Commission**

In this case, commission will be calculated as

Commission = Net Profit before Commission × Rate of Commission

(ii) **When Commission is paid at a Fixed Percentage of Net Profit after Charging such Commission**

In this case, commission is calculated as

$$\text{Commission} = \text{Net Profit before Such Commission} \times \frac{\text{Rate of Commission}}{100 + \text{Rate of Commission}}$$

Accounting Treatment

Adjusting Entry	Profit and Loss Account	Balance Sheet
Manager's Commission A/c Dr To Commission Payable/Outstanding Commission A/c (Being the manager commission adjusted)	Shown on the debit side as a separate item.	Commission payable is shown on the liabilities side.
Profit and Loss A/c Dr To Manager's Commission A/c (Being the commission payable to manager transferred to profit and loss account)		

11. **Abnormal or Accidental Losses** Sometimes losses occur due to some abnormal circumstances such as fire, theft, earthquake, abnormal spoilage/leakage/breakages/pilferage, etc. such losses are called abnormal losses.

    If Given in Adjustment

    Accounting Treatment

Adjusting Entries		Trading Account	Profit and Loss Account	Balance Sheet
Loss of Stock A/c To Trading A/c (Being the loss of stock by fire)	Dr	The total value of abnormal loss is shown on the credit side as a separate item, whether recovered or not.	The total value of irrecovered loss of stock, is shown on the debit side as a separate item. Irrecovered Loss = (Total Loss − Amount Recovered from Insurance Company)	Any amount, which is due from the insurance company is shown on the assets side.
Insurance Claim/Insurance Company A/c Profit and Loss A/c To Loss of Stock A/c (Being the insurance company admitted a partial claim only)	Dr Dr			

    If Given in Trial Balance

    Accounting Treatment

Trading A/c	Profit and Loss Account	Balance Sheet
—	Shown on the debit side	—

12. **Goods Taken for Personal Use** When the goods are taken by the proprietor for his personal use from the business, it is treated as drawings.

    If Given in Adjustment

    Accounting Treatment

Adjusting Entry		Trading Account	Balance Sheet
Drawings A/c To Purchases A/c (Being the goods taken for personal use)	Dr	Deduct drawings of goods (cost) from purchases on the debit side.	Deduct it from capital on the liabilities side.

    If Given in Trial Balance

    Accounting Treatment

Trading A/c	Balance Sheet
—	Deduct it from capital

13. **Goods Distributed as Free Samples** With a view to promote sales, goods are distributed as free samples. When goods are distributed as free samples, the stock gets reduced.

    If Given in Adjustment

    Accounting Treatment

Adjusting Entry		Trading Account	Profit and Loss Account
Advertisement A/c To Purchases A/c (Being the goods distributed as free sample)	Dr	Cost of goods distributed as free samples will be deducted from purchases on the debit side.	Shown on the debit side as advertisement expenses.

If Given in Trial Balance

Accounting Treatment

Trading Account	Profit and Loss Account
—	Shown on the debit side as advertisement expenses

14. **Interest on Capital** The cost of using the capital invested by the proprietor/partner in an enterprise is interest on capital.
If Given in Adjustment

Accounting Treatment

Adjusting Entries		Profit and Loss Account	Balance Sheet
Interest on Capital A/c To Capital A/c (Being the interest on capital provided)	Dr	Shown as an expense on the debit side as a separate item.	Shown on the liabilities side by way of addition to the capital.
Profit and Loss A/c To Interest on Capital A/c (Being the interest on capital transferred to profit and loss account)	Dr		

If Given in Trial Balance

Accounting Treatment

Profit and Loss Account	Balance Sheet
It will be shown on the debit side of profit and loss account.	Nil

15. **Interest on Drawings** When the owner/proprietor withdraws money for his personal use, it is termed as drawings. Interest on drawings is charged from the owner for the withdrawals made by him. Therefore, it is an expense for the owner and an income for the business.
If Given in Adjustments

Accounting Treatment

Adjusting Entries		Profit and Loss Account	Balance Sheet
Drawings A/c To Interest on Drawings A/c (Being the interest on drawings adjusted)	Dr	Shown as a gain on the credit side.	Shown by way of deduction from capital on the liabilities side.
Interest on Drawings A/c To Profit and Loss A/c (Being the interest on drawings transferred to profit and loss account)	Dr		

If Given in Trial Balance

Accounting Treatment

Profit and Loss Account	Balance Sheet
It will be shown in the credit side of profit and loss account.	Nil

16. **Interest on Loan** If the business has taken a loan, then interest on such loan will be an expense for the firm.

If Given in Adjustment

Accounting Treatment

Adjusting Entries		Profit and Loss Account	Balance Sheet
Interest on Loan A/c To Loan A/c (Being the interest on loan provided)	Dr	Shown on the debit side as a separate item.	Outstanding amount of interest will be added to loan account on the liability side.
Profit and Loss A/c To Interest on Loan A/c (Being the interest on loan debited to profit and loss account)	Dr		

If Given in Trial Balance

Accounting Treatment

Profit and Loss Account	Balance Sheet
Shown on the debit side	Nil

17. **Interest on Loan Given** When loan appears on the debit side of trial balance, it means the amount has been lend to outsiders. It is an asset for the firm and interest on such loan will be an income for the firm.

If Given in Adjustment

Accounting Treatment

Adjusting Entries		Profit and Loss Account	Balance Sheet
Loan A/c To Interest on Loan A/c (Being the interest on loan due to be received)	Dr	Shown on the credit side as a separate item.	Accrued interest on such loan will be added to loan account on the assets side.
Interest on Loan A/c To Profit and Loss A/c (Being the interest on loan given credited to profit and loss account)	Dr		

If Given in Trial Balance

Accounting Treatment

Profit and Loss Account	Balance Sheet
Shown on the credit side	Nil

18. **Implied Adjustments** These are also adjusted while preparing final accounts. Sometimes, loan is given on debit or credit side of trial balance carrying a specific rate of interest.

Even if nothing is mentioned in adjustment, we will calculate interest on loan given/loan taken by the business.

- If no amount of interest is shown in trial balance, then full amount of interest will be treated as outstanding/accrued.
- In case some amount of interest is shown in trail balance, then compare the amount of interest calculated with the amount of interest given in the trial balance and the difference if any, will be treated as outstanding/accrued interest.

Solved Examples

Example 1. The following is the trial balance of Ram Krishan Vyas on 31st March, 2021. Prepare trading and profit and loss account and balance sheet after making the following adjustments.

   (i) Value of closing stock ₹ 29,638.

  (ii) Depreciate plant and machinery @ 10%, furniture @ 5% and horses and carts by ₹ 1,000. Also write-off goodwill by ₹ 3,000.

 (iii) Provide 5% for doubtful debts on debtors.

 (iv) Prepaid expenses : Insurance ₹ 300 and taxes ₹ 190.

  (v) $\frac{3}{5}$th of insurance and taxes, rent and general expenses to be charged to factory and the balance to the office.

 (vi) Advertising is to be written-off over 3 years.

(vii) Commission to manager @ 10% on net profit after changing such commission.

Name of Accounts	Amt (₹)	Name of Accounts	Amt (₹)
Plant and Machinery	19,720	Capital	80,000
Manufacturing Wages	34,965	Creditors	50,160
Salaries	10,135	Bank Loan	10,000
Furniture	9,480	Purchases Return	1,140
Freight on Purchases	1,980	Sales	2,46,850
Freight on Sales	2,150	Provision for Bad Debts	6,000
Building	25,000		
Manufacturing Expenses	9,455		
Fuel and Power	1,276		
Electricity (Factory)	986		
Insurance and Taxes	4,175		
Goodwill	30,000		
Rent	2,400		
Debtors	78,140		
Stable Expenses	2,473		
Opening Stock	34,170		
Horses and Carts	5,165		
Purchases	97,165		
Sales Returns	3,170		
General Expenses	8,000		
Bad Debts	1,485		
Interest and Bank Charges	475		
Advertising	4,500		
Bank Balance	7,540		
Cash	145		
	3,94,150		3,94,150

Ans.

Trading and Profit and Loss Account
for the year ended 31st March, 2021

Dr   Cr

Particulars		Amt (₹)	Particulars		Amt (₹)
To Opening Stock		34,170	By Sales	2,46,850	
To Purchases	97,165		(–) Sales Return	(3,170)	2,43,680
(–) Purchases Return	(1,140)	96,025	By Closing Stock		29,638
To Manufacturing Wages		34,965			
To Freight on Purchases		1,980			
To Manufacturing Expenses		9,455			
To Fuel and Power		1,276			
To Electricity (Factory)		986			
To Insurance and Taxes		2,211			
To Rent		1,440			
To General Expenses		4,800			
To Gross Profit c/d		86,010			
		2,73,318			2,73,318
To Salaries		10,135	By Gross Profit b/d		86,010
To Freight on Sales		2,150	By Old Provision for Doubtful Debts		608
To Insurance and Taxes		1,474			
To Rent		960			
To Stable Expenses		2,473			
To General Expenses		3,200			
To Interest and Bank Charges		475			
To Advertising		1,500			
To Depreciation on					
Plant and Machinery	1,972				
Furniture	474				
Horses and Carts	1,000	3,446			
To Goodwill		3,000			
To Manager's Commission		5,255			
To Net Profit Transferred to Capital A/c		52,550			
		86,618			86,618

Balance Sheet
as at 31st March, 2021

Liabilities		Amt (₹)	Assets		Amt (₹)
Bank Loan		10,000	Cash		145
Creditors		50,160	Bank Balance		7,540
Manager's Commission		5,255	Debtors	78,140	
Capital	80,000		(–) New Provision for Doubtful Debts	(3,907)	74,233
(+) Net Profit	52,550	1,32,550	Closing Stock		29,638
			Prepaid Insurance and Taxes		490
			Furniture	9,480	
			(–) Depreciation	(474)	9,006
			Horses and Carts	5,165	
			(–) Depreciation	(1,000)	4,165
			Plant and Machinery	19,720	
			(–) Depreciation	(1,972)	17,748
			Buildings		25,000
			Advertising		3,000
			Goodwill		27,000
		1,97,965			1,97,965

Working Notes

1. Rent to be debited

   (i) in trading account $= 2,400 \times \dfrac{3}{5} = ₹\ 1,440$ (ii) in profit and loss account $= 2,400 \times \dfrac{2}{5} = ₹\ 960$

2. General expenses to be debited

   (i) in trading account $= 8,000 \times \dfrac{3}{5} = ₹\ 4,800$ (ii) in profit and loss account $= 8,000 \times \dfrac{2}{5} = ₹\ 3,200$

3. Insurance and taxes to be debited

   (i) in trading account $= (4,175 - 490) \times \dfrac{3}{5} = ₹\ 2,211$ (ii) in profit and loss account $= (4,175 - 490) \times \dfrac{2}{5} = ₹\ 1,474$

4. Depreciation on

   (i) Plant and machinery $= 19,720 \times \dfrac{10}{100} = ₹\ 1,972$ (ii) Furniture $= 9,480 \times \dfrac{5}{100} = ₹\ 474$

5. Advertising to be debited to profit and loss account $= 4,500 \times \dfrac{1}{3} = ₹\ 1,500$

6. Manager's commission $= 86,618 - 28,813 = 57,805 \times \dfrac{10}{110} = ₹\ 5,255$

7. Calculation of Provision for Doubtful Debts

To Bad Debts	1,485
(+) New Provision	3,907
	5,392
(−) Old Provision	(6,000)
	(608)

When the resultant figure is negative, it will be shown on the credit side of profit and loss account.

Example 2. Tarak Mehta starts business on 1st April, 2020 with a capital of ₹ 3,00,000. The following trial balance was drawn up from his books at the end of the year.

Particulars	Amt (₹)	Particulars	Amt (₹)
Drawings	45,000	Capital	4,00,000
Plant and Fixtures	80,000	Sales	16,00,000
Purchases	11,60,000	Sundry Creditors	1,20,000
Carriage Inward	20,000	Bills Payable	90,000
Returns Inward	40,000		
Wages	80,000		
Salaries	1,00,000		
Printing and Stationery	8,000		
Advertisement	12,000		
Trade Charges	6,000		
Rent and Taxes	14,000		
Sundry Debtors	2,50,000		
Bills Receivable	50,000		
Investments	1,50,000		
Discount	5,000		
Cash at Bank	1,60,000		
Cash in Hand	30,000		
	22,10,000		22,10,000

The value of stock as at 31st March, 2021 was ₹ 2,60,000. You are required to prepare trading and profit and loss account for the year ended 31st March, 2021 and a balance sheet as on that date after taking the following facts into account.

(i) Interest on capital is to be provided at 6% p.a.

(ii) An additional capital of ₹1,00,000 was introduced by Tarak Mehta on 1st October, 2020.

(iii) Plant and fixtures are to be depreciated by 10% per annum.

(iv) Salaries outstanding on 31st March, 2020 amounted to ₹ 5,000.

(v) Accrued interest on investments amounted of ₹ 7,500.

(vi) ₹ 5,000 are bad debts and a provision for doubtful debts is to be created at 5 percent of the balance of debtors.

(vii) Interest charged on drawings at 10%.

Ans.

Trading and Profit and Loss Account

Dr　for the year ending 31st March, 2021　Cr

Particulars		Amt (₹)	Particulars		Amt (₹)
To Purchases		11,60,000	By Sales	16,00,000	
To Wages		80,000	(–) Returns	(40,000)	15,60,000
To Carriage Inward		20,000	By Closing Stock		2,60,000
To Gross Profit c/d		5,60,000			
		18,20,000			18,20,000
To Salaries	1,00,000		By Gross Profit b/d		5,60,000
(+) Outstanding	5,000	1,05,000	By Accrued Interest on Investment		7,500
To Printing and Stationery		8,000	By Interest on Drawings		4,500
To Advertisements		12,000			
To Trade Charges		6,000			
To Rent and Taxes		14,000			
To Discount		5,000			
To Bad Debts	5,000				
(+) Provision for Bad Debts	12,250	17,250			
To Interest on Capital (WN)		21,000			
To Depreciation on Plant and Machinery		8,000			
To Net Profit Transferred to Capital A/c		3,75,750			
		5,72,000			5,72,000

Working Note

$$\text{Interest on Capital} = \left[\left(3,00,000 \times \frac{6}{100} \times \frac{12}{12}\right) + \left(1,00,000 \times \frac{6}{100} \times \frac{6}{12}\right)\right] = ₹\,21,000$$

Balance Sheet

as at 31st March, 2021

Liabilities		Amt (₹)	Assets		Amt (₹)
Sundry Creditors		1,20,000	Cash in Hand		30,000
Bills Payable		90,000	Cash at Bank		1,60,000
Outstanding Salaries		5,000	Bills Receivable		50,000
Capital			Sundry Debtors	2,50,000	
Opening Balance	3,00,000		(–) Further Bad Debts	(5,000)	
(+) Additional Capital	1,00,000		(–) Provision for Doubtful Debts	(12,250)	2,32,750
(+) Interest on Capital	21,000		Investments	1,50,000	
(+) Net Profit	3,75,750		(+) Accrued Interest	7,500	1,57,500
(–) Drawings	(45,000)		Closing Stock		2,60,000
(–) Interest on Drawings	(4,500)	7,47,250	Plant and Fixtures	80,000	72,000
			(–) Depreciation	(8,000)	9,62,250
		9,62,250			9,62,250

Example 3. Arihant & Co has established its business in the rural area of Madhya Pradesh. Prepare the trading and profit and loss account for the year ended 31st March, 2020 and the balance sheet as at 31st March, 2020 from the following information.

Particulars	Amt (₹)	Particulars	Amt (₹)
Sundry Creditors	1,90,000	Bad Debts	1,000
Building	1,50,000	Loan from Ram	25,000
Income Tax	10,250	Sundry Debtors	95,000
Loose Tools	10,000	Investments	65,000
Cash at Bank	1,62,000	Provision for Doubtful Debts	16,000
Sundry Expenses	19,900	Rent and Rates	8,500
Bank Interest (Cr)	750	Furniture	30,000
Purchases	15,70,000	Stock (1st April, 2019)	2,73,500
Wages	1,00,000	Capital	4,73,900
Carriage Inwards	11,200	Discount Allowed	6,300
Sales	18,50,000	Dividends Received	5,350
Motor Van	1,25,000	Drawings	20,000
Cash in Hand	3,350	Bills Payable	1,00,000

Additional Information

(i) Write-off further ₹ 3,000 as bad debts out of sundry debtors and create a provision for doubtful debts at 20% on debtors.

(ii) Dividends accrued and due on investments is ₹ 1,350. Rates paid in advance ₹ 1,000 and outstanding wages ₹ 4,500.

(iii) On 31st March, 2020 stock was valued at ₹ 1,50,000 and loose tools were valued at ₹ 8,000.

(iv) Write-off 5% for depreciation on buildings and 40% on motor van.

(v) Provide for interest at 12% p.a. due on loan taken on 1st June, 2019.

(vi) Income tax paid has to be treated as drawings.

Ans.

Trading and Profit and Loss Account
for the year ending 31st March, 2020

Dr   Cr

Particulars		Amt (₹)	Particulars		Amt (₹)
To Opening Stock		2,73,500	By Sales		18,50,000
To Purchases		15,70,000	By Closing Stock		1,50,000
To Wages	1,00,000				
(+) Outstanding	4,500	1,04,500			
To Carriage Inwards		11,200			
To Gross Profit (transferred to profit and loss account)		40,800			
		20,00,000			20,00,000
To Rent and Rates	8,500		By Gross Profit b/d		40,800
(−) Prepaid	(1,000)	7,500	By Bank Interest		750
To Sundry Expenses		19,900	By Dividends	5,350	
To Interest on Loan (12/100 × 10/12 × 25,000)		2,500	(+) Accrued and Due	1,350	6,700
To Depreciation on			By Old Provision for		
Building	7,500		Doubtful Debts		16,000
Motor Van	50,000		By Net Loss		53,850
Loose Tools	2,000	59,500	(Balancing figure transferred to capital)		
To Discount Allowed		6,300			
To Bad Debts	1,000				
(+) Further Bad Debts	3,000	4,000			
To New Provision for Doubtful Debts		18,400			
(92,000 × 20/100)		1,18,100			1,18,100

Balance Sheet
as at 31st March, 2020

Liabilities	Amt (₹)		Assets		Amt (₹)
Capital			Building	1,50,000	
Opening Balance	4,73,900		(–) Depreciation	(7,500)	1,42,500
(–) Drawings	(20,000)		(5/100 × 1,50,000)		
	4,53,900		Motor Van	1,25,000	
(–) Net Loss	(53,850)		(–) Depreciation	(50,000)	75,000
	4,00,050		(40/100 × 1,25,000)		
(–) Income Tax	(10,250)	3,89,800	Loose Tools	10,000	
Loan from Ram		25,000	(–) Depreciation	(2,000)	8,000
Sundry Creditors		1,90,000	(20/100 × 10,000)		
Interest Outstanding on Loan from Ram		2,500	Furniture		30,000
Bills Payable		1,00,000	Investments	65,000	
Outstanding Wages		4,500	(+) Dividend Accrued and Due	1,350	66,350
			Closing Stock		1,50,000
			Sundry Debtors	95,000	
			(–) Bad Debts (Adjustment)	(3,000)	
				92,000	
			(–) Reserve for Bad Debts	(18,400)	73,600
			(20/100 × 92,000)		
			Cash at Bank		1,62,000
			Cash in Hand		3,350
			Prepaid Rates		1,000
		7,11,800			7,11,800

Example 4. Given below is the trial balance of M/s Kartik and Sons as on 31st March, 2021.

Name of Accounts	Debit Balance (₹)	Credit Balance (₹)
Capital	—	14,40,000
Drawings	80,000	—
Sales	—	20,30,000
Purchases	12,40,000	—
Stock-in-trade (1st April, 2020)	40,000	—
Sales Return	24,000	—
Purchases Return	—	30,000
Sundry Debtors	1,60,000	—
Sundry Creditors	—	60,000
Rent	44,000	—
Electricity	32,000	—
Other Expenses	64,000	—
Wages	2,24,000	—
Cash in Hand	2,44,000	—
Cash at Bank	12,64,000	—
Advance to Supplier	1,44,000	—
Total	35,60,000	35,60,000

Additional Information

(i) On scrutiny, it was found that bank balance as per current account statement on 31st March, 2021 was ₹ 11,56,000. A cheque of ₹ 1,40,000 was collected from a debtor returned dishonoured and a cheque of ₹ 32,000 was deposited by another debtor directly.

(ii) Closing stock as on 31st March, 2021 was ₹ 80,000.

(iii) Purchases return ₹ 4,000 was wrongly posted as sales return but correctly debited to supplier's account.

(iv) Purchases day book was found overcast by ₹ 12,000.

(v) Sales day book was found undercast by ₹ 4,000.

You are required to redraft the trial balance and prepare the final accounts of M/s Kartik and Sons.

Ans.

Rectification Entries in Journal

Date	Particulars	LF	Amt (Dr)	Amt (Cr)
(i)	Debtors Dr		1,40,000	
	To Bank A/c			1,40,000
	(Being the cheque dishonoured)			
(ii)	Bank A/c Dr		32,000	
	To Debtors			32,000
	(Being the amount deposited into bank directly by debtor)			
(iii)	Suspense A/c Dr		8,000	
	To Purchases Return A/c			4,000
	To Sales Return A/c			4,000
	(Being the purchases return wrongly recorded as sales return, now rectified)			
(iv)	Suspense A/c Dr		12,000	
	To Purchases A/c			12,000
	(Being the overcasting in purchases book, now rectified)			
(v)	Suspense A/c Dr		4,000	
	To Sales A/c			4,000
	(Being the undercasting of sales book, now rectified)			

Trial Balance (Redrafted)
as on 31st March, 2021

Name of Accounts	Debit Balance (₹)	Credit Balance (₹)
Capital	—	14,40,000
Drawings	80,000	—
Sales (20,30,000 + 4,000)	—	20,34,000
Purchases (12,40,000 − 12,000)	12,28,000	—
Stock-in-trade (1st April, 2020)	40,000	—
Sales Return (24,000 − 4,000)	20,000	—
Purchases Return (30,000 + 4,000)	—	34,000
Sundry Debtors (1,60,000 + 1,40,000 − 32,000)	2,68,000	—
Sundry Creditors	—	60,000
Rent	44,000	—
Electricity	32,000	—
Other Expenses	64,000	—
Wages	2,24,000	—
Cash in Hand	2,44,000	—
Cash at Bank (12,64,000 − 1,40,000 + 32,000)	11,56,000	—
Advance to Supplier	1,44,000	—
Suspense A/c (8,000 + 12,000 + 4,000)	24,000	—
Total	35,68,000	35,68,000

Note *The existence of suspense account in the rectified trial balance implies that errors still exist.*

Trading and Profit and Loss Account
for the year ended 31st March, 2021

Dr					Cr
Particulars		Amt (₹)	Particulars		Amt (₹)
To Opening Stock		40,000	By Sales	20,34,000	
To Purchases	12,28,000		(−) Sales Return	(20,000)	20,14,000
(−) Purchases Return	(34,000)	11,94,000	By Closing Stock		80,000
To Wages		2,24,000			
To Gross Profit c/d		6,36,000			
		20,94,000			20,94,000
To Rent		44,000	By Gross Profit b/d		6,36,000
To Electricity		32,000			
To Other Expenses		64,000			
To Net Profit Transferred to Capital A/c		4,96,000			
		6,36,000			6,36,000

Balance Sheet
as at 31st March, 2021

Liabilities		Amt (₹)	Assets	Amt (₹)
Sundry Creditors		60,000	Cash in Hand	2,44,000
Capital	14,40,000		Cash at Bank	11,56,000
(+) Net Profit	4,96,000		Sundry Debtors	2,68,000
	19,36,000		Closing Stock	80,000
(−) Drawings	(80,000)	18,56,000	Advance to Supplier	1,44,000
			Suspense A/c	24,000
		19,16,000		19,16,000

Example 5. From the following trial balance of Monika Textiles as at 31st March, 2021. Prepare trading and profit and loss account and balance sheet. Also pass the necessar adjustment entries.

Name of Accounts	Debit Balance (₹)	Credit Balance (₹)
Stock at Commencement	15,00,000	—
Purchases and Sales	1,09,00,000	1,80,00,000
Manufacturing Wages	8,00,000	—
Fuel, Power and Lighting	12,00,000	—
Salaries	11,00,000	—
Income Tax	5,50,000	—
Loan to X @ (10% per annum)	5,00,000	—
Interest on X's Loan	—	30,000
Apprentice Premium	—	4,50,000
Rent	4,00,000	—
Rent Owing	—	60,000
Furniture (Includes furniture of ₹ 1,00,000 purchased on 1st October, 2020)	5,00,000	—
Bills Receivable and Bills Payable	6,00,000	1,60,000
Plant	72,00,000	—
Debtors and Creditors	28,00,000	13,00,000
Capital	—	1,00,00,000
Cash	19,50,000	—
Total	3,00,00,000	3,00,00,000

Additional Information

(i) Closing stock was valued at ₹ 30,00,000.

(ii) Goods worth ₹ 5,00,000 were sold and despatched on 28th March, 2021, but no entry was passed to this effect.

(iii) Goods costing ₹ 7,00,000 were purchased and included into stock but no entry was passed to record the purchases.

(iv) Create a provision of 2% for discount on debtors.

(v) Apprentice premium received on 1st April, 2020 was for 3 years.

(vi) Depreciate furniture by 10% per annum.

(vii) Salaries for the month of March, 2021 are still outstanding.

Ans.

JOURNAL

Date	Particulars		LF	Amt (Dr)	Amt (Cr)
(i)	Closing Stock A/c	Dr		30,00,000	
	To Trading A/c				30,00,000
	(Being the closing stock transferred to trading account)				
(ii)	Debtors A/c	Dr		5,00,000	
	To Sales A/c				5,00,000
	(Being the goods sold but omitted to be recorded)				
(iii)	Purchases A/c	Dr		7,00,000	
	To Creditors A/c				7,00,000
	(Being the goods purchased but omitted to be recorded)				
(iv)	Profit and Loss A/c	Dr		66,000	
	To Provision for Discount on Debtors A/c (WN1)				66,000
	(Being the provision for discount charged from profit and loss account)				
(v)	Apprentice Premium A/c	Dr		3,00,000	
	To Apprentice Premium Received in Advance A/c (WN2)				3,00,000
	(Being the apprentice premium received in advance)				
(vi)	Depreciation A/c (WN3)	Dr		45,000	
	To Furniture A/c				45,000
	(Being the depreciation charged on furniture)				
(vii)	Salary A/c (WN4)	Dr		1,00,000	
	To Salary Outstanding A/c				1,00,000
	(Being the salary outstanding)				

Trading and Profit and Loss Account
for the year ending 31st March, 2021

Dr   Cr

Particulars		Amt (₹)	Particulars		Amt (₹)
To Opening Stock		15,00,000	By Sales	1,80,00,000	
To Purchases	1,09,00,000		(+) Debtors	5,00,000	1,85,00,000
(+) Creditors	7,00,000	1,16,00,000	By Closing Stock		30,00,000
To Manufacturing Wages		8,00,000			
To Fuel, Power and Lighting		12,00,000			
To Gross Profit c/d		64,00,000			
		2,15,00,000			2,15,00,000

Particulars		Amt (₹)	Particulars		Amt (₹)
To Rent		4,00,000	By Gross Profit b/d		64,00,000
To Provision for Discount on Debtors		66,000	By Interest on X's Loan	30,000	
To Depreciation on Furniture		45,000	(+) Accrued Interest (WN5)	20,000	50,000
To Salaries	11,00,000		By Apprentice Premium	4,50,000	
(+) Outstanding Salaries	1,00,000	12,00,000	(−) Received in Advance	(3,00,000)	1,50,000
To Net Profit Transferred to Capital A/c		48,89,000			
		66,00,000			66,00,000

Balance Sheet
as at 31st March, 2021

Liabilities		Amt (₹)	Assets		Amt (₹)
Bills Payable		1,60,000	Cash		19,50,000
Creditors	13,00,000		Bills Receivable		6,00,000
(+) Purchases	7,00,000	20,00,000	Debtors	28,00,000	
Rent Owing		60,000	(+) Sales	5,00,000	
				33,00,000	
Apprentice Premium Received in Advance		3,00,000	(−) Provision for Discount	(66,000)	32,34,000
Salary Outstanding		1,00,000	Closing Stock		30,00,000
Capital	1,00,00,000		Loan to X		5,00,000
(+) Net Profit	48,89,000		Accrued Interest on X's Loan		20,000
	1,48,89,000		Furniture	5,00,000	
(−) Drawings (Income Tax)	(5,50,000)	1,43,39,000	(−) Depreciation	(45,000)	4,55,000
			Plant		72,00,000
		1,69,59,000			1,69,59,000

Working Notes

1. Provision for discount on debtors

Total Debtors $= 28,00,000 + 5,00,000 = ₹\,33,00,000$

Provision for Discount on Debtors $= 33,00,000 \times \dfrac{2}{100} = ₹\,66,000$

2. Apprentice premium for current year $= \dfrac{4,50,000}{3} = ₹\,1,50,000$

Thus, apprentice premium received in advance $= 4,50,000 - 1,50,000 = ₹\,3,00,000$

3. Depreciation on furniture $= \left[4,00,000 \times \dfrac{10}{100} \right] + \left[1,00,000 \times \dfrac{10}{100} \times \dfrac{6}{12} \right] = ₹\,45,000$

4. Salaries for 11 months $= ₹\,11,00,000$

Thus, salary outstanding for March, 2021 $= \dfrac{11,00,000}{11} = ₹\,1,00,000$

5. Interest on Loan $= 5,00,000 \times \dfrac{10}{100} = ₹\,50,000$

Accured Interest $=$ Total Interest on X's Loan $-$ Interest Received $= 50,000 - 30,000 = ₹\,20,000$

PART 1
Objective Questions

• Multiple Choice Questions

1. Need or objective for adjustments in preparation of final accounts is ....
(a) to know the correct financial position
(b) to provide for all losses
(c) to reduce the liability
(d) to increase the assets

Ans. (a) to know the correct financial position

2. Entries which need to be accounted for in the books of accounts at the time of preparing final accounts are called ....
(a) Opening entries   (b) Closing entries   (c) Adjustment entries   (d) Final account entry

Ans. (c) Adjustment entries

3. In case of sole proprietor business, income tax is considered as
(a) business expense   (b) proprietor's expense   (c) capital expense   (d) All of these

Ans. (b) Income tax is considered as a personal expense of the owner in business, so income tax will be added to drawings and subtracted from capital.

4. If the rent of one month is still to be paid, the adjustment entry will be   **(NCERT)**
(a) debit outstanding rent account and credit rent account
(b) debit profit and loss account and credit rent account
(c) debit rent account and credit profit and loss account
(d) debit rent account and credit outstanding rent account

Ans. (d) debit rent account and credit outstanding rent account

5. If the rent received in advance is ₹ 2,000, the adjustment entry will be   **(NCERT)**
(a) debit profit and loss account and credit rent account
(b) debit rent account and credit rent received in advance account
(c) debit rent received in advance account and credit rent account
(d) None of the above

Ans. (b) debit rent account and credit rent received in advance account

6. Goods distributed as free samples. The effect of this entry will be
(a) It is the proprietor's drawings
(b) It is deducted from purchases in the trading account
(c) It will be shown on the debit side of the profit and loss account
(d) Both (b) and (c)

Ans. (d) Both (b) and (c)

7. Manager's commission is always treated as .... expense.

(a) outstanding   (b) accrued   (c) unearned   (d) prepaid

Ans. (a) Manager's commission is calculated on net profit of the firm. It is considered as an outstanding expense for the firm, so it is transferred to liabilities side of balance sheet.

8. If the insurance premium paid ₹ 1,000 and prepaid insurance ₹ 300, the amount of insurance premium shown in profit and loss account will be   **(NCERT)**

(a) ₹ 1,300   (b) ₹ 1,000   (c) ₹ 300   (d) ₹ 700

Ans. (d) Total amount of insurance premium paid = 100

(–) Prepaid insurance	= (300)
	₹ 700

9. Consider the following statement.

(i) Interest on capital is an expense for the proprietor.

(ii) Interest on capital is shown on the debit side of profit and loss account.

(iii) It is added to the capital in the balance sheet.

Alternatives

(a) (i), (ii), (iii) are correct   (b) Both (i) and (ii) are correct

(c) Both (ii) and (iii) are correct   (d) (i), (ii), (iii) are incorrect

Ans. (c) Interest on capital is an expense for business.

10. Match the following.

Column I		Column II
A. Closing stock	(i)	Current liability
B. Manager's commission	(ii)	A court case
C. Depreciation	(iii)	Valued at cost or market price, whichever is lower
D. Contingent liability	(iv)	Allocation of cost

Codes

	A	B	C	D			A	B	C	D
(a)	(iii)	(iv)	(ii)	(i)		(b)	(iii)	(i)	(iv)	(ii)
(c)	(iii)	(iv)	(i)	(ii)		(d)	(iii)	(ii)	(i)	(iv)

Ans. (b) (iii), (i), (iv), (ii)

11. Loan from bank @ 12% per annum is ₹ 8,00,000. Interest on loan is due for the whole year. Amount shown on liabilities side of balance sheet will be

(a) ₹ 8,00,000   (b) ₹ 8,12,000   (c) ₹ 8,90,000   (d) ₹ 8,96,000

Ans. (d) Amount transferred to liability side will be as follows

$$\text{Interest} = \left(\frac{8,00,000 \times 12}{100} \right) = ₹\ 96,000$$

Total amount = 8,00,000 + 96,000 = ₹ 8,96,000

12. On 20th March, 2020 stock worth ₹ 80,000 was destroyed by fire. The stock was insured and the insurance company admitted full claim.

Which of the following journal entry/entries will be passed for above situation?

(i) Loss by Fire A/c	Dr	80,000	
To Trading A/c			80,000
(ii) Insurance Company	Dr	80,000	
To Loss by Fire A/c			80,000

  (iii) Profit and Loss A/c   Dr 80,000

     To Loss by Fire A/c   80,000

Alternatives

(a) Only (i)   (b) Only (ii)   (c) Both (i) and (ii)   (d) Both (ii) and (iii)

Ans. (c) Both (i) and (ii)

13. Consider the following information.

Cost of New Machine Purchased = ₹ 1,20,000   Installation Expenses = ₹ 30,000

Estimated Life of Machine = 5 years   Residual Value after 5 years = ₹ 25,000

Company started the production with this machine from 1st October, 2020. Assuming that the firm closes its accounts on 31st December every year, find the adjusted value of machine on 31st December, 2020?

(a) ₹ 1,43,750   (b) ₹ 1,25,000   (c) ₹ 1,75,000   (d) None of these

Ans. (a) Value of machine = Depreciation on Machine = $\left(\dfrac{1,20,000 + 30,000 - 25,000}{5} \right) \times \dfrac{3}{12} = ₹\ 6,250$

So, adjusted value of machine = (Purchase Value + Installation Expenses − Depreciation)

$$= (1,20,000 + 30,000 - 6,250) = ₹\ 1,43,750$$

14. ABC limited has taken a loan worth ₹ 5,50,000 from Vishal @ 10% per annum for the whole year. Which of the following journal entries will be passed in books of ABC limited to incorprote above adjustment?

  (i) Interest on Loan A/c   Dr   55,000

     To Loan A/c   55,000

  (ii) Profit and Loss A/c   Dr   55,000

     To interest on Loan A/c   55,000

  (iii) Trading A/c   Dr   55,000

     To Interest on Loan A/c   55,000

Alternatives

(a) Only (ii)   (b) Only (iii)

(c) Both (i) and (ii)   (d) Both (i) and (iii)

Ans. (c) Both (i) and (ii)

15 Rahul's trial balance provide you the following information.

Debtors   ₹ 80,000

Bad Debts   ₹ 2,000

Provision for Doubtful Debts   ₹ 4,000

It is desired to maintain a provision for bad debts of ₹ 1,000. State the amount to be debited/credited in profit and loss account. **(NCERT)**

(a) ₹ 5,000 (Debit)   (b) ₹ 3,000 (Debit)   (c) ₹ 1,000 (Credit)   (d) None of these

Ans. (c) Bad Debts   = 2,000

   New Provision = 1,000

        ―――――

        3,000

  (−) Old Provision = (4,000)

       ―――――

       (₹ 1,000)

• Assertion-Reasoning MCQs

Direction (Q. Nos. 1 to 6). *There are two statements marked as Assertion (A) and Reason (R). Read the statements and choose the appropriate option from the options given below.*

(a) Assertion (A) is correct, but Reason (R) is false
(b) Both Assertion (A) and Reason (R) are true
(c) Both Assertion (A) and Reason (R) are false
(d) Assertion (A) is false, but Reason (R) is true

1. Assertion (A) Accrued income given in adjustment is added to respective income on the credit side of profit and loss account and also shown on asset side of balance sheet.

Reason (R) Accrued income is provided as per accrual concept of accounting.

Ans. (b) Under accrual concept of accounting, income is recognised when goods or services have been sold whether the amount has been received or not. Since, it is an income it is credited to profit and loss account and as it is due to the enterprise, thus shown in balance sheet.

2. Assertion (A) Provision for doubtful debts is shown on asset side of balance sheet by way of deduction from sundry debtors.

Reason (R) It is created in accordance to convention of full disclosure.

Ans. (a) It is created in accordance to convention of conservatism.

3. Assertion (A) Bad debts stated in adjustment are debited to trading account and shown on assets side by deducting them from debtors.

Reason (R) Bad debts is an indirect expense which is irrecoverable from debtors.

Ans. (d) Bad debts is an indirect expense, thus are shown on debit side of profit and loss account.

4. Assertion (A) Depreciation specified in adjustment is shown on debit side of trading account and on asset side by way of substraction from value of fixed assets.

Reason (R) Depreciation is a direct and non-cash expense which leads to decrease in value of assets.

Ans. (c) Depreciation is an indirect expense and shown on debit side of profit and loss account.

5. Assertion (A) Goods distributed as free samples are recorded at purchase cost.

Reason (R) Goods distributed as sample is not a sale, but advertisement expense.

Ans. (b) When goods are distributed as free samples to promote sales, then stock will get reduced and it is an advertisement expenditure.

6. Assertion (A) Outstanding salary given in adjustment is added to salary account on debit side of profit and loss account and exhibited on liability side of balance sheet.

Reason (R) Outstanding salary is provided as per accrual concept of accounting.

Ans. (b) Outstanding expenses are provided as per accrual concept of accounting to which all expenses for the year, whether paid or not should be recorded.

• Case Based MCQs

Directions *Read the following text and answer the question no. (i) to (iv) on the basis of the same.*

1. CA Rahul Gupta works as a chartered accountant at Netware clothing in Kamla Nagar. Netware clothing deals in Western clothes and dresses. Rahul gupta is working here for the past 8 years.

On 31st March, 2020, Rahul prepared trial balance after preparation of accounts and subsidiary books. His trial balance total also agreed. But CA Rahul, being a diligent CA checked all the books of accounts again and discovered some of the information which were not taken into consideration.

Following trial balance was prepared by CA Rahul and additional information found by him.

Trial Balance
as on 31st March, 2020

Name of Accounts	Debit Balance (₹)	Credit Balance (₹)
Capital	—	2,70,000
Drawings	19,440	—
Land and Building	75,000	—
Plant and Machinery	42,810	—
Furniture and Fixtures	3,750	—
Carriage Inwards	13,110	—
Wages	64,410	—
Salaries	14,010	—
Provision for Bad Debts	—	7,410
Sales	—	2,73,690
Sales Return	5,280	—
Bank Charges	420	—
Gas and water	2,160	—
Rates and Taxes	2,520	—
Discount	—	360
Purchases	1,26,480	—
Purchases Return	—	25,380
Bills Receivable	3,810	—
Trade Expenses	5,970	—
Sundry Debtors	1,13,400	—
Sundry Creditors	—	36,510
Stock (1st April, 2019)	79,260	—
Apprentice Premium	—	1,500
Fire Insurance	1,470	—
Cash at Bank	39,000	—
Cash in Hand	2,550	—
Total	6,14,850	6,14,850

Adjustments

Charge depreciation on land and building at $2\frac{1}{2}\%$, on plant and machinery at 10% and on furniture and fixtures at 10%. Make provision of 5% on debtors for doubtful debts. Carry forward the following unexpired amounts

(a) Fire insurance ₹ 375   (b) Rates and taxes ₹ 720

(c) Apprentice premium ₹ 1,200   (d) Closing stock ₹ 88,170

CA Rahul immediately incorporated above adjustments while preparing final accounts of Netware clothings.

(i) Which of the undermentioned options reflect correct treatment for following adjustment?

Make provision of 5% on debtors for doubtful debts.

(a) ₹ 5,670 debited to profit and loss account and deducted from sundry debtors in balance sheet.

(b) ₹ 13,080 debited to profit and loss account and deducted from sundry debtors in balance sheet.

(c) ₹ 5,670 debited to trading account and deducted from sundry debtors in balance sheet.

(d) ₹ 13,080 debited to trading account and deducted from sundry debtors in balance sheet.

Ans. (a) Provision for Doubtful Debts $= 1,13,400 \times \dfrac{5}{100} = ₹\,5,670$

(ii) Which of the following will be the amount of rates and taxes shown in profit and loss account?

(a) ₹ 1,800   (b) ₹ 2,520   (c) ₹ 3,240   (d) ₹ 720

Ans. (a) Rent and taxes   2,520
     (–) Unexpired rent and taxes   (720)
                                 ₹ 1,800

₹1,800 will be the amount of rates and taxes shown in profit and loss account.

(iii) At what amount, land and building will be shown in balance sheet?

(a) ₹ 75,000   (b) ₹ 76,800   (c) ₹ 73,125   (d) ₹ 76,875

Ans. (c) Land and building = 75,000

     (–) Depreciation   = (1,875)

$$\left[\frac{25}{100} \times 75,000\right] \qquad ₹\,73,125$$

(iv) Which of the undermentioned amount is correct answer for apprentice premium to be shown in profit and loss account?

(a) ₹ 300   (b) ₹ 1,500   (c) ₹ 1,200   (d) ₹ 1,800

Ans. (a) Apprentice Premium =   1,500
        (–) Unexpired   = (1,200)
                     ₹ 300

2. **Direction** *Read the following text and answer the question no. (i) to (iv) on the basis of the same.*

Aman Mathur recently cleared his final CA exam in his 1st attempt. He is now appointed as a CA in Gopal Das Textiles, Chandni Chowk. On 31st March, 2020, he prepared trial balance whose total also agreed. But later he discovered some additional information which has to be taken into account while preparing final accounts. After taking into account few adjustments, he prepared final accounts of Gopal Das Textiles. Following trial balance was prepared by CA Aman Mathur and undermentioned adjustments were discovered by him.

Name of Accounts	Debit Balance (₹)	Credit Balance (₹)
Cash in Hand	20,000	—
Cash at Bank	1,80,000	—
Purchase and Sales	22,00,000	35,00,000
Return Inwards	60,000	—
Return Outwards	—	75,000
Carriage on Purchases	44,000	—
Carriage on Sales	21,000	—
Fuel and Power	1,55,000	—
Stock (1st April, 2019)	3,60,000	—
Bad Debts	62,000	—
Bad Debts Provision	—	25,000
Debtors and Creditors	8,20,000	3,00,000
Capital	—	21,70,000
Investments	2,00,000	—
Interest on Investments	—	20,000
Loan from X (@ 18% per annum)	—	1,00,000
Repairs	15,200	—
General Expenses	1,06,000	—
Land and Buildings	18,00,000	—
Wages and Salaries	1,80,000	—
Miscellaneous Receipts	—	1,200
Bills Payable	—	52,000
Stationery	20,000	—
Total	**62,43,200**	**62,43,200**

Additional Information

(a) Written-off ₹ 20,000 as bad debts and provision for doubtful debts is to be maintained at 5% on debtors.

(b) Loan from X was taken on 1st August, 2018. No interest has been paid so far.

(c) Included in general expenses is insurance premium ₹ 12,000, paid for one year ending 30th June, 2020.

(d) $\frac{1}{3}$ of wages and salaries is to be charged to trading account and the balance to profit and loss account.

(e) Entire stationery was used by the proprietor for his personal purpose.

(f) Closing stock was valued at ₹ 5,00,000.

(i) Which of the following amount of loan will be shown in balance sheet?

(a) ₹ 1,12,000   (b) ₹ 88,000   (c) ₹ 1,00,000   (d) ₹ 1,24,000

Ans. (a) Interest on loan $= 1,00,000 \times \dfrac{8}{12} \times \dfrac{18}{100}$

$$= ₹ \, 12,000$$

Amount of interest shown in balance sheet $= 1,00,000 + 12,000$

$$= ₹ \, 1,12,000$$

(ii) Calculate the amount of wages and salaries to be debited to profit and loss account?

(a) ₹ 60,000   (b) ₹ 1,80,000   (c) ₹ 1,20,000   (d) ₹ 3,00,000

Ans. (c) Amount of wages and salaries

Shown in profit and loss account $= \left[1,80,000 - \dfrac{1}{3} \times 1,80,000 \right]$

$$= ₹ \, 1,20,000$$

(iii) Which of the following will be the correct treatment for entire stationery used by proprietor for his personal purpose?

(a) Only shown in balance sheet as drawings.

(b) Shown as expense in profit and loss account and drawings in balance sheet.

(c) Shown as expense in trading account and drawings in balance sheet.

(d) None of the above

Ans. (a) Only shown in balance sheet as drawings.

(iv) Which of the following amount of prepaid insurance premium will be shown in balance sheet?

(a) ₹ 6,000   (b) ₹ 5,000   (c) ₹ 4,000   (d) ₹ 3,000

Ans. (d) Prepaid insurance premium $= 12,000 \times \dfrac{3}{12} = ₹ \, 3,000$

PART 2
Subjective Questions

• Short Answer (SA) Type Questions

1. What are the adjusting entries? Why are they necessary for preparing final accounts?

Or

Why is it necessary to record the adjusting entries in the preparation of final accounts? **(NCERT)**

Ans. It is the entry passed to record expenses and incomes that relate to the accounting period but are yet to be paid or received.

The need of making various adjustments are stated below

(i) To ascertain the true profit or loss of the business.

(ii) To determine the true financial position of the business.

(iii) To make a record of the transactions earlier omitted in the books.

(iv) To rectify the errors committed in the books.

(v) To complete the incomplete transactions.

2. State the meaning of **(NCERT)**

(i) Outstanding expenses   (ii) Prepaid expenses

(iii) Income received in advance

Ans. (i) **Outstanding Expenses** Those expenses whose benefit have been derived during the current year but payment is not made at the end of the year are known as outstanding expenses.

(ii) **Prepaid Expenses** Those expenses which have been paid in current year but the benefit of which will be available in the next accounting year are known as prepaid expenses.

(iii) **Income Received in Advance** The income or portion of income which is received during the current accounting year but has not been earned is called unearned income.

3. What is meant by closing stock? Show its treatment in final accounts. **(NCERT)**

Ans. Closing stock implies the value of unsold goods at the end of an accounting period. Closing stock is valued at cost or net realisable value, whichever is lower.

If closing stock is given in adjustment, it will be shown on the credit side of trading account and will also be shown on the assets side of balance sheet under current assets. If closing stock is given in trial balance, it will only be shown on the assets side of balance sheet under current assets.

4. What is meant by provision for doubtful debts? Why is it necessary to create a provision for doubtful debts at the time of preparation of final accounts?

Ans. The provision for doubtful debts is estimated amount of bad debts that will arise from amount receivable from debtors. In order to bring an element of certainty in amount of debtors, a provision for doubtful debts is created to cover the loss of possible bad debts as per the principle of prudence or conservatism.

5. Consider the following extract of trial balance

Extract of Trial Balance
as on 31st March, 2021

Name of Accounts	Debit Balance (₹)	Credit Balance (₹)
Commission Received		9,000

Additional Information

Commission earned but not received ₹ 1,800.

Pass an adjusting entry and show how will this appear in final accounts.

Ans. **Adjustment Entry**

JOURNAL

Particulars		Amt (Dr)	Amt (Cr)
Accrued Commission A/c	Dr	1,800	
To Commission A/c			1,800
(Being commission receivable)			

Effect on Final Accounts

Profit and Loss Account

Dr for the year ended 31st March, 2021 Cr

Particulars	Amt (₹)	Particulars		Amt (₹)
		By Commission	9,000	
		(+) Accrued Commission	1,800	10,800

Balance Sheet
as at 31st March, 2021

Liabilities	Amt (₹)	Assets	Amt (₹)
		Accrued Commission	1,800

6. Consider the following extract of trial balance taken from Prakhar's Books

Extract of Trial Balance
as at 31st March, 2021

Name of Accounts	Debit Balance (₹)	Credit Balance (₹)
Rent Received		15,600

Additional Information
Rent received but not earned ₹ 1,200.
Pass an adjusting entry and show how will this appear in final accounts.

Ans. **Adjustment Entry**

JOURNAL

Particulars		Amt (Dr)	Amt (Cr)
Rent A/c	Dr	1,200	
To Rent Received in Advance A/c			1,200
(Being adjustment entry for unearned rent)			

Effect on Final Accounts

Profit and Loss Account

Dr for the year ended 31st March, 2021 Cr

Particulars	Amt (₹)	Particulars		Amt (₹)
		By Rent	15,600	
		(−) Unearned Rent	(1,200)	14,400

Balance Sheet
as at 31st March, 2021

Liabilities	Amt (₹)	Assets	Amt (₹)
Unearned Rent	1,200		

7. Consider the following extract of trial balance taken from books of Harshit Enterprises.

Extract of Trial Balance
as on 31st March, 2021

Name of Accounts	Debit Balance (₹)	Credit Balance (₹)
Bad Debts	10,800	—
Provision for Bad and Doubtful Debts (1st April, 2020)	—	22,500
Sundry Debtors	6,00,000	—

Additional Information

(i) Write-off further bad debts ₹ 6,000.

(ii) Provision for doubtful debts to be maintained at 5% on sundry debtors.

(iii) Create a provision for discount on sundry debtors at 3%.

Show effect on profit and loss account and balance sheet.

Ans. **Effect on Final Acccounts**

Profit and Loss Account

Dr   for the year ended 31st March, 2021   Cr

Particulars		Amt (₹)	Particulars	Amt (₹)
To Bad Debts	10,800			
(+) Further Bad Debts	6,000			
	16,800			
(+) New Provision	29,700			
	46,500			
(−) Old Provision	(22,500)	24,000		
To Provision for Discount on Debtors		16,929		

Balance Sheet
as at 31st March, 2021

Liabilities	Amt (₹)	Assets		Amt (₹)
		Sundry Debtors	6,00,000	
		(−) Further Bad Debts	(6,000)	
			5,94,000	
		(−) New Provision for Doubtful Debts	(29,700)	
		(5% on 5,94,000)	5,64,300	
		(−) Provision for Discount on Debtors	(16,929)	5,47,371
		(3% on 5,64,300)		

8. Consider the following extract of trial balance taken from books of Mehta Limited.

Extract of Trial Balance
as at 31st March, 2021

Name of Accounts	Debit Balance (₹)	Credit Balance (₹)
Purchases	1,00,000	—
Capital	—	3,00,000

Additional Information

During the year, the proprietor, Mr Mehta withdrew goods worth ₹ 5,000.

Pass an adjusting entry and show effect on financial statements.

Ans. **Adjusting Entry**

JOURNAL

Date	Particulars		LF	Amt (Dr)	Amt (Cr)
	Drawings A/c	Dr		5,000	
	To Purchases A/c				5,000

Effect on Financial Statements

Trading Account

Dr   for the year ended 31st March, 2021   Cr

Particulars		Amt (₹)	Particulars	Amt (₹)
To Purchases	1,00,000			
(–) Goods withdrawn by Proprietor	(5,000)	95,000		

Balance Sheet
as at 31st March, 2021

Liabilities		Amt (₹)	Assets	Amt (₹)
Capital	3,00,000			
(–) Goods Withdrawn by Proprietor	(5,000)	2,95,000		

9. Consider the following trial balance of Rohan Limited.

Extract of Trial Balance
as at 31st March, 2021

Name of Accounts	Debit Balance (₹)	Credit Balance (₹)
Purchases	1,00,000	—

Additional Information

During the year the proprietor, Mr Rohan distributed goods worth ₹ 10,000 as free samples.

Pass an adjusting entry and show effect on financial statements.

Ans. **Adjusting Entry**

JOURNAL

Date	Particulars	LF	Amt (Dr)	Amt (Cr)
	Advertisement A/c　　　　　　　　Dr		10,000	
	To Purchases A/c			10,000

Effect on Financial Statements

Trading Account

Dr　　　　　　　　　　for the year ended 31st March, 2021　　　　　　　　　　Cr

Particulars	Amt (₹)		Particulars	Amt (₹)
To Purchases	1,00,000			
(–) Goods Distributed as				
Free Sample	(10,000)	90,000		

Profit and Loss Account

Dr　　　　　　　　　　for the year ended 31st March, 2021　　　　　　　　　　Cr

Particulars	Amt (₹)	Particulars	Amt (₹)
To Avertisement Expenses	10,000		

10. Consider the following extract of trial balance taken from books of Manisha Enterprises.

Extract of Trial Balance
as at 31st March, 2020

Name of Accounts	Debit Balance (₹)	Credit Balance (₹)
Creditors	—	18,26,400
Debtors	40,00,000	—
Purchases	7,22,500	—
Sales	—	7,98,920

Additional Information

(i) Credit sales of ₹ 9,000 were not recorded in books of accounts.

(ii) Received ₹ 98,000 worth of goods on 29th March, 2020 but the invoice of purchases was not recorded.

Ans.

Trading Account

Dr　　　　　　　　　　for the year ended 31st March, 2020　　　　　　　　　　Cr

Particulars	Amt (₹)		Particulars	Amt (₹)	
To Purchases	7,22,500		By Sales	7,98,920	
(+) Omitted Purchases	98,000	8,20,500	(+) Credit Sales	9,000	8,07,920

Balance Sheet
as on 31st March, 2020

Liabilities	Amt (₹)		Assets	Amt (₹)	
Creditors	18,26,400		Debtors	40,00,000	
(+) Omitted Purchases	98,000	19,24,400	(+) Credit Sales Not Recorded	9,000	40,09,000

11. Following trial balance is prepared on 31st March, 2019 from a trader's book

Particulars	Dabit Balance (₹)	Credit Balance (₹)
Cash in Hand	22,000	—
Wages	20,000	—
Sales	—	5,02,000
Furniture	2,00,000	—
Bills Receivable	45,000	—
Opening Stock	84,000	—
Creditors	—	33,000
Purchases	3,60,000	—
Sales Return	6,000	—
Rent	32,000	—
Debtors	90,000	—
Insurance	22,000	—
Bad Debts	6,000	—
Carriage	4,800	—
Capital	—	3,50,000
Commission	—	6,800
Total	**8,91,800**	**8,91,800**

Taking into consideration the adjustments given below. Pass the journal entries for the same.

  (i) Closing stock ₹ 1,00,000

 (ii) Outstanding rent ₹ 4,200 and outstanding wages ₹ 9,000

(iii) Prepaid insurance ₹ 7,900 and accrued commission ₹ 1,200

(iv) Charge depreciation on furniture @ 10% p.a.

Ans.

JOURNAL

Date	Particulars		LF	Amt (Dr)	Amt (Cr)
(i)	Closing Stock A/c	Dr		1,00,000	
	To Trading A/c				1,00,000
	(Being the closing stock recorded)				
(ii)	Rent A/c	Dr		4,200	
	Wages A/c	Dr		9,000	
	To Rent Outstanding A/c				4,200
	To Wages Outstanding A/c				9,000
	(Being the outstanding rent and wages recorded)				
(iii)	Prepaid Insurance Premium A/c	Dr		7,900	
	To Insurance Premium A/c				7,900
	(Being the adjustment for prepaid insurance premium recorded)				
	Accrued Commission A/c	Dr		1,200	
	To Commission A/c				1,200
	(Being the adjustment made for accrued commission)				
(iv)	Depreciation A/c	Dr		20,000	
	To Machinery A/c				20,000
	(Being the depreciation charged on machinery)				

Working Note

$$\text{Depreciation of Machinery} = 2,00,000 \times \frac{10}{100} = ₹\ 20,000$$

12. The net profit of a firm amounts to ₹ 31,500 before charging commission. The manager of the firm is entitled to a commission of 5% on the net profits. Calculate the commission payable to the manager in each of the following alternative cases and also show its effect on final accounts.

  (i) If the manager is allowed commission on the net profit before charging such commission.

  (ii) If the manager is allowed commission on the net profit after charging such commission.

    Also, show its treatment in final accounts ending on 31st March, 2021.

Ans. (i) Manager's Commission = Net Profit before Charging such Commission $\times \dfrac{\text{Rate of Commission}}{100}$

$$= 31,500 \times \frac{5}{100} = ₹1,575$$

(ii) Manager's Commission = Net Profit before Charging such Commission $\times \dfrac{\text{Rate of Commission}}{100 + \text{Rate of Commission}}$

$$= 31,500 \times \frac{5}{105} = ₹1,500$$

Effect on Final Accounts

Profit and Loss Account

Dr		for the year ended 31st March, 2021		Cr
Particulars	**Amt (₹)**	**Particulars**		**Amt (₹)**
To Manager's Commission	1,500			

Balance Sheet
as at 31st March, 2021

Liabilities	**Amt (₹)**	**Assets**	**Amt (₹)**
Current Liabilities			
Manager's Commission Outstanding	1,500		

13. Consider the following extract of trial balance of ABC Limited

Extract of the Trial Balance
as on 31st December, 2020

Name of Accounts	**Debit Balance (₹)**	**Credit Balance (₹)**
Loan to Kartik	16,000	

Adjustment Interest on Kartik's loan is due to be received @ 12% per annum for the whole year. Pass an adjusting entry and show effect on financial statements.

Ans. Adjustment Entries

JOURNAL

Date	Particulars		LF	Amt (Dr)	Amt (Cr)
	Kartik's Loan A/c	Dr		1,920	
	To Interest on Loan A/c				1,920
	(Being the interest on Kartik's loan due to be received)				
	Interest on Loan A/c	Dr		1,920	
	To Profit and Loss A/c				1,920
	(Being the interest on loan credited to profit and loss account)				

Working Note

Interest of Loan $= 16,000 \times \dfrac{12}{100} = ₹ 1,920$

Effect on Final Accounts

Profit and Loss Account

Dr   for the year ended 31st December, 2020   Cr

Particulars	Amt (₹)	Particulars	Amt (₹)
		By Interest on Loan	1,920

Balance Sheet
as at 31st December, 2020

Liabilities	Amt (₹)	Assets		Amt (₹)
		Kartik's Loan	16,000	
		(+) Interest	1,920	17,920

14. Consider the following extract of trial balance from books of Prateek Limited.

Extract of Trial Balance
as at 31st March, 2021

Particulars	Debit Balance (₹)	Credit Balance (₹)
Capital A/c	—	10,00,000
Drawings A/c	1,60,000	—

Adjustment Charge ₹ 6,000 as interest on drawings.

Pass an adjusting entry and show effect on financial statements.

Ans. **Adjustment Entries**

JOURNAL

Date	Particulars		LF	Amt (Dr)	Amt (Cr)
	Drawings A/c	Dr		6,000	
	To Interest on Drawings A/c				6,000
	(Being the interest charged on drawings)				
	Interest on Drawings A/c	Dr		6,000	
	To Profit and Loss A/c				6,000
	(Being the interest on drawings credited to profit and loss account)				

Effect on Final Accounts

Profit and Loss Account

Dr   for the yearded 31st March, 2021   Cr

Particulars	Amt (₹)	Particulars	Amt (₹)
		By Interest on Drawings	6,000

Balance Sheet
as at 31st March, 2021

Liabilities		Amt (₹)	Assets	Amt (₹)
Capital	10,00,000			
(−) Drawings	(1,60,000)			
	8,40,000			
(−) Interest on Drawings	(6,000)	8,34,000		

• Long Answer (LA) Type Questions

1. From the following trial balance of Sh. Prakash, prepare trading and profit and loss account for the year ended 31st March, 2020 and balance sheet as at that date.

Particulars	Debit Balance (₹)	Credit Balance (₹)
Purchases and Sales	5,50,000	10,40,000
Return Inwards	30,000	—
Return Outwards	—	18,000
Carriage	24,800	—
Wages and Salaries	1,17,200	—
Trade Expenses	4,400	—
Rent	—	26,000
Insurance	4,000	—
Audit Fees	2,400	—
Debtors and Creditors	2,20,000	1,24,200
Bills Receivable and Bills Payable	6,600	4,400
Printing and Advertising	11,000	—
Commission	—	2,000
Opening Stock	72,000	—
Cash in Hand	25,600	—
Cash at Bank	53,600	—
Bank Loan	—	40,000
Interest on Loan	3,000	—
Capital	—	5,00,000
Drawings	30,000	—
Fixed Assets	6,00,000	—
	17,54,600	17,54,600

Additional Information

(i) Stock at the end ₹ 1,20,000.　　(ii) Depreciation to be charged on fixed assets @ 10%.

(iii) Commission earned but not received amounting to ₹ 800.

(iv) Rent received in advance ₹ 2,000.

(v) 8% interest to be allowed on capital and ₹ 1,800 to be charged as interest on drawings.

Ans.

Trading and Profit and Loss Account

Dr　　for the year ending 31st March, 2020　　Cr

Particulars		Amt (₹)	Particulars		Amt (₹)
To Opening Stock		72,000	By Sales	10,40,000	
To Purchases	5,50,000		(–) Return Inwards	(30,000)	10,10,000
(–) Return Outwards	(18,000)	5,32,000	By Closing Stock		1,20,000
To Carriage		24,800			
To Wages and Salaries		1,17,200			
To Gross Profit (transferred to profit and loss account)		3,84,000			
		11,30,000			11,30,000
To Trade Expenses		4,400	By Gross Profit b/d		3,84,000
To Insurance		4,000	By Commission	2,000	
To Audit Fees		2,400	(+) Accrued		
To Printing and Advertising		11,000	Commission	800	2,800
To Interest on Loan		3,000	By Rent	26,000	
To Depreciation on Fixed Assets		60,000	(–) Received in		
To Interest on Capital		40,000	Advance	(2,000)	24,000
To Net Profit (transferred to capital account)		2,87,800	By Interest on Drawings		1,800
		4,12,600			4,12,600

Balance Sheet
as at 31st March, 2020

Liabilities	Amt (₹)		Assets	Amt (₹)	
Bank Loan		40,000	Cash in Hand		25,600
Bills Payable		4,400	Cash at Bank		53,600
Creditors		1,24,200	Bills Receivable		6,600
Rent Received in Advance		2,000	Debtors		2,20,000
Capital	5,00,000		Closing Stock		1,20,000
(+) Interest on Capital	40,000		Accrued Commission		800
(+) Net Profit	2,87,800		Fixed Assets	6,00,000	
	8,27,800		(–) Depreciation	(60,000)	5,40,000
(–) Drawings	(30,000)				
(–) Interest on Drawings	(1,800)	7,96,000			
		9,66,600			9,66,600

2. Following balances have been extracted from the trial balance of M/s Keshav Electronics Ltd. You are required to prepare the trading and profit and loss account and balance sheet as on 31st December, 2019.

Particulars	Amt (₹)	Particulars	Amt (₹)
Opening Stock	2,26,000	Sales	6,80,000
Purchases	4,40,000	Return Outwards	15,000
Drawings	75,000	Creditors	50,000
Buildings	1,00,000	Bills Payable	63,700
Motor Van	30,000	Interest Received	20,000
Freight Inwards	3,400	Capital	3,50,000
Sales Return	10,000		
Trade Expenses	3,300		
Heat and Power	8,000		
Salary and Wages	5,000		
Legal Expenses	3,000		
Postage and Telegram	1,000		
Bad Debts	6,500		
Cash in Hand	79,000		
Cash at Bank	98,000		
Sundry Debtors	25,000		
Investments	40,000		
Insurance	3,500		
Machinery	22,000		
	11,78,700		11,78,700

The following additional information is available

(i) Stock on 31st December, 2019 was ₹ 30,000.
(ii) Depreciation is to be charged on building @ 5% and motor van @ 10%.
(iii) Provision for doubtful debts is to be maintained @ 5% on sundry debtors.
(iv) Unexpired insurance was ₹ 600.
(v) The manager is entitled to commission @ 5% on net profit after charging such commission.

Ans.

Trading and Profit and Loss Account
for the year ending 31st December, 2019

Dr   Cr

Particulars		Amt (₹)	Particulars		Amt (₹)
To Opening Stock		2,26,000	By Sales	6,80,000	
To Purchases	4,40,000		(−) Return	(10,000)	6,70,000
(−) Return outwards	(15,000)	4,25,000	By Closing Stock		30,000
To Freight Inward		3,400			
To Heat and Power		8,000			
To Gross Profit		37,600			
(transferred to profit and loss account)					
		7,00,000			7,00,000
To Depreciation on			By Gross Profit b/d		37,600
Building	5,000		By Interest Received		20,000
Motor Car	3,000	8,000			
To Bad Debts	6,500				
(+) Provision on Debtors	1,250	7,750			
To Insurance	3,500				
(−) Prepaid Insurance	(600)	2,900			
To Trade Expenses		3,300			
To Salary and Wages		5,000			
To Legal Expenses		3,000			
To Postage and Telegram		1,000			
To Manager's Commission $\left(26,650 \times \dfrac{5}{105}\right)$		1,269			
To Net Profit (transferred to capital account)		25,381			
		57,600			57,600

Balance Sheet
as at 31st December, 2019

Liabilities		Amt (₹)	Assets		Amt (₹)
Capital	3,50,000		Building	1,00,000	
(+) Net Profit	25,381		(−) Depreciation	(5,000)	95,000
	3,75,381		Motor Car	30,000	
(−) Drawings	(75,000)	3,00,381	(−) Depreciation	(3,000)	27,000
Manager's Commission		1,269	Debtors	25,000	
Bills Payables		63,700	(−) Provision on Debtors	(1,250)	23,750
Creditors		50,000	Prepaid Insurance		600
			Cash in Hand		79,000
			Cash at Bank		98,000
			Investment		40,000
			Machinery		22,000
			Closing Stock		30,000
		4,15,350			4,15,350

3. The following is the trial balance of Mr Chidambram on 31st March, 2020.

Particulars	Debit Balance (₹)	Credit Balance (₹)
Cash in Hand	10,800	—
Cash at Bank	52,600	—
Purchases/Sales	8,13,500	19,75,600
Returns	13,600	10,000
Wages	2,09,600	—
Power	94,600	—
Carriage on Sales	64,000	—
10% Bank Loan	—	1,00,000
Carriage on Purchases	40,800	—
Stock (on 1st April, 2019)	1,15,200	—
Buildings	6,00,000	—
Freehold Land	2,00,000	—
Machinery	4,00,000	—
Salaries	3,00,000	—
Patents	1,50,000	—
General Expenses	60,000	—
Insurance	12,000	—
Drawings/Capital	1,04,900	14,20,000
Sundry Debtors/Creditors	2,90,000	26,000
	35,31,600	35,31,600

Taking into account the following adjustments, prepare trading and profit and loss account and the balance sheet.

(i) Stock in hand on 31st March, 2020 is ₹ 1,36,000.

(ii) Machinery is to be depreciated at the rate of 10% p.a. and patent at the rate of 20% p.a.

(iii) Salaries for the month of March, 2020 amounting to ₹ 30,000 were unpaid.

(iv) Insurance includes a premium of ₹ 1,700 for 2020-21.

(v) Wages include a sum of ₹ 40,000 spent on the erection of a cycle shed for employees and customers.

(vi) A provision for doubtful debts is to be created to the extent of 5% on sundry debtors.

(vii) Bank loan was taken on 1st October, 2019.

Ans.

Dr   **Trading and Profit and Loss Account**   Cr
for the year ended 31st March, 2020

Particulars	Amt (₹)		Particulars	Amt (₹)	
To Opening Stock		1,15,200	By Sales	19,75,600	
To Purchases	8,13,500		(–) Return	(13,600)	19,62,000
(–) Return	(10,000)	8,03,500	By Closing Stock		1,36,000
To Wages	2,09,600				
(–) Wages Paid on Erection of a Cycle Shed	(40,000)	1,69,600			
To Carriage Inward		40,800			
To Power		94,600			
To Gross Profit		8,74,300			
(Transferred to profit and loss account)					
		20,98,000			20,98,000
To Carriage Outward		64,000	By Gross Profit b/d		8,74,300
To Salaries	3,00,000				
(+) Outstanding	30,000	3,30,000			
To General Expenses		60,000			

Particulars	Amt (₹)		Particulars	Amt (₹)
To Insurance	12,000			
(–) Prepaid	(1,700)	10,300		
To Depreciation on				
Machinery	40,000			
Patents	30,000	70,000		
To Provision for Doubtful Debts		14,500		
To Outstanding Interest on Bank Loan (for 6 months)		5,000		
To Net Profit Transferred to Capital A/c		3,20,500		
		8,74,300		8,74,300

Balance Sheet
as at 31st March, 2020

Liabilities	Amt (₹)		Assets	Amt (₹)	
Bank Loan	1,00,000		Cash in Hand		10,800
(+) Outstanding Interest	5,000	1,05,000	Cash at Bank		52,600
Creditors		26,000	Debtors	2,90,000	
Outstanding Salaries		30,000	(–) Provision	(14,500)	2,75,500
Capital	14,20,000		Prepaid Insurance		1,700
Opening Balance			Closing Stock		1,36,000
(+) Net Profit	3,20,500		Building (6,00,000 + 40,000)		6,40,000
	17,40,500		Land		2,00,000
(–) Drawings	(1,04,900)	16,35,600	Machinery	4,00,000	
			(–) Depreciation	(40,000)	3,60,000
			Patents	1,50,000	
			(–) Depreciation	(30,000)	1,20,000
		17,96,600			17,96,600

4. From the following ledger balances of Mr Navjot Singh, prepare the trading and profit and loss account for the year ended 31st March, 2020 and the balance sheet as at that date after making the necessary adjustments.

Particulars	Amt (₹)	Particulars	Amt (₹)
Trade Expenses	1,600	Purchases	1,64,000
Freight and Duty	4,000	Stock (1st April, 2019)	30,000
Carriage Outwards	1,000	Plant and Machinery (1st April, 2019)	40,000
Sundry Debtors	41,200	Plant and Machinery	10,000
Furniture and Fixtures	10,000	(additions on 1st October, 2019)	
Return Inwards	4,000	Drawings	12,000
Printing and Stationery	800	Capital	1,60,000
Rent, Rates and Taxes	9,200	Provision for Doubtful Debts	1,600
Sundry Creditors	20,000	Rent for Premises Sublet	3,200
Sales	2,40,000	Insurance Charges	1,400
Return Outwards	2,000	Salaries and Wages	42,600
Postage and Telegraphs	1,600	Cash in Hand	12,400
		Cash at Bank	41,000

Additional Information

(i) Stock on 31st March, 2020 was ₹ 28,000.

(ii) Write-off ₹ 1,200 as bad debts.

(iii) Provision for doubtful debts is to be maintained @ 5%.

(iv) Provision for depreciation on furniture and fixtures at 5% p.a. and on plant and machinery at 20% p.a.

(v) Insurance prepaid was ₹ 200.

(vi) A fire occurred in the godown and stock of the value of ₹ 10,000 was destroyed. It was insured and the insurance company admitted full claim.

Ans.

Trading and Profit and Loss Account

Dr   for the year ending 31st March, 2020   Cr

Particulars		Amt (₹)	Particulars		Amt (₹)
To Opening Stock		30,000	By Sales	2,40,000	
To Purchases	1,64,000		(−) Return Inwards	(4,000)	2,36,000
(−) Return Outwards	(2,000)	1,62,000	By Loss of Stock by Fire		10,000
To Freight and Duty		4,000	By Closing Stock		28,000
To Gross Profit (Transferred to profit and loss account)		78,000			
		2,74,000			2,74,000
To Trade Expenses		1,600	By Gross Profit b/d		78,000
To Carriage Outwards		1,000	By Rent for Premises		3,200
To Depreciation on Furniture and Fixtures		500			
To Depreciation on Plant and Machinery					
$(40,000 \times 20/100)$	8,000				
$(10,000 \times 20/100 \times 6/12)$	1,000	9,000			
To Printing and Stationery		800			
To Rent, Rates and Taxes		9,200			
To Insurance	1,400				
(−) Prepaid	(200)	1,200			
To Salaries and Wages		42,600			
To Postage and Telegraphs		1,600			
To Provision for Doubtful Debts	2,000				
(Closing) $(40,000 \times 5/100)$					
(+) Further Bad Debts	1,200				
	3,200				
(−) Provision for Doubtful Debts (Opening)	(1,600)	1,600			
To Net Profit (transferred to capital account)		12,100			
		81,200			81,200

Balance Sheet
as at 31st March, 2020

Liabilities		Amt (₹)	Assets		Amt (₹)
Sundry Creditors		20,000	Cash in Hand		12,400
Capital			Cash at Bank		41,000
Opening Balance	1,60,000		Sundry Debtors	41,200	
(+) Net Profit	12,100		(−) Further Bad Debts	(1,200)	
	1,72,100			40,000	
(−) Drawings	(12,000)	1,60,100	(−) Provision for Doubtful Debts	(2,000)	38,000
			Closing Stock		28,000
			Insurance Claim		10,000
			Prepaid Insurance		200
			Furniture and Fixtures	10,000	
			(−) Depreciation	(500)	9,500
			Plant and Machinery	50,000	
			(−) Depreciation	(9,000)	41,000
		1,80,100			1,80,100

Note *Sometimes, the balance in the provision for doubtful debts account is more than sufficient to meet the bad debts and the new provision required. Thus, remaining amount is then credited to the profit and loss account.*

5. Prepare a trading and profit and loss account for the year ending 31st December, 2020 from the balances extracted from M/s Rahul and Sons. Also prepare a balance sheet at the end of the year.

Name of Accounts	Amt (₹)	Name of Accounts	Amt (₹)
Stock	50,000	Sales	1,80,000
Wages	3,000	Purchase return	2,000
Salary	8,000	Discount received	500
Purchases	1,75,000	Provision for bad debts	2,500
Sales return	3,000	Capital	3,00,000
Sundry debtors	82,000	Bills payable	22,000
Discount allowed	1,000	Commission received	4,000
Insurance	3,200	Rent	6,000
Rent, rates and taxes	4,300	Loan	34,800
Fixtures and fittings	20,000		
Trade expenses	1,500		
Bad debts	2,000		
Drawings	32,000		
Repair and renewals	1,600		
Travelling expenses	4,200		
Postage	300		
Telegram expenses	200		
Legal fees	500		
Bills receivable	50,000		
Building	1,10,000		
	5,51,800		5,51,800

Adjustments

(i) Commission received in advance ₹ 1,000.

(ii) Rent received ₹ 2,000.

(iii) Salary outstanding ₹ 1,000 and insurance prepaid ₹ 800.

(iv) Further bad debts ₹ 1,000 and provision for bad debts @ 5% on debtors and discount on debtors @ 2%.

(v) Closing stock ₹ 32,000.

(vi) Depreciation on building @ 6% p.a.

Ans.

Trading and Profit and Loss Account

Dr
as at 31st December, 2020
Cr

Particulars		Amt (₹)	Particulars		Amt (₹)
To Opening Stock		50,000	By Sales	1,80,000	
To Purchases	1,75,000		(−) Sales Return	(3,000)	1,77,000
(−) Purchases Return	(2,000)	1,73,000	By Closing Stock		32,000
To Wages		3,000	By Gross Loss (Transferred to profit and loss account)		17,000
		2,26,000			2,26,000
To Gross Loss b/d		17,000	By Discount Received		500
To Salary	8,000		By Commission Received	4,000	
(+) Outstanding Salary	1,000	9,000	(−) Advance	(1,000)	3,000
To Discount Allowed		1,000	By Rent Received	6,000	
To Insurance	3,200		(+) Accrued Rent	2,000	8,000
(−) Prepaid Insurance	(800)	2,400	By Net Loss (Transferred		43,189
To Rent, Rates and Taxes		4,300	to capital account)		
To Trade Expenses		1,500			
To Bad Debts	2,000				
(+) Further Bad Debts	1,000				
(+) New Provision	4,050				
(+) Discount	1,539				
(−) Old Provision	(2,500)	6,089			
To Postage		300			
To Telegram Expenses		200			
To Repair and Renewals		1,600			
To Travelling Expenses		4,200			
To Legal Fees		500			
To Depreciation on Building		6,600			
		54,689			54,689

Balance Sheet
as at 31st December, 2020

Liabilities		Amt (₹)	Assets		Amt (₹)
Capital	3,00,000		Sundry Debtors (WN)		75,411
(−) Net Loss	(43,189)		Bills Receivable		50,000
	2,56,811		Fixture and Fitting		20,000
(−) Drawings	(32,000)	2,24,811	Prepaid Insurance		800
Bills Payable		22,000	Building	1,10,000	
Loan		34,800	(−) Depreciation @ 6%	(6,600)	1,03,400
Advance Commission		1,000	Rent (Accrued)		2,000
Outstanding Salary		1,000	Closing Stock		32,000
		2,83,611			2,83,611

Working Note

	Amt (₹)
Sundry Debtors	82,000
(–) Further Bad Debts	(1,000)
	81,000
(–) Provision (5%)	(4,050)
	76,950
(–) Discount (2%)	(1,539)
	75,411

6. From the books of M/s Aggarwal, the following trial balance has been prepared on 31st March, 2020

Trial Balance
as on 31st March, 2020

Name of Accounts	Debit Balance (₹)	Name of Accounts	Credit Balance (₹)
Purchases	19,35,000	Sales	30,00,000
Wages	2,32,500	Sales Tax Collected	2,45,000
Carriage on Purchases	1,80,000	Interest on Investment	7,000
Prepaid Insurance (1st April, 2019)	6,250	Provision for Doubtful Debts	25,000
Bad Debts	6,000	Cash Discount	45,000
Rent and Insurance	77,500	Capital	7,11,750
Salary	1,35,000	Creditors	1,87,500
Debtors	3,75,000	Outstanding Wages	9,000
Stock (31st March, 2020)	2,05,000	(31st March, 2020)	
Investment	1,00,000		
Cash	1,45,000		
Accrued Interest (31st March, 2020)	8,000		
Furniture	1,05,000		
Plant of Factory	5,00,000		
Income Tax	2,20,000		
	42,30,250		42,30,250

Prepare the trading and profit and loss account for the year ended 31st March, 2020 and the balance sheet as at that date, taking into consideration the adjustments given below

 (i) On 1st October, 2019, plant worth ₹ 1,00,000 was purchased on credit but no entry has been passed.
 (ii) Outstanding expenses rent ₹ 5,000 and salary ₹ 6,000.
(iii) Prepaid expenses insurance ₹ 2,500 and wages ₹ 4,000.
(iv) Goods worth ₹ 27,500 were taken for personal use by the owner but no entry has been made.
 (v) Write-off depreciation on plant and furniture @ 10% p.a.
(vi) Write-off ₹ 5,000 from debtors as bad debts and create provision for doubtful debts @ 5% and 2% provision for discount on debtors.

Ans.

Trading and Profit and Loss Account
for the year ending 31st March, 2020

Dr | | | | Cr

Particulars	Amt (₹)		Particulars	Amt (₹)
To Purchases	19,35,000		By Sales	30,00,000
(–) Goods Taken for Personal Use	(27,500)	19,07,500		
To Wages	2,32,500			
(–) Prepaid Wages	(4,000)	2,28,500		
To Carriage on Purchases		1,80,000		

Particulars	Amt (₹)	Particulars	Amt (₹)
To Gross Profit (Transferred to profit and loss account)	6,84,000		
	30,00,000		30,00,000
To Rent and Insurance 77,500		By Gross Profit b/d	6,84,000
(+) Outstanding Rent 5,000		By Interest on Investment	7,000
82,500		By Discount Received	45,000
(−) Prepaid Insurance (2,500)			
80,000			
(+) Prepaid Insurance Last Year 6,250	86,250		
To Bad Debts 6,000			
(+) Further Bad Debts 5,000			
(+) Provision on Debtors 18,500			
29,500			
(−) Old Provision (25,000)	4,500		
To Depreciation on Plant 50,000			
(+) New Plant 5,000	55,000		
To Salary 1,35,000			
(+) Outstanding 6,000	1,41,000		
To Depreciation on Furniture	10,500		
To Provision for Discount on Debtors	7,030		
To Net Profit (transferred to capital account)	4,31,720		
	7,36,000		7,36,000

Balance Sheet
as at 31st March, 2020

Liabilities	Amt (₹)	Assets	Amt (₹)
Capital 7,11,750		Plant (old) 5,00,000	
(+) Net Profit 4,31,720		(−) Depreciation (50,000)	4,50,000
11,43,470		New Plant (1st October, 2019) 1,00,000	
(−) Drawings (27,500)		(−) Depreciation (for 6 months) (5,000)	95,000
11,15,970		Prepaid Wages	4,000
(−) Income Tax Paid (2,20,000)	8,95,970	Prepaid Insurance	2,500
Sales Tax Collected	2,45,000	Furniture 1,05,000	
Outstanding wages	9,000	(−) Depreciation (10,500)	94,500
Creditors	1,87,500	Debtors 3,75,000	
Outstanding Rent	5,000	(−) Further Bad Debts (5,000)	
Outstanding Salary	6,000	3,70,000	
Creditors for Plant	1,00,000	(−) Provision for Doubtful Debts (18,500)	
		3,51,500	
		(−) Provision for Discount (7,030)	3,44,470
		Investment	1,00,000
		Cash	1,45,000
		Accrued Interest	8,000
		Closing Stock	2,05,000
	14,48,470		14,48,470

Chapter Test

Multiple Choice Questions

1. Which of the following is the journal to record accrued income?

(a) Accrued Income A/c   Dr
       To Concerned Income   A/c

(b) Concerned Income A/c   Dr
       To Accrued Income A/c

(c) Cash A/c   Dr
       To Concerned Income A/c

(d) Cash A/c   Dr
       To Accrued Income A/c

2. Debtors given in trial balance of Rajeev Enterprises are ₹ 30,000. After creating a provision for doutbful debts @ 5% on debtors, at what value the debtors will be shown in balance sheet?

(a) ₹ 30,000   (b) ₹ 28,500   (c) ₹ 31,500   (d) Nil

3.

Extract of Trial Balance
as on 31st March, 2020

Name of Accounts	Debit Balance (₹)	Credit Balance (₹)
12% Bank Loan	—	40,000
Interest Paid	3,800	—

Amount of outstanding interest will be ....

(a) ₹ 4,800   (b) ₹ 5,000   (c) ₹ 5,500   (d) ₹ 1,000

4. Net profit of a firm before charging manager's commission is ₹ 21,000. If manager is entitled to 5% commission after charging such commission, how much manager will get as commission?

(a) ₹ 1,050   (b) ₹ 1,000   (c) ₹ 2,100   (d) ₹ 2,000

5. Goods worth ₹ 3,00,000 were burnt by fire and claim of ₹ 1,80,000 has been accepted by insurance company. .... will be shown on the debit side of profit and loss account.

(a) ₹ 1,80,000   (b) ₹ 1,20,000   (c) ₹ 3,00,000   (d) Nil

6. Which of the following statement(s) is/are true?

(i) Goods taken for personal use by proprietor will be shown on debit side of profit and loss account.

(ii) Goods taken for personal use by proprietor will be deducted from purchases.

(iii) Goods taken for personal use by proprietor will be deducted from capital.

Alternatives

(a) Both (i) and (ii)   (b) Both (ii) and (iii)   (c) Both (i) and (iii)   (d) All of the these

Short Answer (SA) Type Questions

1. What will be the treatment of the following at the time of preparation of final accounts if given as an adjustment outside trial balance?

(i) Provision for discount on creditors @ 10%   (ii) Bad debts @ ₹ 5,500

Creditors and debtors given in trial balance are ₹ 3,00,000 and ₹ 2,35,000 respectively.

2. On 28th March, 2021 stock worth ₹ 80,000 were destroyed by fire. The stock was insured and the insurance company admitted a claim of ₹ 60,000 only. Give the necessary journal entries and show how it will be treated in the final accounts.

3. Consider the following extract of trial balance taken from books of Raghu Enterprises.

Extract of Trial Balance
as on 31st March, 2021

Name of Accounts	Debit Balance (₹)	Credit Balance (₹)
Sundry Debtors	32,000	—
Bad Debts	2,000	—
Provision for Doubtful Debts	—	3,500

Additional Information

Write-off further bad debts ₹ 1,000 and create a provision for doubtful debts @ 5% on debtors.

Pass necessary journal entries and show relevant accounts (excluding final accounts)

4. Consider the following extract of trial balance taken from books of Dolly Limited and show their effect on financial statements.

Extract of Trial Balance
as at 31st March, 2020

Name of Accounts	Debit Balance (₹)	Credit Balance (₹)
10% loan (1st October, 2019)	—	2,50,000

5. Consider the following extract of trial balance taken from books of Jain Enterprises and show their effect on financial statements.

Extract of Trial Balance
as at 31st March, 2019

Name of Accounts	Debit Balance (₹)	Credit Balance (₹)
Insurance	3,000	

(i) Insurance includes an annual premium of ₹ 600 on a policy expiring on 30th September, 2019.

(ii) Closing stock included goods costing ₹ 5,600 which were sold and recorded as sales but not delivered to the customer.

(iii) Closing stock ₹ 28,000.

Long Answer (LA) Type Questions

1. Prepare trading and profit and loss account for the year ended 31st March, 2021 and a balance sheet as on that date from the following trial balance.

Name of Accounts	Amt (₹)	Name of Accounts	Amt (₹)
Stock on 1st April, 2020	16,000	Sales Less Return	1,10,000
Purchases Less Return	38,000	Sundry Creditors	15,000
SP Kumar	1,500	Capital	33,900
Wages	7,700	Mortgage and Interest Due	7,800
Carriage Inwards	1,300	Rent Outstanding	500
Carriage Outwards	750		
Salaries	20,000		
Advertisements	4,500		
Trade Expenses	2,400		
Rent	6,000		
Establishment	2,700		
Stable Expenses	1,050		
Mortgage Interest	300		
Sundry Debtors	20,000		
Cash in Hand	1,250		
Machinery	43,750		
	1,67,200		1,67,200

Additional Adjustments

(i) Closing stock was ₹ 23,000.

(ii) Provision for doubtful debts be created on sundry debtors @ 5% and a provision for discount on sundry debtors at 2%.

(iii) Salary of ₹ 1,500 paid to SP Kumar, an employee of the firm, stands debited to his personal account and it is to be corrected.

(iv) A stationery bill for ₹ 100 remains unpaid and unrecorded.

(v) Write-off one-third of advertisement expenses.

(vi) Sundry creditors include ₹ 5,000 loan taken from Mr Sudhir on 1st September, 2020 bearing interest @ 12% per annum.

2. The following trial balance has been extracted from the books of Shri Manjul Kumar on 31st March, 2020.

Particulars	Debit Balance (₹)	Credit Balance (₹)
Plant and Machinery	10,00,000	—
Furniture and Fixtures	1,20,000	—
Capital Account/Drawings Account	20,000	17,60,000
Loose Tools	2,00,000	—
Goodwill	1,00,000	—
Opening Stock (1st April, 2019)	2,00,000	—
Returns	80,000	40,000
Discount	—	60,000
Purchases/Sales	21,20,000	46,80,000
Wages and Other Expenses	10,00,000	—
Provision for Doubtful Debts	—	20,000
Carriage Inwards	1,20,000	—
Salaries	4,16,000	—
General Expenses and Insurance	7,20,000	—
Rent and Taxes	1,44,000	—
Postage and Telegrams	40,000	—
Bank Overdraft	—	2,00,000
Sundry Debtors/Creditors	5,60,000	2,40,000
K Maheshwari	20,000	—
Cash and Bank Balances	1,40,000	—
	70,00,000	70,00,000

The following additional information is available

(i) Stock on 31st March, 2020 was ₹ 3,08,000.

(ii) Depreciation is to be charged on plant and machinery at 5% p.a. and furniture and fixtures at 6% p.a. Loose tools are revalued at ₹ 1,60,000.

(iii) Provision for doubtful debts is to be maintained at 5% on sundry debtors.

(iv) Remuneration of ₹ 20,000 paid to Mr K Maheshwari, a temporary employee, stands debited to his personal account and it is to be corrected.

(v) Unexpired insurance was ₹ 4,000.

Prepare trading and profit and loss account for the year ended 31st March, 2020 and a balance sheet as on that date.

Answers

Multiple Choice Questions

1. (a)   2. (b)   3. (d)   4. (b)   5. (b)   6. (b)

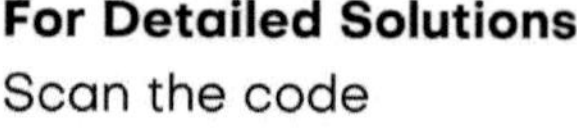

Accounts From Incomplete Records

In this Chapter...

- Meaning of Incomplete Records
- Statement of Affairs or Net Worth Method

Meaning of Incomplete Records

Accounting records which are not maintained in accordance with the principles of double entry system are known as accounts from incomplete records or single entry system of accounting.

Under this system, both the aspects are recorded for certain transactions only, while for others only one aspect is recorded. Some transactions are ignored and not recorded at all.

Features of Incomplete Records

- It is an inaccurate, unscientific and unsystematic method of recording business transactions.
- Generally, records for cash transactions and personal accounts are properly maintained and there is no information regarding revenues and/or gains, expenses and/or losses, assets and liabilities.
- This system is suitable for small size business where the number of transactions are less.

Advantages/Uses of Incomplete Records

- Single entry system can be adopted even by people who do not have the proper knowledge of accounting principles.
- As specialised accountants are not required, it is an inexpensive mode of maintaining records.
- As only few books are maintained, time consumed in maintaining records is also less.
- It is a convenient mode of maintaining records as the owner may record only important transactions according to the need of a business.

Limitations of Incomplete Records

- Arithmetical accuracy of accounts under single entry system cannot be ensured as trial balance cannot be prepared.
- Correct ascertainment and evaluation of financial results of business operations cannot be made.
- A problem in raising funds from outsiders and planning for future business activities may arise as analysis of profitability, liquidity and solvency of the business cannot be done.
- Filing of insurance claim with an insurance company by the owner in case of loss of inventory by fire or theft becomes difficult.

- Convincing the income tax authorities about the reliability of the computed income becomes difficult.
- Avoiding misappropriation of assets may become difficult as assets accounts are not maintained and it may be difficult to keep full control.
- Correct profit earned or loss incurred during the accounting period is not known as trading and profit and loss account cannot be prepared.

Ascertainment of Profit or Loss under Incomplete Records

Every business firm wishes to ascertain the results of its operations to assess its efficiency, success and failures. This gives rise to the need for preparing the financial statements to disclose

- the profit made or loss sustained by the firm during a given period.
- the amount of assets and liabilities as at the closing date of the accounting period.

This can be done in two ways

- By preparing the statement of affairs as at the beginning and at the end of the accounting period, called **statement of affairs** or **net worth method**.
- By **conversion method**, i.e. by preparing trading and profit and loss account and the balance sheet by putting the accounting records in proper order.

Note *'Conversion Method' is not covered in latest syllabus, therefore not explained.*

Statement of Affairs or Net Worth Method

A statement of affairs is a statement of all assets and liabilities. It is a statement in which assets are shown on one side and the liabilities on the other, just as in case of a balance sheet. The difference between the totals of the two sides is the capital. Under this method, statement of assets and liabilities as at the beginning and at the end of the relevant accounting period is prepared to ascertain the amount of change in the capital during the period.

It is based on the accounting equation as

$$\text{Capital} = \text{Assets} - \text{Liabilities}$$

A statement of affairs is similar to, though not the same as a balance sheet.

Format of Statement of Affairs

Statement of Affairs
as at ...

Liabilities	Amt (₹)	Assets	Amt (₹)
Bank Overdraft	...	Cash in Hand	...
Bills Payable	...	Cash at Bank	...
Sundry Creditors	...	Bills Receivable	...
Outstanding Expenses	...	Sundry Debtors	...
Incomes Received in Advance	...	Stock Prepaid Expenses	...
Capital (Balancing figure)	...	Accrued Income	...
		Furniture	...
		Plant and Machinery, etc.	...
	...		...

Preparation of Statement of Profit and Loss

Once the amount of capital, both at the beginning and at the end is computed with the help of statement of affairs, a statement of profit and loss is prepared to ascertain the exact amount of profit or loss made during the year.

The difference between the opening and closing capital represents its increase or decrease which is to be adjusted for withdrawals made by the owner or any fresh capital introduced by him during the accounting period in order to arrive at the amount of profit or loss made during the period.

Format of Statement of Profit and Loss

Statement of Profit and Loss
for the year ending…

Particulars	Amt (₹)
Capital as at the End of the Year (Computed from statement of affairs as at the end of the year)	…
(+) Drawings During the Year	…
(–) Additional Capital Introduced During the Year	(…)
Adjusted Capital at the End of the Year	…
(–) Capital as at the Beginning of the Year	(…)
(Computed from statement of affairs as at the beginning of the year)	
Profit or Loss Made During the Year	…

The same computation can be done in the form of an equation as follows

Profit or Loss = Capital at the End – Capital at the Beginning + Drawings During the Year

– Capital Introduced During the Year

Solved Examples

Example 1. Panwar commenced business on 1st January, 2020 with a capital of ₹ 10,000, which he paid into bank account opened for the purpose. On the same date, he brought furniture which cost ₹ 2,000 and made purchases of goods worth ₹ 6,500. He kept his books on single entry system. On 31st December, 2020, stock was valued at ₹ 8,300. There were book debts amounting to ₹ 3,400 out of which ₹ 200 represented debts which were irrecoverable.

Creditors amounted to ₹ 3,600 and bank passbook showed a balance of ₹ 1,450. Panwar withdrew three times from business for his private expenses, each time he withdrew ₹ 600 and in addition he used ₹ 500 worth of goods from his shop. He took ₹ 1,000 as loan from his wife during the year. He gave ₹ 200 to his son from business, which he omitted to enter. You are required to prepare a statement showing profit or loss in the business for the year ending 31st December, 2020 from the above information.

Ans.

Statement of Affairs
as at 31st December, 2020

Liabilities	Amt (₹)	Assets		Amt (₹)
Creditors	3,600	Bank		1,450
Loan from Wife	1,000	Stock		8,300
Capital (Balancing Figure)	10,350	Debtors	3,400	
		(–) Bad Debts	(200)	3,200
		Furniture		2,000
	14,950			14,950

Statement Showing Profit or Loss
for the year ending 31st December, 2020

Particulars		Amt (₹)
Closing Capital as on 31st December, 2020		10,350
(+) Drawings During the Year		
Drawings in Cash (600 × 3)	1,800	
Drawings in Goods	500	
Drawings in Cash (To Son)	200	2,500
Adjusted Capital at the End		12,850
(–) Opening Capital		(10,000)
Profit For the Year		2,850

Example 2. Mr Girdhari Lal does not keep full double entry records. His balance as on 1st January, 2021 is as

Liabilities	Amt (₹)	Assets	Amt (₹)
Sundry Creditors	35,000	Cash in Hand	5,000
Bills Payable	15,000	Cash at Bank	20,000
Capital	40,000	Sundry Debtors	18,000
		Stock	22,000
		Furniture	8,000
		Plant	17,000
	90,000		90,000

His position at the end of the year is

Items	Amt (₹)
Cash in Hand	7,000
Stock	8,600
Debtors	23,800
Furniture	15,000
Plant	20,350
Bills Payable	20,200
Creditors	15,000

He withdrew ₹ 500 per month out of which he spent ₹ 1,500 for business purpose. Prepare the statement of profit or loss.

(NCERT)

Ans.

Statement of Affairs
as at 31st December, 2021

Liabilities	Amt (₹)	Assets	Amt (₹)
Bills Payable	20,200	Cash in Hand	7,000
Creditors	15,000	Stock	8,600
Capital (Balancing Figure)	39,550	Debtors	23,800
		Furniture	15,000
		Plant	20,350
	74,750		74,750

Statement Showing Profit or Loss
for the year ended 31st December, 2021

Particulars	Amt (₹)
Capital at the End of the Year as on 31st December, 2021	39,550
(+) Drawings During the Year [(500 × 12) − 1,500]	4,500
Adjusted Capital at the End	44,050
(−) Capital in the Beginning of the Year as on 1st January, 2021	(40,000)
Profit for the Year	4,050

Example 3. Roop Prakash keeps his books on incomplete records. Following is the information available

Particulars	1st April, 2020 (₹)	31st March, 2021 (₹)
Plant and Machinery	1,40,000	1,85,000
Cash in Hand	40,800	2,31,500
Stock	65,800	1,70,600
Furniture	75,000	90,000
Building	1,60,000	1,80,000
Creditors	37,000	16,800
Debtors	24,600	86,200
10% Investment	2,00,000	2,00,000

During the year, he sold his personal investment of ₹ 5,00,000 and 80% of it introduced into his business. He withdrew ₹ 30,000 quarterly. Calculate profit after making following adjustments

 (i) Provide depreciation on building and furniture at 10% and 20% respectively.

(ii) Create provision on debtors at 5%.   (iii) Rent paid in advance ₹ 5,800.

(iv) Interest on investment accrued for 6 months.   (v) Salary due but not paid ₹ 2,200.

Ans.

Statement of Affairs
as at 1st April, 2020

Liabilities	Amt (₹)	Assets	Amt (₹)
Creditors	37,000	Plant and Machinery	1,40,000
Opening Capital (Balancing figure)	6,69,200	Cash in Hand	40,800
		Stock	65,800
		Furniture	75,000
		Building	1,60,000
		Debtors	24,600
		10% Investment	2,00,000
	7,06,200		7,06,200

Statement of Affairs (Before Adjustments)
as at 31st March, 2021

Liabilities	Amt (₹)	Assets	Amt (₹)
Creditors	16,800	Plant and Machinery	1,85,000
Closing Capital (Balancing figure)	11,26,500	Cash in Hand	2,31,500
		Stock	1,70,600
		Furniture	90,000
		Building	1,80,000
		Debtors	86,200
		10% Investment	2,00,000
	11,43,300		11,43,300

Statement of Profit and Loss
for the year ending 31st March, 2021

Particulars		Amt (₹)
Closing Capital		11,26,500
(+) Drawings (30,000 × 4)		1,20,000
		12,46,500
(−) Additional Capital (5,00,000 × 80%)		(4,00,000)
Adjusted Capital		8,46,500
(−) Opening Capital		(6,69,200)
Profit before Adjustment		1,77,300
(−) Provision on Debtors	(4,310)	
(−) Depreciation on Building	(18,000)	
(−) Depreciation on Furniture	(18,000)	
(−) Salary Outstanding	(2,200)	
	(42,510)	
(+) Interest on Investment (Accrued)	10,000	
(+) Rent Paid in Advance	5,800	15,800
Net Profit after Adjustment		1,50,590

Statement of Affairs (After Adjustments)
as at 31st March, 2021

Liabilities	Amt (₹)	Amt (₹)	Assets	Amt (₹)	Amt (₹)
Opening Capital	6,69,200		Plant and Machinery		1,85,000
(+) Additional Capital	4,00,000		Cash in Hand		2,31,500
(+) Net Profit	1,50,590		Stock		1,70,600
(−) Drawings	(1,20,000)	10,99,790	Furniture	90,000	
Creditors		16,800	(−) Depreciation	(18,000)	72,000
Salary Outstanding		2,200	Building	1,80,000	
			(−) Depreciation	(18,000)	1,62,000
			Debtors	86,200	
			(−) Provision on Debtors	(4,310)	81,890
			10% Investment	2,00,000	
			(+) Accrued Interest	10,000	2,10,000
			Rent Paid in Advance		5,800
		11,18,790			11,18,790

Chapter Practice

Objective Questions

• Multiple Choice Questions

1 Generally accounts under single entry system are maintained by ………. .
(a) small businesses   (b) company   (c) partnership firm   (d) government undertakings

Ans. (a) Single entry system is adopted by the small business organisations where transactions are limited and most of them are on cash basis.

2. In single entry system of accounting,
(a) dual aspect of a transaction is recorded   (b) single aspect of transaction is recorded
(c) important transactions are recorded   (d) All of these

Ans. (d) It is a system of recording business transactions. In some of the transactions, both aspects are recorded while in others one aspect is recorded or it is not recorded at all.

3. Single entry system can only provide ………… degree of ………… as no proper method of accounting is followed in preparation of profit and loss.
(a) low, accuracy   (b) low, record   (c) high, accuracy   (d) high, record

Ans. (a) Profit and loss for the year cannot be ascertained under single entry system with high degree of accuracy, as only estimation of the profit earned or loss incurred can be made.

4. What are the common objectives between the double entry system and single entry system?
(a) To determine profit/loss during the year   (b) To ascertain amount due from the debtors
(c) To know the financial position of the business   (d) Both (a) and (c)

Ans. (d) Both (a) and (c)

5. Incomplete record mechanism of book keeping is
(a) scientific   (b) unscientific   (c) unsystematic   (d) Both (b) and (c)

Ans. (d) Both (b) and (c)

6. Consider the following statements regarding single entry system of accounting and identify correct statement(s).
 (i) Only cash transactions and personal accounts are maintained.
 (ii) There is huge dependence on original vouchers for determining total credit sales, credit purchases etc.
(iii) Financial position of current year can be easily compared with previous years.
Alternatives
(a) Only (i)   (b) Both (ii) and (iii)   (c) Both (i) and (ii)   (d) All of these

Ans. (c) Both (i) and (ii)

7. Which among the following transactions will be ignored under single entry system?
(a) Depreciation on fixed asset   (b) Cash paid to acquire a fixed asset
(c) Interest paid on loan   (d) None of these

Ans. (a) Depreciation on fixed asset comprise of effect on nominal and real account which are not prepared under single entry system as only cash and personal accounts are prepared. Thus, this transaction will be ignored under single entry system.

8. Which of the following is not a method of ascertainment of profit or loss under single entry system?
   (i) Conversion method   (ii) Net worth method
   (iii) Alteration method   (iv) Conservation method
Alternatives
(a) Only (i)   (b) Both (ii) and (iii)   (c) Both (iii) and (iv)   (d) Only (iv)

Ans. (c) Both (iii) and (iv)

9. Statement of financial position produced from incomplete accounting record is called ………. .
(a) Balance sheet   (b) Statement of events
(c) Statement of affairs   (d) None of these

Ans. (c) Statements of affairs

10. What will be the correct sequence of events under net worth method?
   (i) Prepare statement of affairs at the end to calculate closing capital.
   (ii) Prepare statement of profit or loss to find profit earned or loss incurred during the year.
   (iii) Prepare statement of affairs at the beginning of year for calculating opening capital.

Alternatives
(a) (i), (ii), (iii)   (b) (ii),(iii), (i)   (c) (iii), (ii), (i)   (d) (iii), (i), (ii)

Ans. (d) (iii), (i), (ii)

11. Opening capital = ₹ 60,000; Drawings = ₹ 5,000; Capital added during the year = ₹ 10,000; Closing capital = ₹ 90,000. Find profit/loss for the year.
(a) ₹ 15,000   (b) ₹ 25,000   (c) ₹ 18,000   (d) ₹ 10,000

Ans (b) Profit = Closing Capital + Drawings – Opening Capital – Additional Capital
$$= 90,000 + 5,000 - 60,000 - 10,000 = ₹\, 25,000$$

12. What will be the opening capital, if drawings are ₹ 15,000, profit for the year ₹ 25,000 and closing capital ₹ 70,000?
(a) ₹ 80,000   (b) ₹ 60,000   (c) ₹ 95,000   (d) ₹ 55,000

Ans. (b) Opening Capital = Closing Capital + Drawings – Profit – Additional Capital = $70,000 + 15,000 - 25,000$
$$= ₹\, 60,000$$

13. Closing Capital = ₹ 1,20,000
Drawing was 25% of closing capital
Additional capital was ₹ 34,000.
Opening capital was ₹ 20,000.
What will be the amount of profit?
(a) ₹ 80,000   (b) ₹ 90,000   (c) ₹ 96,000   (d) ₹ 1,20,000

Ans. (c) Profit = Closing Capital + Drawings – Additional Capital – Opening Capital
$$= 1,20,000 + 30,000\ (25\%\ \text{of}\ 1,20,000) - 34,000 - 20,000 = ₹\, 96,000.$$

• Assertion-Reasoning MCQs

Direction *(Q. Nos. 1 to 4) There are two statements marked as Assertion (A) and Reason (R). Read the statements and choose the appropriate option from the options given below.*
   (a) Both Assertion (A) and Reason (R) are true, but Reason (R) is not the correct explanation of Assertion (A)
   (b) Both Assertion (A) and Reason (R) are true and Reason (R) is the correct explanation of Assertion (A)
   (c) Both Assertion (A) and Reason (R) are false
   (d) Assertion (A) is false, but Reason (R) is true

1. Assertion (A) Single entry system is incomplete method of maintaining accounting records.

Reason (R) Both aspects of a transaction i.e., debit and credit are not recorded.

Ans. (b) Single entry system is incomplete method in which very few books are maintained and both aspects of transactions are not recorded.

2. Assertion (A) Single entry system is very expensive mode of maintaining books of accounts.

Reason (R) Specialised accountants are required to maintain accounts under single entry system.

Ans. (c) It is an inexpensive mode of maintaining records as no specialised accountants are required to prepare it.

3. Assertion (A) Arithmetical accuracy cannot be checked under single entry system.

Reason (R) A trial balance is not prepared under single entry system.

Ans. (b) Trial balance is not prepared under single entry system as both aspects of transactions are not recorded. Thus, arithmetical accuracy cannot be checked.

4. Assertion (A) Accounts of various organisations are comparable under single entry system.

Reason (R) There is uniformity between books of accounts maintained under single entry system.

Ans. (c) Accounts of different organisations are not comparable as there is no uniformity in maintenance and preparation of accounts.

• Case Based MCQs

Direction *Read the following case study and answer the question no. (i) to (iv) on the basis of the same.*

1. Rohan, B.Com Hons. graduate from SRCC, has now started his own business of furniture near Gurugram. His business transactions are very less, therefore he maintains books of accounts on single entry system. As being a commerce graduate, Rohan is maintaining books of accounts himself.

Following information is available

Particulars	1st April, 2020 (₹)	31st March, 2021 (₹)
Sundry Debtors	1,20,000	1,70,000
Sundry Creditors	35,000	44,000
Buildings	2,25,000	3,65,000
Furniture	50,000	60,000
Stock	21,600	19,500
Cash in Hand	1,17,600	11,09,600
Land	5,00,000	5,00,000
Machinery	1,65,000	2,70,000

During the year, he introduced additional capital of ₹ 5,60,000 and withdrew ₹ 2,000 p.m. for household expenses.

At the end of year 31st March, 2021, he noticed few adjustments which are as follows

(a) Provision on debtors created @ 10%.

(b) Building and furniture depreciated by 10% and 5% respectively.

(c) Fire insurance paid in advance ₹ 10,000.

(d) Outstanding salary ₹ 5,000.

(i) Amount of opening capital will be ....

(a) ₹ 11,99,200

(b) ₹ 10,44,200

(c) ₹ 11,64,200

(d) ₹ 11,29,200

Ans. (c)

Statement of Affairs
as at 1st April, 2020

Liabilities	Amt (₹)	Assets	Amt (₹)
Sundry Creditors	35,000	Sundry Debtors	1,20,000
Opening Capital (Balancing figure)	11,64,200	Building	2,25,000
		Furniture	50,000
		Stock	21,600
		Cash in Hand	1,17,600
		Land	5,00,000
		Machinery	1,65,000
	11,99,200		11,99,200

(ii) What will be the net profit after all adjustments?

(a) ₹ 6,98,400   (b) ₹ 6,88,400   (c) ₹ 6,94,600   (d) None of these

Ans. (a)

Statement of Profit and Loss
for the year ending 31st March, 2021

Particulars		Amt (₹)
Capital at the End		24,50,100
(+) Drawings (2,000 × 12)		24,000
		24,74,100
(−) Additional Capital		(5,60,000)
Adjusted Capital		19,14,100
(−) Opening Capital		(11,64,200)
Profit before Adjustment		7,49,900
(−) Provision on Debtors	(17,000)	
(−) Depreciation on Building	(36,500)	
(−) Depreciation on Furniture	(3,000)	
(−) Outstanding Salary	(5,000)	(61,500)
Prepaid Expenses		10,000
Net Profit after Adjustment		6,98,400

(iii) Which of the following will be the amount of closing capital after taking into consideration all adjustments?

(a) ₹ 24,50,100   (b) ₹ 24,47,600   (c) ₹ 21,54,200   (d) ₹ 23,98,600

Ans. (d) Amount of Closing Capital

Opening Capital	11,64,200
(+) Additional Capital	5,60,000
(+) Net Profit	6,98,400
(−) Drawings	(24,000)
	₹ 23,98,600

(iv) What is the amount of closing capital before taking into account any of the above adjustments?

(a) ₹ 24,94,100   (b) ₹ 23,98,600

(c) ₹ 24,50,100   (d) ₹ 25,38,100

Ans. (c)

Statement of Affairs
as at 31st March, 2021

Liabilities	Amt (₹)	Assets	Amt (₹)
Sundry Creditors	44,000	Sundry Debtors	1,70,000
Closing Capital (Balancing figure)	24,50,100	Building	3,65,000
		Furniture	60,000
		Stock	19,500
		Cash in Hand	11,09,600
		Land	5,00,000
		Machinery	2,70,000
	24,94,100		24,94,100

PART 2
Subjective Questions

• Short Answer (SA) Type Questions

1. Mention any three features of single entry system.

Ans. Features of single entry system are as follows
   (i) It is an inaccurate, unscientific and unsystematic method of recording business transactions.
   (ii) Generally records for cash transactions and personal accounts are properly maintained and there is no information regarding revenues and/or gains, expenses and/or losses, assets and liabilities.
   (iii) This system is suitable for small size business where the number of transactions are less.

2. What are the possible reasons for keeping incomplete records?   (NCERT)

Ans. It is observed that many businessmen keep incomplete records because of the following reasons
   (i) Single entry system can be adopted by people who do not have the proper knowledge of accounting principles.
   (ii) As specialised accountants are not required, it is an inexpensive mode of maintaining records.
   (iii) As only a few books are maintained, time consumed in maintaining records is also less.
   (iv) It is a convenient mode of maintaining records as the owner may record only important transactions according to the need of a business.
   (v) It is suitable for organisations which have limited number of transactions and very few assets and liabilities.

3. What practical difficulties are encountered by a trader due to incompleteness of accounting records? (NCERT)

Ans. The practical difficulties encountered by a trader due to incompleteness of accounting records are
   (i) As the accounts are incomplete in nature, there are strong chances of fraud to take place.
   (ii) Arithmetical accuracy of accounts under single entry system cannot be checked, as trial balance cannot be prepared.
   (iii) Correct ascertainment and evaluation of financial results of business operations cannot be made.
   (iv) Correct profit earned or loss incurred during the accounting period is not known as trading and profit and loss cannot be prepared.

4. Books maintained under double entry system are more reliable as compared to when maintained under single entry system. Comment.

Ans. Double entry system of accounting records both aspects of a transaction. Thus it provides accurate information as to profit, liabilities, etc. On the other hand, single entry system of accounting does not record transactions in some cases, while in certain others, it records both aspects and in some only one aspect. Thus, double entry system is more reliable than single entry system.

5. Distinguish between statement of affairs and balance sheet on any four basis.

Ans. The differences between statement of affairs and balance sheet are (any four)

Basis	Statement of Affairs	Balance Sheet
Objective	The objective of preparing statement of affairs is to estimate the capital on a particular date.	The objective of preparing balance sheet is to show the true financial position of an entity on a particular date.
Accounting Method	When accounts are prepared under single entry system of accounting, statement of affairs is prepared.	When accounts are prepared under double entry system of accounting, balance sheet is prepared.
Reliability	It is less reliable as it is prepared from incomplete records.	It is more reliable as it is prepared from double entry records.
Omission	Omission of assets or liabilities cannot be discovered easily.	Omission of assets or liabilities can be discovered easily and can be traced from accounting records.
Trial Balance	Statement of affairs is not based on trial balance.	Balance sheet is based on the trial balance.
Arithmetical Accuracy	Statement of affairs does not prove in any sense the arithmetical accuracy of accounting.	Tallying of balance sheet implies arithmetical accuracy.
Missing of Facts	There is always a possibility of missing of facts. The reason is neither all transactions nor both aspects of every transactions are recorded in the book of accounts.	Since both the aspects of all transactions are duly recorded, possibility of missing of facts from accounts, hardly remains.

6. What is meant by statement of affairs? Prepare its format as used for ascertaining profit or loss under incomplete records.

Or

What is meant by statement of affairs? How can the profit or loss of a trader be ascertained with the help of a statement of affairs?

(NCERT)

Ans. A statement of affairs is a statement of all assets and liabilities. It is a statement in which assets are shown on one side and the liabilities on the other, just as in case of a balance sheet. Under this method, profits or losses of the business are ascertained by comparing capital at the end, and capital at the beginning of the accounting period.

Capital in the beginning is calculated by preparing 'opening statement of affairs' and capital at the end is calculated by preparing 'closing statement of affairs'. After calculating opening and closing capital, a statement showing profit and loss is prepared to ascertain the profit or loss of the period.

Statement Showing Profit or Loss
for the year ended ......

Particulars	Amt (₹)
Capital at the End of the Year (Computed from statement of affairs as at the end of year)	...
(+) Drawings During the Year	...
(−) Additional Capital Introduced During the Year	(...)
Adjusted Capital at the End of Year	...
(−) Capital in the Beginning of Year (Computed from statement of affairs as at the beginning of year)	(...)
Profit or Loss Made During the Year	...

7. Differentiate between double entry system and single entry system on any four basis.

Ans. The differences between statement of affairs and balance sheet are (any four)

Basis	Double Entry System	Single Entry System
Recording of Aspects	This system records both the aspects of a transaction.	This system does not record both the aspects of a transaction, for some transactions two aspects, for some other, one aspect and yet for others, no aspect at all are recorded.
Type of Accounts	Under double entry system, all accounts i.e., personal, real and nominal are maintained.	Under single entry system, only personal accounts and cash book are maintained.
Arithmetical Accuracy	Under this system, arithmetical accuracy of books of accounts can be checked by preparing a trial balance.	Under this system, arithmetical accuracy of books of accounts cannot be checked, as a trial balance cannot be prepared.
Authenticity	This system is considered authentic by the court.	The court does not consider this system as authentic.
Use	Double entry system is used by almost all business.	Single entry system is used by only small business and institutions.
Adjustments	Under this system, adjustments are made at the time of preparing final accounts.	Due to incompleteness of accounts, there is no provision to make adjustments.
Reliability	Books maintained in this system are reliable because they are based on scientific principles.	Books maintained in this system are less reliable because they are based on estimates.

8. Rishant keeps incomplete records of his business. He gives you the following information; capital at the beginning of the year ₹ 8,00,000; capital at the end of the year ₹ 6,20,000. ₹ 2,50,000 was withdrawn by him for his personal use. As Rishant needed money for expansion of his business, he asked his wife for help, his wife allowed him to sell her ornaments and invest that amount into the business which comes to ₹ 30,000.

You are required to calculate profit or loss made during the year.

Ans.
Statement Showing Profit or Loss
for the year ended ....

Particulars	Amt (₹)
Capital at the End	6,20,000
(+) Drawings	2,50,000
	8,70,000
(–) Additional Capital Introduced	(30,000)
Adjusted Capital at the End	8,40,000
(–) Capital in the Beginning	(8,00,000)
Profit Made During the Year	40,000

9. From the following information, calculate capital at the beginning.

Items	Amt (₹)
Capital at the End of the Year	4,00,000
Drawings Made During the Year	60,000
Fresh Capital Introduced During the Year	1,00,000
Profit of the Current Year	80,000

Ans.

Statement Showing Capital
at the beginning of the year

Particulars	Amt (₹)
Capital at the End of the Year	4,00,000
(+) Drawings Made During the Year	60,000
	4,60,000
(–) Fresh Capital Introduced During the Year	(1,00,000)
	3,60,000
(–) Profit of the Current Year	(80,000)
Capital in the Beginning of the Year	2,80,000

10. Raghav, who keeps his books on single entry system, tells you that his capital on 31st March, 2020 is ₹ 3,74,000 and his capital on 1st April, 2019 was ₹ 3,84,000. He further informs you that during the year, he withdrew for his household purpose ₹ 1,68,400. He sold his personal investment of ₹ 40,000 @ 2% premium and brought that money into the business.

You are required to prepare statement of profit or loss.

Ans.

Statement Showing Profit or Loss
for the year ended 31st March, 2020

Particulars	Amt (₹)
Capital at the End	3,74,000
(+) Drawings Made During the Year	1,68,400
	5,42,400
(–) Capital Introduced During the Year (102/100 × ₹ 40,000)	(40,800)
Adjusted Capital at the End	5,01,600
(–) Capital in the Beginning	(3,84,000)
Net Profit for the Year	1,17,600

11. Raja Ram keeps his books under single entry system. His assets and liabilities were as under

Particulars	31st March, 2020 (₹)	31st March, 2021 (₹)
Cash	2,000	1,800
Sundry Debtors	78,000	90,000
Stock	68,000	64,000
Plant and Machinery	1,20,000	1,60,000
Sundry Creditors	30,000	29,800
Bills Payable	—	10,000

Prepare statement of affairs for year ending 31st March, 2020 and 2021.

Ans.

Statement of Affairs
as at 31st March, 2020

Liabilities	Amt (₹)	Assets	Amt (₹)
Sundry Creditors	30,000	Cash	2,000
Capital (Balancing figure)	2,38,000	Sundry Debtors	78,000
		Stock	68,000
		Plant and Machinery	1,20,000
	2,68,000		2,68,000

Statement of Affairs
as at 31st March, 2021

Liabilities	Amt (₹)	Assets	Amt (₹)
Sundry Creditors	29,800	Cash	1,800
Bills Payable	10,000	Sundry Debtors	90,000
Capital (Balancing figure)	2,76,000	Stock	64,000
		Plant and Machinery	1,60,000
	3,15,800		3,15,800

12. Kartik started a firm on 1st April, 2019 with a capital of ₹ 30,000. On 1st July, 2019, he borrowed from his wife a sum of ₹ 12,000 @ 9% per annum (interest not yet paid) for business and introduces a further capital of his own amounted to ₹ 4,500. On 31st March, 2020 his position was, cash ₹ 1,800, stock ₹ 28,200, debtors ₹ 21,000 and creditors ₹ 18,000.

Ascertain his profit or loss taking into account ₹ 6,000 for his drawings during the year.

Ans.

Statement of Affairs
as at 31st March, 2020

Liabilities		Amt (₹)	Assets	Amt (₹)
Creditors		18,000	Cash	1,800
Mrs Kartik's Loan	12,000		Stock	28,200
(+) Interest on Loan $\left(12,000 \times \dfrac{9}{100} \times \dfrac{9}{12}\right)$	810	12,810	Debtors	21,000
Capital (Balancing figure)		20,190		
		51,000		51,000

Statement Showing Profit or Loss
for year ended 31st March, 2020

Particulars	Amt (₹)
Capital at the End	20,190
(–) Capital Introduced During the Year	(4,500)
	15,690
(+) Drawings	6,000
Adjusted Capital at the End	21,690
(–) Capital in the Beginning	(30,000)
Net Loss for the Year	(8,310)

Note *Loan from wife along with interest on loan is a liability for the business and not an additional capital.*

13. Mr A started business with a capital ₹ 5,00,000. At the end of the year his position was

Items	Amt (₹)
Cash in Hand	15,000
Cash at Bank	70,000
Sundry Debtors	1,20,000
Stock	2,40,000
Furniture	75,000
Machinery	2,00,000

Sundry creditors on this date totalled ₹ 80,000. During the year, he introduced a further capital of ₹ 1,50,000 and withdrew for household expenses ₹ 90,000.

You are required to calculate profit or loss during the year.

Ans.

Statement of Affairs
as at the end of the year

Liabilities	Amt (₹)	Assets	Amt (₹)
Sundry Creditors	80,000	Cash in Hand	15,000
Capital (Balancing Figure)	6,40,000	Cash at Bank	70,000
		Sundry Debtors	1,20,000
		Stock	2,40,000
		Furniture	75,000
		Machinery	2,00,000
	7,20,000		7,20,000

Statement Showing Profit or Loss
for the year ended…

Particulars	Amt (₹)
Capital at the End	6,40,000
(+) Drawings (Household expenses)	90,000
	7,30,000
(–) Additional Capital Introduced	(1,50,000)
Adjusted Capital at the End	5,80,000
(–) Capital in the Beginning	(5,00,000)
Profit for the Year	80,000

• Long Answer (LA) Type Questions

1. Mr Arun has extracted the following information relating to his business.

Particulars	1st January, 2020 (₹)	31st December, 2020 (₹)
Sundry Creditors	45,000	39,000
Loan from Wife	66,000	75,000
Sundry Debtors	22,500	10,300
Land & Building	89,600	45,000
Cash in Hand	15,000	7,700
Bank Overdraft	12,500	—
Furniture	1,100	2,000
Stock	50,000	12,500

Draw up the statement of affairs and find the profit or loss.

Ans.

Statement of Affairs
as at 1st January, 2020

Liabilities	Amt (₹)	Assets	Amt (₹)
Sundry Creditors	45,000	Sundry Debtors	22,500
Loan from Wife	66,000	Land & Building	89,600
Bank Overdraft	12,500	Cash in Hand	15,000
Capital (Balancing figure)	54,700	Furniture	1,100
		Stock	50,000
	1,78,200		1,78,200

Statement of Affairs
as at 31st December, 2020

Liabilities	Amt (₹)	Assets	Amt (₹)
Sundry Creditors	39,000	Land & Building	45,000
Loan from Wife	75,000	Cash in Hand	7,700
		Sundry Debtors	10,300
		Furniture	2,000
		Stock	12,500
		Capital (Balancing figure)	36,500
	1,14,000		1,14,000

Working Note

Profit/(Loss) = Capital at the End – Capital in the Beginning = (36,500) – 54,700

∴   Loss = ₹ 91,200

2. Mr Akshat keeps his books on incomplete records, following information is given below.

Particulars	1st April, 2020 (₹)	31st March, 2021 (₹)
Cash in Hand	1,000	1,500
Cash at Bank	15,000	10,000
Stock	1,00,000	95,000
Debtors	42,500	70,000
Business Premises	75,000	1,35,000
Furniture	9,000	7,500
Creditors	66,000	87,000
Bills Payable	44,000	58,000

During the year, he withdrew ₹ 45,000 and introduced ₹ 25,000 as further capital in the business. Compute the profit or loss of the business.

Ans.

Statement of Affairs
as at 1st April, 2020

Liabilities	Amt (₹)	Assets	Amt (₹)
Creditors	66,000	Cash in Hand	1,000
Bills Payable	44,000	Cash at Bank	15,000
Capital (Balancing figure)	1,32,500	Stock	1,00,000
		Debtors	42,500
		Business Premises	75,000
		Furniture	9,000
	2,42,500		2,42,500

Statement of Affairs
as at 31st March, 2021

Liabilities	Amt (₹)	Assets	Amt (₹)
Sundry Creditors	87,000	Cash in Hand	1,500
Bills Payable	58,000	Cash at Bank	10,000
Capital (Balancing figure)	1,74,000	Stock	95,000
		Debtors	70,000
		Business Premises	1,35,000
		Furniture	7,500
	3,19,000		3,19,000

Statement of Profit and Loss
for the year ending 31st March, 2021

Particulars	Amt (₹)
Capital at the End of the Year as at 31st March, 2021	1,74,000
(+) Drawings During the Year	45,000
	2,19,000
(−) Additional Capital Introduced During the Year	(25,000)
Adjusted Capital at the End	1,94,000
(−) Capital at the Beginning of the Year as at 1st April, 2020	(1,32,500)
Profit Earned During the Year	61,500

3. Barkat Lal maintains his account on single entry system. Calculate his profit on 31st March, 2021 from the following information

Items	1st April, 2020 (₹)	31st March, 2021 (₹)
Cash in Hand	3,000	1,000
Bank Balance	9,000	7,000
Furniture	4,000	4,000
Stock	2,000	6,000
Creditors	8,000	6,000
Debtors	6,000	8,000

During the year, his drawings were ₹ 2,000 and additional capital invested was ₹ 4,000. Furniture appreciated by 20% and create a provision on debtors at 5%.

Ans.

Statement of Affairs
as at 1st April, 2020

Liabilities	Amt (₹)	Assets	Amt (₹)
Creditors	8,000	Cash in Hand	3,000
Capital (Balancing figure)	16,000	Bank Balance	9,000
		Furniture	4,000
		Stock	2,000
		Debtors	6,000
	24,000		24,000

Statement of Affairs (Before Adjustments)
as at 31st March, 2021

Liabilities	Amt (₹)	Assets	Amt (₹)
Creditors	6,000	Cash in Hand	1,000
Capital (Balancing figure)	20,000	Bank Balance	7,000
		Furniture	4,000
		Stock	6,000
		Debtors	8,000
	26,000		26,000

Statement showing Profit and Loss
for the year ended 31st March, 2021

Particulars	Amt (₹)
Capital at the End	20,000
(+) Drawings During the Year	2,000
	22,000
(−) Additional Capital Invested	(4,000)
Adjusted Capital at the End	18,000
(−) Opening Capital	(16,000)
Profit Made During the Year (Before adjustment), i.e. Gross Profit	2,000
(−) Provision on Debtors (400)	
(+) Appreciation on Furniture 800	400
Net Profit (After adjustments)	2,400

Statement of Affairs (After adjustments)
as at 31st March, 2021

Liabilities	Amt (₹)		Assets	Amt (₹)	
Capital on 1st April, 2020	16,000		Cash in Hand		1,000
(+) Additional Capital	4,000		Bank Balance		7,000
(+) Net Profit	2,400		Furniture	4,000	
(−) Drawings	(2,000)	20,400	(+) Appreciation	800	4,800
Creditors		6,000	Stock		6,000
			Debtors	8,000	
			(−) Provision on Debtors	(400)	7,600
		26,400			26,400

4. Vijay Sharma keeps incomplete records. The statement of affairs of his business as at 1st April, 2020 was as follows

Statement of Affairs
as at 1st April, 2020

Liabilities	Amt (₹)	Assets	Amt (₹)
Creditors	10,000	Cash in Hand	800
Capital	1,40,000	Cash at Bank	3,200
		Debtors	34,000
		Stock	40,000
		Furniture	12,000
		Plant and Machinery	60,000
	1,50,000		1,50,000

His position on 31st March, 2021 was Cash in Hand ₹ 2,000; Bills Receivable ₹ 8,000; Stock ₹ 64,000; Plant and Machinery ₹ 80,000; Cash at Bank ₹ 4,000; Debtors ₹ 42,000; Furniture ₹ 16,000 and Creditors ₹ 36,000. He withdrew ₹ 60,000 during the year, out of which he used ₹ 36,000 for purchasing a scooty for the business. Calculate his net profit for the year after the following adjustments and prepare a final statement of affairs as at 31st March, 2021

(i) Depreciate furniture and scooty @ 20%.

(ii) Make a provision of 5% on bills receivable.

(iii) 5% of the debtors are doubtful and ₹ 1,600 are absolutely bad.

Ans.

Statement of Affairs
as at 31st March, 2021 (Before Adjustments)

Liabilities	Amt (₹)	Assets	Amt (₹)
Creditors	36,000	Cash in Hand	2,000
Capital (Balancing Figure)	2,16,000	Cash at Bank	4,000
		Bills Receivable	8,000
		Debtors	42,000
		Stock	64,000
		Furniture	16,000
		Scooty	36,000
		Plant and Machinery	80,000
	2,52,000		2,52,000

Statement of Profit and Loss
for the year ending 31st March, 2021

Particulars		Amt (₹)
Closing Capital as on 31st March, 2021		2,16,000
(+) Drawings during the year (60,000 − 36,000)		24,000
		2,40,000
(−) Opening Capital as on 1st April, 2020		(1,40,000)
Profit before adjustments		1,00,000
(−) Depreciation on Furniture	(3,200)	
(−) Depreciation on Scooty	(7,200)	
(−) Provision on Bills Receivable	(400)	
(−) Bad Debts	(1,600)	
(−) Provision for Doubtful Debts @ 5% on 40,400 (42,000 − 1,600)	(2,020)	(14,420)
Profit Made During the Year 2020-21		85,580

Final Statement of Affairs (After Adjustments)
as at 31st March, 2021

Liabilities		Amt (₹)	Assets		Amt (₹)
Creditors		36,000	Cash in Hand		2,000
Opening Capital	1,40,000		Cash at Bank		4,000
(+) Net Profit	85,580		Bills Receivable	8,000	
	2,25,580		(−) Provision @ 5%	(400)	7,600
(−) Drawings	(24,000)	2,01,580	Debtors	42,000	
			(−) Bad Debts	(1,600)	
				40,400	
			(−) Provision for Doubtful Debts	(2,020)	38,380
			Stock		64,000
			Furniture	16,000	
			(−) Depreciation	(3,200)	12,800
			Scooty	36,000	
			(−) Depreciation	(7,200)	28,800
			Plant and Machinery		80,000
		2,37,580			2,37,580

Multiple Choice Questions

1. Which of the following is not a disadvantage of single entry system?
(a) Expensive
(b) Difficult to keep control over assets
(c) Internal check is not possible
(d) Lack of uniformity between accounts of different organsiations

2. In the single entry system .... is not possible, hence there are always the chances of errors and frauds.
(a) internal check
(b) internal control
(c) cash credit
(d) None of these

3. Opening capital is ascertained by preparing
(a) total debtors account
(b) total creditors account
(c) cash account
(d) opening statement of affairs

4. Which of the following statement(s) is/are not true about statement of affairs?
(i) It is prepared to know profit or loss at a point of time.
(ii) It is prepared only under single entry system of accounting.
(iii) Trial balance is not prepared.
(iv) It is prepared on the basis of ledger accounts.

Alternatives
(a) Only (i)
(b) Both (i) and (iv)
(c) Both (ii) and (iii)
(d) Only (ii)

5. Capital at the end of year exceeds the capital that in the beginning, it represents
(a) loss
(b) profit
(c) expense
(d) income

6. Opening Capital = ₹ 70,000
Profit for the year = ₹ 20,000
Drawings = ₹ 7,000
During the year, proprietor sold ornaments of his wife for ₹ 20,000 and invested the same in business. What will be the amount of closing capital?
(a) ₹ 1,03,000
(b) ₹ 83,000
(c) ₹ 63,000
(d) ₹ 97,000

Short Answer (SA) Type Questions

1. Mention any three advantages of accounts from incomplete records.

2. Why is statement of affairs prepared under single entry system not referred to as balance sheet?

3. Mrs Anu started a firm with a capital ₹ 4,00,000 on 1st July, 2020. She borrowed from her friends a sum ₹ 1,00,000 @ 10% p.a. (interest paid) for business and brought a further amount to capital ₹ 75,000. On 31st December, 2020, her position was as follows

Items	Amt (₹)
Cash	30,000
Stock	4,70,000
Debtors	3,50,000
Creditors	3,00,000

She withdrew ₹ 8,000 per month for the year. Calculate profit or loss for the year and show your working clearly.

4. Miss Priyanka runs a small bakery business. On 1st April, 2020 she had started the business with a capital of ₹ 78,000. On 31st March, 2021 her incomplete records provide the following data
(i) Amount due to suppliers of raw materials ₹ 17,500.
(ii) Stock of raw materials ₹ 2,000 and finished products ₹ 2,500.
(iii) Fixed assets ₹ 34,000.
(iv) Amount due from customers ₹ 42,000.
(v) She had withdrawn ₹ 2,500 per month for meeting her personal expenses.
(vi) She had introduced ₹ 7,000 as capital during the year.
(vii) She has cash at bank ₹ 21,000 and cash in hand ₹ 1,800.
(viii) Outstanding electricity bill ₹ 2,250
Calculate the profit/loss of her business during the year using statement of affairs method.

5. Jofra states his capital on 31st December, 2020 as ₹ 1,10,000. He further informs that his capital on 1st January, 2020 was ₹ 1,20,000. He gave a loan of ₹ 40,000 to his brother on private account and withdrew ₹ 7,000.

He lives in a flat, the rent (₹ 1,500 per month) and the electricity charges (₹ 500 per month) being paid from business account.

During the year, he sold his 10% government bonds of ₹ 15,000 at 4% premium and brought that money into business. He asks you to ascertain his business profit or loss.

Long Answer (LA) Type Questions

1. Gauri keeps incomplete records. Following information is available from her books.

Particulars	1st April, 2020 (₹)	31st March, 2021 (₹)
Sundry Debtors	60,000	1,24,000
Stock	1,28,000	76,000
Loan from Wife	30,000	30,000
Sundry Creditors	45,200	33,600
Office Equipment	30,000	25,000
Building	1,20,000	1,20,000
Cash Balance	4,200	9,000
Bank Overdraft	27,000	50,000

During the year Gauri received ₹ 2,000 per month as pension, of which she invested ₹ 15,000 into the business. She also sold her private house for ₹ 50,000 and invested this amount into the business.

Gauri withdrew from the business ₹ 2,000 per month upto 31st August, 2020 and thereafter ₹ 4,000 per month as drawings. In addition, she withdrew from the business ₹ 8,400 for paying Income Tax and ₹ 6,000 to pay the legal expenses in private suit.

The following adjustments should also be considered.

  (i) Outstanding expenses ₹ 3,600 and prepaid expenses ₹ 1,000.

 (ii) Commission earned but not received ₹ 4,000.

(iii) Depreciate office equipment by 20%.

(iv) Provide 4% on debtors for doubtful debts.

Prepare a statement to ascertain the profit or loss and also prepare the final statement of affairs as at 31st March, 2021.

2. M/s Saniya Sports Equipment does not keep proper records. From the following information, find out profit or loss and also prepare balance sheet for the year ended 31st December, 2021.

Items	31st December, 2020 (₹)	31st December, 2021 (₹)
Cash in Hand	6,000	24,000
Bank Overdraft	30,000	—
Stock	50,000	80,000
Sundry Creditors	26,000	40,000
Sundry Debtors	60,000	1,40,000
Bills Payable	6,000	12,000
Furniture	40,000	60,000
Bills Receivable	8,000	28,000
Machinery	50,000	1,00,000
Investment	30,000	80,000

Drawings ₹ 10,000 per month for personal use, fresh capital introduced during the year ₹ 2,00,000. A bad debts ₹ 2,000 and a provision of 5% to be made on debtors. Outstanding salary ₹ 2,400, prepaid insurance ₹ 700, depreciation charged on furniture and machinery @ 10% per annum.

Answers

Multiple Choice Questions

1. (a)   *2. (a)*   *3. (d)*   *4. (b)*   *5. (b)*   *6. (a)*

For Detailed Solutions

Scan the code

CHAPTER 07

Computers in Accounting

In this Chapter...

- Introduction to Computer
- Information System
- Computerised Accounting System
- Sourcing of Accounting Software

Introduction to Computer

A computer is an electronic device which is capable of performing a variety of operations in accordance with a set of instructions called a computer program or software. It is useful for processing raw data into meaningful information.

Characteristics/Capabilities of a Computer System

A computer system possesses some characteristics, which, in comparison to human beings, turn out to be its capabilities. These are as follows

1. **Speed** The amount of time, a computer takes to complete a task or an operation refers to its speed. In comparison to human beings, computers require far less time to perform a task.

2. **Accuracy** Computers perform job with high degree of accuracy. It cannot make mistakes if proper instructions are given. Most of the errors in **Computer Based Information System** (CBIS) occur because of bad software programming and deviation from procedures.

3. **Reliability** Unlike human beings, computer systems are immune to tiredness, boredom or fatigue and can perform jobs of repetitive nature any number of times, therefore they are more reliable.

4. **Versatility** Computer is a versatile machine which can do variety of tasks; from simple calculations to complex and logical operations. It is used in various fields for various purposes.

5. **Storage and Retrieval** The computer system have huge capacity to store data in a very small physical space. A typical mainframe computer system is capable of storing and providing one billion of characters and thousands of graphic images.

Limitations of a Computer System

Inspite of possessing many capabilities, computers suffer from various limitations as are discussed below

1. **Lack of Common Sense** A computer system does not have common sense of its own like a human being has. Therefore, they only work according to a set of instructions known as program or software.

2. **Lack of Decision-making** A computer does not possess the quality of decision-making like a human being does. Computers can be programmed to take only those decisions which are procedure-oriented.

3. **Lack of Intelligence** A computer system does not possess intelligence of its own. It cannot visualise and think what exactly to do under a particular situation. It operates on the basis of instructions given by human beings.

4. **Lack of Feeling** Computers do not have feelings like human beings because they are machines. No computer possesses the equivalence of a human heart and soul.

5. **High Cost** Besides the high cost of computer system, huge money is required to get the trained specialised staff to ensure effective and efficient use of computer system.

Functional Components of Computer System

The functional components of a computer are as follows

1. **Input Unit** It is the unit which controls the input devices used for data entry. The input devices used for entering the data into the computer system are keyboard, mouse, light pen, optical scanner, etc.

2. **Output Unit** The output unit is used to communicate the information, (after processing the data) to the users in a human readable and understandable form. The commonly used output devices include monitor also called Visual Display Unit (VDU), printer, magnetic storage devices, etc.

3. **Central Processing Unit** (CPU) This is the main part of a computer system. It is also called the brain of the computer. It processes the given data according to the instructions and arranges the information in a manner which provides easier retrieval of the data when required by the user.

   It has two main units as described below

   (i) **Arithmetic and Logic Unit** (ALU) It is responsible for performing all the arithmetic calculations.

   (ii) **Control Unit** This unit is responsible for controlling and coordinating the activities of all other units of the computer system.

4. **Memory Unit** In this unit, data is stored before being actually processed. The processing of data is accomplished either through batch processing or real-time processing, which are explained below

   (i) **Batch Processing** It applies to large and voluminous data that is accumulated off-line from various units i.e., branches or departments.

   (ii) **Real-time Processing** It provides online outcome in the form of information and reports without time lag between the transaction and its processing.

Elements of a Computer System

There are six elements of a computer system which are as follows

1. **Hardware** Computer hardware consists of physical components such as keyboard, mouse, monitor and processor. These components can be physically touched. These are electronic and electromechanical components. These are the basic components of a computer that collectively form a system.

These parts are necessary for a computer to perform the basic functions. These are as follows

(i) **Motherboard** The main electronic division of the computer with the help of which other components or peripherals, that are also a part of the operating system, communicate with each other, is motherboard.

(ii) **Processor** It is the processing unit that controls all the components attached to the computer system. It is also known as CPU (Central Processing Unit).

(iii) **Primary Storage Memory** Alternatively referred to as volatile memory, internal memory and main memory.

It is a storage location that holds memory for short period of time while the computer is running.

(iv) **Secondary Storage Devices** These devices are meant for storing the data permanently on the computer, i.e., the data will stay on the device until the user erases it or the device gets damaged.

(v) **Keyboard** It is an input device which is used to input text into the computer in the CUI (Character User Interface). On the keyboard, keys are placed in a special sequence.

(vi) **Sound Card and Speakers** Computers are also equipped with a sound card and speakers. With the help of these, music stored as digital data in the computer is converted into analog data of sound waves.

(vii) **Monitor and Liquid Crystal Display** (LCD) **Panel** It is an output device on which the user can see the work done.

(viii) **Printers** Printers are devices used for producing information as a hard copy, i.e., in a printed form.

2. **Software** It is the set of instructions that makes the computer work. Software is held on the computer's hard disk, CD-ROM, DVD or on a diskette (floppy disk) and is loaded from the disk into the computer's RAM (Random Access Memory), as and when required.

Some of the important softwares are as follows

(i) **Operating System** An integrated set of specialised programmes that is meant to manage the resources of a computer and also facilitate its operation is called operating system.

It creates a necessary interface that is an interactive link between the user and the computer hardware.

(ii) **Utility Programmes** These are a set of computer programmes which are designed to perform certain supporting operations.

It is also known as system utility. Most major operating systems come with several pre-installed utilities like, disk storage, disk cleaners, disk space analysers, disk and data compression, file managers, anti-virus, etc.

(iii) **Application Softwares** These are user oriented programmes designed and developed for performing certain specified tasks, such as payroll accounting, inventory accounting, financial accounting, etc.

Some examples of application softwares are

   (a) **Word Processing Software** MS-word, wordpad, notepad.

   (b) **Spreadsheet Software** Excel, lotus 1-2-3, apple numbers.

   (c) **Database Software** MS access, My SQL oracle.

   (d) **Presentation Graphic Software** MS power point.

3. **Humanware/People** It constitutes the most important part of a computer system. It basically refers to the individual or the users who interact with the computer through the use of hardware or software. People who respond to the procedures instituted for executing the computer programs are also a part of **humanware/live-ware**.

They are as follows

(i) **System Analysts** These are the people who design data processing systems.

(ii) **Programmers** These are the people who write programs to implement the data processing system design.

(iii) **Operators** These are the people who participate in operating the computers.

4. **Procedures** A specified series of actions or operations which have to be executed in a certain manner, in order to always achieve the desired result in same circumstances is referred to as procedure.

There are three types of procedures which constitute part of computer system

(i) **Hardware-oriented Procedure** It provides details about components and their method of operation.

(ii) **Software-oriented Procedure** It provides a set of instructions required for using the software of computer system.

(iii) **Internal Procedure** It helps to ensure smooth flow of data to computers by sequencing the operation of each sub-system of overall computer system.

5. **Data** Data are the facts which are gathered and entered into a computer system. Data may comprise of numbers, texts, graphics, etc.

The computer system processes and organises data to create information that is relevant and can be used for decision-making.

6. **Connectivity** It is the sixth element of the computer system. It refers to the manner in which a particular computer system is connected to other electronic devices, say through telephone lines, microwave transmission, satellite link, etc.

Information System

It is an integrated set of components for collecting, storing and processing data for delivering information, knowledge and digital products.

There are number of information systems which have evolved to fulfil the diverse needs of organisations of which two systems are described as follows

1. **Transaction Processing System** (TPS) It is an information processing system for business transactions involving the collection, modification and retrieval of all transaction data. Characteristics of a TPS include performance, reliability and consistency. It is among the earliest computerised system catering to the requirements of large business enterprises.

The purpose of a typical TPS is to record, process, validate and store transactions that occur in the various functional areas of a business for subsequent retrieval and usage, e.g. cash withdrawal at an ATM.

TPS involves following steps in processing transaction

- Data collection
- Data editing
- Data validation
- Data manipulation
- Data storage
- Report generation
- Query support

2. **Management Information System** (MIS) It is the most commonly used form of information system. MIS is a system that provides the necessary information required for managing an organisation effectively and in taking various decisions. MIS is viewed and used by management at many levels such as operational, tactical and strategic. MIS is supportive of the institution's long-term strategic goals and objectives.

MIS is basically concerned with processing data into information which is then communicated to various departments in an organisation for appropriate decision-making.

Data → Information → Communication → Decision

The purpose of management information system is to provide the right information, to the right person, at the right place, at the right time, in the right form and at the right cost.

Accounting Information System (AIS)

It is a sub-system of management information system. It identifies, collects, processes economic information about an entity and communicates it to a wide variety of users. Such information is organised in a manner that correct decisions can be based on it.

It is a collection of resources (people and equipment), designed to transform financial and other data into information. This information is communicated to a wide variety of decision-makers. Accepting information systems perform this transformation whether they are essentially manual systems or thoroughly computerised.

MIS and AIS

- Every accounting system is essentially a part of the Accounting Information System (AIS) which in turn is a part of the broader system, i.e., organisation's management information system.
- A management information system generates accurate, timely and organised information to help managers make decisions, control process, solve problems, supervise activities and track progress.
- Accounting information system identifies, collects, processes and communicates economic information of an organisation to a wide variety of users.
- Accounting information system is one of the function organisation systems and management information system has a link with all the function information systems of an organisation.

Computerised Accounting System

An accounting information system that processes the financial transactions and events as per Generally Accepted Accounting Principles (GAAP) to produce reports as per user requirements is referred to as a computerised accounting system. In this system, the framework of storage and processing of data is called **operating environment**.

Features of Computerised Accounting System

Typically, computerised accounting system offers the following features

- Online input and storage of accounting data.
- Printout of purchase and sales invoices.
- Logical scheme for codification of accounts and transactions. Every account and transaction is assigned a unique code.
- Grouping of accounts is done from the very beginning.

- Instant reports for management, e.g. stock statement, trial balance, trading and profit and loss account, balance sheet, stock valuation, Goods & Services Tax (GST), returns, payroll report, etc.

Basic Requirements of Computerised Accounting System

Every computerised accounting system has two basic requirements

1. **Accounting Framework** It consists of set of principles, coding and grouping structure of accounting.
2. **Operating Procedure** It is a well-defined operating procedure blended suitably with the operating environment of the organisation.

The use of computers in any database oriented application has four basic requirements as mentioned below

1. **Front-end Interface** It is an interactive link between the user and database oriented software through which the user communicates to the back-end database.
2. **Back-end Database** It is the data storage system that is hidden from the user and responds to the requirement of the user to the extent the user is authorised to access.
3. **Data Processing** It is a sequence of actions that are taken to transform the data into decision useful information.
4. **Reporting System** It is an integrated set of objects that constitute the report.

Advantages of Computerised Accounting System

Computerised accounting system offers several advantages which are as follows

- Speed
- Accuracy
- Reliability
- Scalability
- Legibility
- Efficiency
- Storage and retrieval

Limitations of a Computerised Accounting System

Computerised accounting system has many limitations which are as follows

- Cost of training
- Staff opposition
- Disruption
- System failure
- Inability to check unanticipated errors
- Ill-effects on health
- Breach of security

Comparison between Manual and Computerised Accounting

The comparison between manual and computerised accounting is stated in the points below

1. **Identifying** Identification of transactions, based on application of accounting principles is common to both manual and computerised accounting system.

2. **Recording** In a manual accounting system, financial transactions are recorded through books of original entries. While in computerised accounting system, the data content of such transactions is stored in a well-designed accounting database.

3. **Classification** In a manual accounting system, transactions recorded are classified by posting them into the ledger accounts which results in data duplicity of transactions. Whereas, in a computerised accounting system, the posting process is carried out by internal sorting of data, i.e., with the help of application and utility software without any further process.

4. **Summarising** In a manual accounting system, the transactions are summarised to produce trial balance by ascertaining the balances of various accounts. In a computerised accounting software, generation of ledger is not a necessary condition for producing trial balance, a transaction or event once recorded, is stored in the database and can be processed to produce a trial balance directly.

5. **Adjusting Entries** In a manual accounting system, adjusting entries are made to adhere to the principle of cost matching revenue. These entries are recorded to match the expenses of the accounting period with the revenues generated by them. Some other adjusting entries may be made as part of errors and rectification. However, in computerised accounting, journal vouchers are prepared and stored to follow the principle of cost matching revenue.

6. **Grouping of Accounts** In a manual accounting system, the account is grouped as an asset, a liability, an income or an expense at the time of preparing the financial statements. However, in a computerised accounting system, it is decided at the time, when a transaction takes place. It is also defined whether the particular head of account shall be shown as an asset or liability or an income or an expense.

7. **Financial Statements** Availability of trial balance is essential to prepare financial statements in a manual accounting system. Whereas, in a computerised accounting system, the generation of financial statements is independent of producing the trial balance because such statements can be prepared by direct processing of originally stored transaction data.

8. **Closing the Books** In manual accounting system, the accountants make preparations for the next accounting period, after the preparation of financial reports which is achieved by posting of closing and reversing journal entries. However, in a computerised accounting system, there is year end processing to create and store opening balances of accounts in database.

Sourcing of Accounting Software

Accounting software is an integral part of the computerised accounting system. An important factor to be considered before acquiring accounting software is the accounting expertise of people responsible in organisation for accounting work. The need for accounting software arises in two situations

- When the computerised accounting system is implemented to replace the manual system.
- When the current computerised system needs to be replaced with a new one in view of changing needs.

Classification of Accounting Software

Software can also be classified as

1. **Ready-to-use/Readymade Software** These softwares are developed not for only specific user but for the users in general.
   These softwares are suited for organisations running small/conventional business where the frequency or volume of transactions is very low. e.g., Tally, EX-Busy, etc.

2. **Customised Software** The term 'customised software' means making changes in the readymade software to suit the specific requirement of the user i.e., make it user specific.

   These softwares are available off-the-shelf and are changed to suit the requirements of the user. Customised software are best suited for large and medium businesses and can be linked to the other information systems.

3. **Tailored Software** These softwares are developed to meet the requirement of the user on the basis of discussions between the user and developers. These softwares are suited for large business organisations with multi-users and geographically scattered locations.

Generic Considerations before Sourcing an Accounting Software

The following factors are usually taken into consideration before sourcing an accounting software

- Flexibility
- Cost of installation and maintenance
- Size of organisation
- Ease of adaptation and training needs

- Utilities/MIS reports
- Expected level of secrecy (software and data)
- Exporting/Importing data facility
- Vendors reputation and capability

Automation of Accounting Process

It means performing the accounting function with the help of an accounting software. The purpose of automation is to reduce human intervention to the minimum so as to reduce manual errors i.e., errors committed in manual accounting. Although the human intervention cannot be completely eliminated, it can be reduced to the minimum. Automation of accounting can save a great deal of time when posting debits and credits.

Stages of Automation

The automation process can be divided into following stages

Stage 1 Planning

Stage 2 Selection of accounting software

Stage 3 Selection of accounting hardware

Stage 4 Classification and grouping of accounts

Stage 5 Generating reports

Creation of Accounts Group and Hierarchy

- Accounts groups are a collection of ledgers of the same nature which are maintained to determine the hierarchy of ledger accounts.
- The group behaviour is classified into capital or revenue and more specifically into assets, liabilities, income and expenditure.
- The groups ascertain whether the same will affect profit and loss account which is revenue in nature or balance sheet which is capital in nature.
- Groups can be sub-classified to practically unlimited levels. But at the lowest level would be the ledger account.

Accounting Reports

- Accounting reports are the scorecard by which a business's financial health is measured.
- Business owners, investors, suppliers and banks use accounting reports to understand the financial position, financial performance and cash flows of business.
- Every report is prepared with a definite objective. The three main accounting reports for any business are the trial balance, the income statement (also called the profit and loss statement) and balance sheet.
- Every accounting report must be able to fulfil the following criterion
  - (a) Relevance
  - (b) Timeliness
  - (c) Accuracy
  - (d) Completeness
  - (e) Summarisation
- Accounting reports can be classified as summary reports, demand reports, customer reports, exception reports, responsibility reports and debtor's reports.

Steps Involved in Designing Accounting Reports

The various steps involved in designing accounting reports from accounting data are as follows

Step 1 **Definition of Objectives** The reports should clearly define the objectives, who are the users of the report and the decision to be taken on the basis of report.

Step 2 **Structure of the Report** The information to be contained therein and the style of presentation.

Step 3 **Querying with the Database** The accounting information queries must be clearly defined and the methodology to be adopted while interacting with the database.

Step 4 **Finalising the Report** The report should have complete ending with proper analysis and suggestion.

Chapter Practice

Objective Questions

• Multiple Choice Questions

1. Which characteristic of a computer is reflected in the following statement?

"Error in computer based information system occurs because of poor software programming".

(a) Versatility   (b) Accuracy
(c) Reliability   (d) Speed

Ans. (b) Accuracy

2. Which unit of CPU controls the operations of a computer system?

(a) ALU   (b) CU
(c) Memory   (d) RAM

Ans. (b) CU

3. A set of instructions in the computer is called
....

(a) Program/Software   (b) System
(c) Internal plan   (d) Raw device

Ans. (a) Program/Software

4. A computer system consists of ...... elements.

(a) hardware   (b) software
(c) humanware   (d) All of these

Ans. (d) All of these

5. Which of the following is the oldest information system, used in profit making as well as non-profit organisations?

(a) AIS   (b) TPS
(c) ESS   (d) MIS

Ans. (a) AIS

6. Which of the following is the security measure that protects sensitive data of AIS?

(a) Technology   (b) Data
(c) Procedures   (d) Control

Ans. (d) Control sub-system is mainly responsible for controlling AIS, that can be a manual system.

7. Applications that collect and process order from clients by mail is ....

(a) order processing
(b) decision processing
(c) Both (a) and (b)
(d) None of the above

Ans. (a) Order processing is an example of application of TPS which collects and processes order from clients by e-mail.

8. The way in which a computer system is connected to other electronic devices and link ups such as satellite link, telephone lines is

(a) electronic way   (b) processor
(c) connectivity   (d) None of these

Ans. (c) connectivity

9. Name the software used for controlling internal functions, such as reading data from input devices.

(a) System software
(b) Application software
(c) Connectivity software
(d) None of the above

Ans. (a) System software

10. Consider the following statements.

(i) Batch processing applies to large and voluminous data.

(ii) Real time processing provides online outcome in the form of information.

Alternatives

(a) (i) is correct   (b) (ii) is correct
(c) Both are correct   (d) Both are incorrect

Ans. (c) Batch processing applies to large and voluminous data i.e., is accumulated offline from various units. Real time processing provides online outcome in the form of information and reports without any delay of time.

11. Match the following.

	Column I		Column II
A.	Front-end interface	(i)	Data can be retrieved by user (Authorised)
B.	Back-end database	(ii)	Link between user and database
C.	Data processing	(iii)	Transferring data into information
D.	Reporting system	(iv)	System composing information

Codes

	A	B	C	D
(a)	(ii)	(i)	(iii)	(iv)
(b)	(ii)	(i)	(iv)	(iii)
(c)	(i)	(ii)	(iii)	(iv)
(d)	(iii)	(iv)	(ii)	(i)

Ans. (a) (ii), (i), (iii), (iv)

12. Modern computerised accounting system is based on the concept of ....
(a) database level   (b) operating level
(c) system level   (d) working level

Ans. (a) database level

13. .... reports are the user specific reports.
(a) Debtors   (b) Exception
(c) Demand   (d) Responsibility

Ans. (a) Debtors

14. Which of the following is/are limitation(s) of computerised accounting system?
(a) Staff opposition   (b) High cost of training
(c) System failure   (d) All of these

Ans. (d) All of these

15. Tailor made software is important because
(a) they are available of the shelf
(b) they are used by the number of users
(c) they are user specific and trained user use it
(d) All of these

Ans. (c) they are user specific and trained user use it

16. Accounting information system is a sub-system of
(a) ESS   (b) MIS
(c) DSS   (d) MPS

Ans. (b) MIS

17. Automation of accounting process depends on certain criteria, which is/are
(a) size of the organisation
(b) number of transactions
(c) cost of automation
(d) All of these

Ans. (d) All of these

18. Automation of accounting can save time of posting .... and .... entries.
(a) debit, credit   (b) starting, final
(c) secrecy, reputation   (d) exporting, importing

Ans. (a) debit, credit

19. The automation process can be divided into following stages.
(i) Planning
(ii) Generating reports
(iii) Selection of accounting hardware
(iv) Selection of accounting software
(v) Classification and grouping of accounts.

Alternatives
(a) (i), (iv), (iii), (v), (ii)   (b) (iv), (i), (iii), (v), (ii)
(c) (ii), (i), (iii), (iv), (v)   (d) (i), (ii), (iii), (iv), (v)

Ans. (a) (i), (iv), (iii), (v), (ii)

• Assertion-Reasoning MCQs

Direction *(Q. Nos. 1 to 3) There are two statements marked as Assertion (A) and Reason (R). Read the statements and choose the appropriate option from the options given below.*
(a) Assertion (A) is correct, but Reason (R) is wrong
(b) Both Assertion (A) and Reason (R) are correct
(c) Assertion (A) is wrong, but Reason (R) is correct
(d) Both Assertion (A) and Reason (R) are wrong

1. Assertion (A) System software create and control a connection between a computer and a server.
Reason (R) System software enable computer to share and communicate the resources of server and other connected computers.

Ans. (d) Connectivity software create and control a connection between a computer and a server so that the computer is able to communicate and share the resources of server and other connected computers.

2. Assertion (A) Computer work according to a set of instructions known as program or software.
Reason (R) Computer does not have common sense of its own.

Ans. (b) Computers work according to set of instructions known as program or software as it does not have any common sense of its own.

3. Assertion (A) Language processors translate machine language into programming language.
Reason (R) Computers understand only programming language.

Ans. (d) Computers understand only machine language. Language processors are used to translate or interpret the program written in a programming language into machine language.

• Case Based MCQs

1. Direction *Read the following text and answer question no. (i) to (iv) on the basis of the same.*

Riddhima, class 11th student of commerce in Saraswati School has got an assignment on "Computers in accounting". She hates studying theory of computers and has never understood technical terms used in computers. To complete her assignment, she took help of her sister Karishma, who is an engineer. Karishma not only helped her to complete the assignment, but also taught her all the theory with the help of interesting examples.

Following are some of the questions asked in her assignment

(i) Which of the following is an output device?
(a) Scanner   (b) Printer
(c) Smart card reader   (d) Keyboard

Ans. (b) Printer

(ii) ……… are used for giving instructions to the computer.
(a) Input devices
(b) Primary storage memory
(c) Output devices
(d) Secondary storage memory

Ans. (a) Input devices

(iii) On which language is CPU dependent?
(a) C   (b) Assembly
(c) Java   (d) All except Java

Ans. (d) C is a high level programming language while assembly is a low level computer programming language on which CPU is dependent.

(iv) Which of the following information systems support the operations, management and decision-making functions in an organisation?
(a) AIS   (b) TIS   (c) MIS   (d) None of these

Ans. (a) AIS

2. Direction *Read the following text and answer question no. (i) to (iv) on the basis of the same.*

Sameer, who lives in Laxminagar, Delhi owns a showroom of opticals in Chirag, Delhi. He has hired Shamita, B.Com hons. graduate from Dyal Singh College who maintains his computerised books of accounts.

Due to computerised accounting system, Sameer has been effectively and efficiently able to optimise resources, able to make quick decisions for success of his venture.

(i) The framework of storage and processing of data in a computerised accounting system is

(a) software environment
(b) operating environment
(c) functional environment
(d) accounting environment

Ans. (b) operating environment

(ii) Which of the following is an interactive link between the user and database oriented software through which the user communicates to the back end database?
(a) Front-end interface   (b) Back-end interface
(c) Data processing   (d) Reporting system

Ans. (a) Front-end interface

(iii) DBMS stands for ……… .
(a) Data Based Management System
(b) Device Based Methodology Structure
(c) Device Based Mandatory System
(d) Data Based Manual System

Ans. (a) Data Based Management System

(iv) In computerised accounting, ……… and ……… of adjustment entries are done manually and their posting is done by software.
(a) identification, recording   (b) classify, summarising
(c) interpretating, analysis   (d) system, sub-system

Ans. (a) identification, recording

PART 2
Subjective Questions

• Short Answer (SA) Type Questions

1. Briefly explain any four limitations of a computer system.

Ans. Following are the limitations of computer system

(i) **Lack of Decision-making** Decision-making involves a lot of understanding, information intelligence and ability to decide making it a complex process which can't be performed by computer.

(ii) **Lack of Emotions** Computer do not have any feelings as they are devoid of human heart or soul, since it is a machine.

(iii) **Lack of Common Sense** Computers fail to understand the logical aspect of problem and just keep on working as per it's programming.

(iv) **Lack of Intelligence Quotient** Computers cannot think themselves and need to be directed before each and every step.

They operate on the basis of instructions given by human beings.

2. Explain briefly the functions of a computer.

Ans. Computer performs following functions which are as follows

(i) **Input** Information or data that is entered into a computer is called input. It sends data and instructions to the CPU.

(ii) **Processing** It is sequence of actions taken on data to convert it into information which is meaningful to the user.

(iii) **Output** It makes processed data available to the user. It is mainly used to display the desired result to the user as per input instructions.

3. Define memory unit along with its types.

Ans. **Memory Unit** In this unit, data is stored before being actually processed. The processing of data is accomplished either through batch processing or real-time processing, which are explained below

(i) **Batch Processing** It applies to large and voluminous data that is accumulated off-line from various units i.e., branches or departments. The entries accumulated data is processed in one shot to generate the desired reports according to the requirement.

(ii) **Real-time Processing** It provides online outcome in the form of information and reports without time lag between the transaction and its processing.

4. Write a short note on CPU.

Ans. Central Processing Unit (CPU) is the main part of a computer system. It is also called the brain of the computer. It processes the given data according to the instructions and arranges the information in a manner which provides easier retrieval of the data when required by the user.

It has two main units as described below

(i) **Arithmetic and Logic Unit** (ALU) It is responsible for performing all the arithmetic calculations such as addition, subtraction, division, multiplication and exponentiation. In addition to this, it also performs logical operations involving comparisons among variables and data items.

(ii) **Control Unit** This unit is responsible for controlling and coordinating the activities of all other units of the computer system.

5. Mention any four components of a computer system.

Ans. The four elements/components of a computer system are

(i) **Hardware** Computer hardware consists of physical components such as keyboard, mouse, monitor and processor. These components can be physically touched.

These are electronic and electromechanical components. These are the basic components of a computer that collectively form a system.

(ii) **Software** It is the set of instructions that makes the computer work. Software is held on the computer's hard disk, CD-ROM, DVD or on a diskette (floppy disk) and is loaded from the disk into the computer's RAM (Random Access Memory), as and when required. It is the hypothetical or imaginary part of computer which is used with hardware to make computer perform operations.

(iii) **Humanware/People** People interacting with the computer and executing the program or software are known as humanware. They constitute the most important part of the computer system and they are system analyst programmers and operators.

(iv) **Procedures** A specified series of actions or operations, which have to be executed in the same manner, in order to always achieve the desired result in same circumstances. There are three types of procedures which constitute part of computer system and they are hardware oriented procedure, software oriented procedure and internal procedure.

6. Briefly explain any four components of a computer hardware.

Ans. The various components of a computer hardware are

(i) **Motherboard** The main electronic division of the computer with the help of which other components or peripherals, that are also a part of the operating system, communicate with each other is motherboard.

(ii) **Processor** It is the processing unit that controls all the components attached to the computer system. It is also known as CPU (Central Processing Unit).

(iii) **Primary Storage Memory** Alternatively referred to as volatile memory, internal memory and main memory. It is a storage location that holds memory for short period of time while the computer is running, e.g. RAM.

(iv) **Keyboard** It is an input device which is used to input text into the computer in the CUI. On the keyboard, keys are placed in a special sequence.

7. Write a short note on secondary storage devices.

Ans. Secondary storage devices refers to storage devices that serve as an addition to the computer's primary storage, RAM and cache memory. It consists of non-volatile memory that allow users to permanently store data even if computer is turned off or there is a power cut. It is also known as backup storage device, external storage, etc.

Secondary storage devices are as follows
(i) Online storage media
(ii) Near line storage device
(iii) Offline storage media or distribution media

8. Write a short note on the following
(i) Operating system   (ii) Utility programme

Ans. (i) **Operating System** It is an integrated set of specialised programmes that is meant to manage the resources of a computer and also facilitate the operation. It creates a necessary interface that is an interactive link between the user and the computer hardware.

(ii) **Utility Programme** It is a set of computer programmes which are designed to perform certain supporting operations. It is also known as system utility. Most major operating systems come with several pre-installed utilites like disk storage, disk cleaners, disk space analysers, etc.

9. Define procedures as an element/component of computer system. Also, discuss the types of procedures.

Ans. A specified series of actions or operations which have to be executed in the same manner, in order to always achieve the desired result in same circumstances are referred to as procedures.

There are three types of procedures which constitute part of computer system

(i) **Hardware-oriented Procedure** It provides details about components and their method of operation.

(ii) **Software-oriented Procedure** It provides a set of instructions required for using the software of computer system.

(iii) **Internal Procedure** It is instituted to ensure smooth flow of data to computers by sequencing the operation of each sub-system of overall computer system.

10. What is a management information system?

Ans. It is the most commonly used form of information system. Management Information System (MIS) is a system that provides the necessary information required for managing an organisation effectively and in taking various decisions.

MIS is viewed and used by management at many levels such as operational, tactical and strategic. MIS is supportive of the institution's long-term strategic goals and objectives.

Management information system is basically concerned with processing data into information which is then communicated to various departments in an organisation for appropriate decision-making.

Data → Information → Communication → Decision

The purpose of management information system is to provide the right information, to the right person, at the right place, at the right time, in the right form, at the right cost.

11. Write a short note on accounting information system.

Ans. AIS is a subsystem of management information system. It enables users to collect, store, manage, process, retrive and report financial data to its internal and external users.

AIS can be used by following
(i) Business analyst
(ii) CEO/CFO
(iii) Accountants
(iv) Regulators
(v) Auditors
(vi) Managers

This system allow its users to track all accounting and business activities of an entity. It helps to manage the organisation efficiently and effectively by combining modern technology resources together with traditional accounting controls and methods.

12. With the help of a diagram, show the relationship of the accounting system with the other functional management information system.

Ans. Every accounting system is essentially a part of the Accounting Information System (AIS) which in turn is a part of the broader system viz. the organisation's management information system.

Inspite of the accounting information system, other functional management information systems are manufacturing information system, human resource information system and marketing information system.

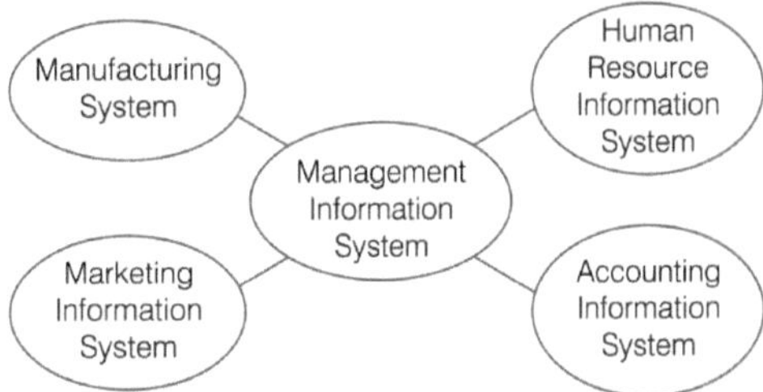

The diagram shown above entails the four widely recognised functional areas of management. An organisation operates in a given environment surrounded by the suppliers and customers. The informational needs emerge from the business processes stratified into functional areas where accounting is one of them. The Accounting Information System (AIS) receives and provides information to the various sub-systems of the institutional/integrated MIS.

13. Briefly explain the need of computers in accounting.

Ans. The advent of globalisation has resulted in the rise in business operations. Consequently, every medium and large size organisation requires well established information system in order to generate information required for decision-making and achieving the organisational objectives.

This made information technology to play vital role in supporting business operations.

14. Define computerised accounting system. Also, mention any three features of this system.

Ans. An accounting information system that processes the financial transactions and events as per Generally Accepted Accounting Principles (GAAP) to produce reports as per user requirements is referred to as a computerised accounting system.

Features of computerised accounting system are as follows (any three)
  (i) Online input and storage of accounting data.
  (ii) Printout of purchases and sales invoices.
  (iii) Logical scheme for codification of accounts and transactions. Every account and transaction is assigned a unique code.
  (iv) Grouping of accounts is done from the very beginning.

15. Mention any four disadvantages of computerised accounting system.

Ans.
  (i) **Cost of Training** In a computerised accounting system, the use of complicated accounting softwares generally require specialised staff. It also involves huge training cost to understand use of hardware and software on a continuous basis.
  (ii) **Staff Opposition** Whenever the accounting system is computerised, a high degree of objection is observed from the existing accounting staff.
  (iii) **Ill Effects on Health** Various health problems like bad backs, eye strain, muscular pains, etc are developed due to the extensive use of computer systems.
  (iv) **Inability to Check Unanticipated Errors** Computers are not capable to detect unanticipated errors as they lack the capability to judge.

16. The use of computers in any database oriented application has four basic requirements. Briefly discuss them.

Ans. The use of computers in any database oriented application has four basic requirements as mentioned below

  (i) **Front-end Interface** It is an interactive link between the user and database oriented software through which the user communicates to the back-end database.
  (ii) **Back-end Database** It is the data storage system that is hidden from the user and responds to the requirement of the user to the extent the user is authorised to access.
  (iii) **Data Processing** It is a sequence of actions that are taken to transform the data into useful information for decision-making.
  (iv) **Reporting System** It is an integrated set of objects that constitute the report.

17. An organisation can choose from number of softwares available. What are the factors taken in consideration before sourcing an accounting software?

Ans. The following factors are usually taken in consideration before sourcing an accouning software
  (i) **Flexibility** The software system must be flexible in respect of data handling and report preparing.
  (ii) **Maintenance Cost** The accounting software must be such which has less maintenance cost.
  (iii) **Size of Organisation** The accounting software must be according to need and size of the organisation.
  (iv) **Easy to Adaptation** The accounting software must be such which is easy to apply in organisation.

18. Mention the steps involved in designing accounting reports.

Ans. The various steps involved in designing accounting reports from accounting data are as follows

  Step 1 Definition of Objectives The reports should clearly define the objectives, who are the users of the report and the decision to be taken on the basis of report.

  Step 2 Structure of Report The information to be contained therein and the style of presentation.

  Step 3 Querying with the Data Base The accounting information queries must be clearly defined and the methodology to be adopted while interacting with the database.

  Step 4 Finalising the Report The report should be completely ending with proper analysis and suggestion.

19. What do you mean by codification of accounts?

Ans. Each account is given a separate code based on the group and sub-group to which it belongs. The account can be classified as belonging to incomes group, expenses group, assets group or liabilities group.

The process of grouping can be better understood with the following example

Main Code	Sub-Code	Account Code	Main Head	Sub-head	Account Head
1			→ Assets		
	1			→ Fixed Assets	
		001			→ Land
		002			→ Buildings
		003			→ Plant and Machinery
		004			→ Electrical Installation
		005			→ Vehicles
		006			→ Furniture and Fixtures
		007			→ Computers

Thus, code for land account will be 11001 and for building account it will be 11002 and so on.

20. Give two examples each of the organisation where ready-to-use, customised and tailored accounting packages respectively are suitable to perform the accounting activity. **(NCERT)**

Ans. (i) Ready-to-use accounting packages are best suitable for small and conventional business.

(ii) Customised accounting packages are best suitable for large and medium business.

(iii) Tailored accounting packages are best suitable for large and typical business.

• Long Answer (LA) Type Questions

1. "A computer system possesses some characteristics, which in comparison to human beings, turn out to be its capabilities." In the light of this statement, discuss the characteristics/capabilities of a computer system.

Ans. The above said statement is correct. The characteristics/capabilities of a computer system are as follows (any four)

(i) **Speed** The amount of time, a computer takes to accomplish a task or an operation refers to its speed.

In comparison to human beings, computers require far less time to perform a task. Generally, human beings take into account a second or minute as unit of time. But computers have such a fast operating capability that the relevant unit of time is fraction of a second.

Modern computers are capable of performing a 100 million calculations per second and that is why the industry has developed Million Instructions Per Second (MIPS) as the criterion to classify different computers according to speed.

(ii) **Accuracy** The degree of exactness with which computations are made and operations are performed is referred to as its accuracy. Most of the errors in Computer Based Information System (CBIS) occurs because of bad programming, erroneous data and deviation from procedures, which are caused by human beings. Errors attributable to hardware are normally detected and corrected by the computer system itself.

(iii) **Reliability** It refers to the ability with which the computers remain functional to serve the user. Computer systems are more reliable than human beings as they are well-adapted to perform repetitive operations and are immune to tiredness, boredom or fatigue. However, there can be failures of computer system due to various internal and external reasons.

(iv) **Versatility** The ability of computers to perform a variety of tasks is referred to as versatility. Task can be simple as well as complex. Computers are usually versatile unless designed for a specific application. A general purpose computer is capable of being used in any area of applications such as business, industry, scientific, statistical, technological, communications and so on and when installed in an organisation, can take over the jobs of several specialists because of its versatility.

(v) **Storage and Retrieval** It refers to the amount of data, which a computer system can store and access.

The computer systems, besides having instant access to data, have huge capacity to store such data in a very small physical space, e.g. CD-ROM. A typical mainframe computer system is capable of storing and providing one billion of characters and thousands of graphic images.

2. "An organisation is a collection of interdependent decision-making units that exists to pursue organisational objectives". In the light of this statement, explain the relationship between information and decisions. Also, explain the role of transaction processing system in facilitating the decision-making process in business organisations. **(NCERT)**

Ans. An organisation consists of various interdependent decision-making units at every level of management and department. All these separate departments take decisions for their respective fields to achieve the desired common organisational objectives.

The organisation as a whole needs to set its targets, draft plans and formulate various policies. These activities are based on the information (in the form of data) regarding the past experiences and expected future conditions. It is on the basis of this information that an organisation allocates its resources and attempts to accomplish its determined targets. Thus, it can be said that on one hand, information facilitates the decision-making process while on the other hand, past decisions act as a pool of information in the future.

In this aspect, information forms the most crucial part of today's business environment. In this context, Transaction Processing System (TPS) has emerged as crucial component of the business operations.

Transaction Processing System (TPS) refers to a computerised system that records, processes, validates and stores routine transactions that occur in various functional areas of a business on daily basis. This system facilitates the decision-making in a business organisation through the following processes

  (i) **Data Collection** It refers to the collection of data.
  (ii) **Data Editing** It refers to checking data for correctness.
  (iii) **Data Validation** It refers to verifying data for any errors and rectifying those errors.
  (iv) **Data Manipulation** It refers to processing and analysing data on a pre-set design.
  (v) **Data Storage** It refers to the processing of stored data in the database.
  (vi) **Report Generation** It refers to generating reports in hard copy or soft copy in a pre-designed format.
  (vii) **Query Support** It refers to the process whereby the user of TPS can raise a query and extract the data to get report.

3. What are the components of an accounting information system?

Ans. Accounting information system generally has following main components

  (i) **People** The people in an AIS are simply the system users.

  (ii) **Procedure** It is the methods and instructions of collecting, storing, retrieving, processing data and communicating information to its users.
  (iii) **Data** All relevant financial and business information required by the users is data. Data included in an AIS depend on the nature of business. Generally, it includes information relating to purchases and sales, debtors and creditors, revenues and expenses, assets and liabilities. These are used to prepare accounting information that are relevant for its users.
  (iv) **Information Technology Infrastructure** It includes the hardware and software programmes used to operate AIS. Quality, reliability, flexibility and security are the key components of an effective AIS software.
  (v) **Internal Control** It refers to the security measures that protect data against unauthorised computer access and to limit access of data only to an authorised user. AIS must have internal controls system.

4. Describe the various types of accounting software along with their advantages and limitations. **(NCERT)**

Ans. Types of accounting software are

  (i) **Readymade Softwares** These are the softwares that are developed not for any specific user but for the users in general e.g., Tally, Ex, Busy.

Advantages of readymade software are
  (a) The cost of installation of these softwares is generally low and number of users is limited.
  (b) Ready-to-use software is relatively easier to learn and people (accountant) adaptability is very high.
  (c) The training needs are simple and sometimes the vendor (supplier of software) offers the training on the software free.
  (d) As these softwares are available off-the-shelf, time required in developing a 'tailor made software' is saved.

Limitations of readymade software are
  (a) The level of secrecy is relatively low and the software is prone to data frauds.
  (b) These softwares offer little scope of linking to other information systems.
  (c) These softwares use laser printers which are costly than dot matrix printers.

  (ii) **Customised Softwares** Customised softwares means modifying the readymade softwares to suit the specific requirements of the user.

Advantages of customised softwares are
  (a) Secrecy of data and software is high in customised software.
  (b) Linkage to other information system is available on the basis of need of the enterprise.

Limitations of customised softwares are
(a) The cost of installation and maintenance is relatively high because the high cost is to be paid to the vendor for customisation.
(b) Since the need to train the software users is important, the training costs are therefore high.
(iii) **Tailored Softwares** The softwares that are developed to meet the requirement of the user on the basis of discussion between the user and developers.
Advantages of tailored softwares are
(a) The secrecy and authenticity checks are robust in such softwares.
(b) Such softwares offer high flexibility in terms of number of users.
(c) As these softwares are developed according to specification of the user, it takes care of the specific needs of the enterprise.
(d) These softwares can be effectively linked to some other information system.
Limitations of tailored softwares are
(a) These softwares require specialised training to the users.
(b) The cost of maintenance and development of such softwares is much higher as compared to readymade and customised software.
(c) The results will be misleading, in case the accounts are grouped in an incorrect manner.

5. Define a computerised accounting system. Distinguish between a manual and computerised accounting system. **(NCERT)**

Ans. A computerised accounting system is that accounting information system that processes the financial transactions and events as per Generally Accepted Accounting Principles (GAAP) to produce reports as per requirements of the user.

The differences between a manual and computerised accounting system are

Basis	Manual Accounting System	Computerised Accounting System
Recording	In a manual accounting system, financial transactions are recorded through books of original entries.	While in computerised accounting system, the data content of such transactions is stored in a well-designed accounting database.
Classification	In a manual accounting system, transactions recorded are classified by positng them into the ledger accounts.	In a computerised accounting system the data stored are processed automatically by the application and utility software to give ledger accounts.
Summarising	In a manual accounting system, the transactions are summarised to produce trial balance by ascertaining the balances of various accounts.	In a computerised system a transaction or event once recorded, is stored in the database which will be processed to produce a trial balance directly.
Adjusting Entries	In a manual accounting system, adjusting entries are made to adhere to the matching principle. Some other adjusting entries may be made as part of errors and rectification.	However, in computerised accounting, journal vouchers are prepared and stored to follow the matching principle.
Grouping of Accounts	In a manual accounting system, the account is grouped as an asset, a liability, an income or an expense at the time of preparing the financial statements.	However, in a computerised accounting system, it is decided at the time, when a transaction takes place. It is also defined whether the particular head of account shall be shown as an asset or a liability or an income or an expense.
Financial Statements	Preparation of trial balance is essential, to prepare financial statements in a manual accounting system.	In a computerised accounting system financial statements can be prepared by direct processing of originally stored data. There is no need to prepare trial balance.
Closing the Books	In manual accounting system, closing of books of accounts and transferring of opening balance is done by recording journal entries.	In a computerised accounting system, closing of books of accounts is done through the software and opening balances are stored in the database.

Chapter Test

Multiple Choice Questions

1. Raw facts that form a logical meaning is known as
(a) Logical unit   (b) Data   (c) Performance   (d) System

2. Which among the following is not a limitation of a computer system?
(a) Lack of decision-making   (b) Lack of common sense   (c) Lack of intelligence   (d) Lack of validity

3. Primary storage memory are
(a) REM and RSM   (b) ROM and RAM   (c) REM and RAM   (d) ROM and RSM

4. Which of the following is said to be the brain of a computer?
(a) CPU   (b) Monitor   (c) MS excel   (d) Keyboard

5. MIS stands for Management .... System.
(a) Information   (b) Instruction   (c) Input   (d) Intelligence

6. Which one of the following is an accounting software?
(a) Microsoft office   (b) Coral draw   (c) Tally and busy   (d) Word and excel

7. Consider the following statements.
(i) ALU (Arithmetic and Logical Unit) is capable of performing programs of control.
(ii) In memory unit, each memory is called a register and ALU gets data from these registers.

Alternatives
(a) Both are incorrect   (b) Both are correct   (c) (i) is correct   (d) (ii) is correct

8. Which of the following is not a subsystem of management information system?
(a) Manufacturing Information System   (b) Marketing Information System
(c) Human Resource Information System   (d) Finance Information System

Short Answer (SA) Type Questions

1. Explain input units and output units of computer.

2. Write a short note on primary storage memory.

3. What do you understand by Transaction Processing System (TPS)?

4. Write about any four accounting reports.

5. A scorecard is prepared to check the financial health of the business which is used by its users to understand financial position and financial performance. Identify the scorecard referred to in the above statement. Also write a note on the same.

6. Identify the need for creation of accounts group and hierarchy in automation process.

Long Answer (LA) Type Questions

1. "Accounting function is performed with the help of an accounting software to reduce human intervention and to minimise errors". Identify the process discussed in above statement. Also, enumerate about its stages.

2. Distinguish between ready-to use, customised and tailored software.

Answers

Multiple Choice Questions

1. *(b)*   2. *(d)*   3. *(b)*   4. *(a)*   5. *(a)*   6. *(c)*   7. *(d)*   8. *(d)*

For Detailed Solutions
Scan the code

Practice Paper 1*
(Solved)

Instructions

- Time : 2 Hours
- Max. Marks : 40

1. There are 14 questions in the question paper. All questions are compulsory.
2. Question no. 1-4 and 10 are Short Answer Type Questions. Each question carries 3 marks.
3. Question no. 5-9 are Case Based MCQs. Each question carries 1 mark.
4. Question no. 11-14 are Long Answer Type Questions. Each question carries 5 marks.
5. There is no overall choice. However, internal choices have been provided in some questions. Students have to attempt only one of the alternatives in such question.

*** As exact Blue-print and Pattern for CBSE Term II exams is not released yet. So the pattern of this paper is designed by the author on the basis of trend of past CBSE Papers. Students are advised not to consider the pattern of this paper as official, it is just for practice purpose.**

Part A
Financial Accounting–I

Short Answer (SA) **Type Questions** (3 Marks)

1. State any three features of trial balance.

Or From the following information, draw up a trial balance in the books of Shri Manmohan as on 31st March, 2021. Capital ₹ 1,12,000; purchases ₹ 28,800; discount allowed ₹ 960; carriage inwards ₹ 6,960; carriage outwards ₹ 1,840; sales ₹ 48,000; return inwards ₹ 240; return outwards ₹ 560; rent and taxes ₹ 960; plant and machinery ₹ 64,560; stock on 1st April, 2020 ₹ 12,400; sundry debtors ₹ 16,160; sundry creditors ₹ 9,600; investments ₹ 2,880; commission received ₹ 1,440; cash in hand ₹ 80; cash at bank ₹ 8,080; motor cycle ₹ 27,680 and stock on 31st March, 2021 (not adjusted) ₹ 16,400.

2. Who is a notary public? Enumerate the facts which are noted by notary public when a bill is dishonoured.

Or On 1st January, 2020, Rao sold goods worth ₹ 20,000 to Reddy. Half of the payment was made immediately and for the remaining half, Rao drew a bill of exchange upon Reddy payable after 30 days. Reddy accepted the bill and returned it to Rao. On the due date, Rao presented the bill to Reddy and received the payment. Journalise the above transactions in the books of Rao and prepare Rao's account in the books of Reddy.

3. Name the errors, which affect the trial balance.

4. Give journal entries to rectify the following errors.

  (i) ₹ 65,000 paid for furniture purchased has been debited to purchases account.

  (ii) ₹ 10,000 paid to Golu for salary were debited to his personal account.

  (iii) An amount of ₹ 64,000 spent on annual white-washing was debited to building account.

Part B
Financial Accounting–II

Case Based MCQs ($1 \times 5 = 5$ Marks)

Shubhangi Jain, PGT commerce at Jain Public School gave assignment on financial statements (without adjustments) to all weak students during remedial class.

All the students were able to correctly solve all questions except Mohak Bansal.

She decided to observe Mohak's behaviour during the class and analysed his assignment carefully

Following errors were done by Mohak

(i) He has wrongly shown items in debit and credit side of trading account and profit and loss account.

(ii) He has copied wrong formulae of adjusted purchases from the book.

(iii) He don't know about the items to be shown in balance sheet

(iv) He has done mistakes in totalling.

Shubhangi, after analysing his assignment again, discovered that he has visual dyslexia.

5. Which of the following is correct formula of adjusted purchases?

  (a) Adjusted Purchases   = Purchases + Opening Stock + Direct Expenses – Closing Stock
  (b) Adjusted Purchases   = Net Purchases + Opening Stock – Closing Stock
  (c) Adjusted Purchases   = Net Purchases + Closing Stock – Opening Stock
  (d) Adjusted Purchases   = Net Purchases + Closing Stock + Direct Expenses – Opening Stock

6. Can you identify where contingent liabilities are shown while preparing financial statements.
  (a) They are shown on liabilities side of balance sheet
  (b) They are shown as a footnote below the balance sheet
  (c) They are shown on debit side of profit and loss account
  (d) They are added to capital in balance sheet

7. Which of the following item(s) is/are not shown in profit and loss account?

  (i) Royalty   (ii) Export duties
  (iii) Warehousing expenses   (iv) Consumable stores

Alternatives

(a) Only (i)   (b) Only (ii) and (iii)   (c) Only (ii)   (d) Only (i) and (iv)

8. Sales during the year 2021 ₹ 2,85,000 and Gross profit is 25% on sales. Cost of goods sold in given question is

(a) ₹ 2,13,750   (b) ₹ 3,56,250   (c) ₹ 2,22,750   (d) ₹ 3,57,250

9. Identify the correct arrangement of assets listed in order of liquidity in a balance sheet.
  (a) Land and Building, Plant and Machinery, Bills Receivable, Cash in Hand.
  (b) Bills Receivable, Cash in Hand, Land and Building, Plant and Machinery.
  (c) Cash in Hand, Bills Receivable, Plant and Machinery, Land and Building.
  (d) Cash in Hand, Bills Receivable, Plant and Machinery, Land and Building.

Short Answer (SA) **Type Question** (3 Marks)

10. Mention main components/parts of a computer and draw a block diagram depicting the same.

Or Explain any three types of software.

Long Answer (LA) Type Questions (5 Marks)

11. State whether the following expenditures are capital or revenue in nature.
   (i) Payment of rent ₹ 50,000
   (ii) Custom duty ₹ 10,000 paid on import of a machinery.
   (iii) Air conditioning of the office of director ₹ 1,00,000.
   (iv) Annual Insurance premium paid on car ₹ 1,000.
   (v) Electricity bill of office ₹ 50,000

Or From the following trial balance and additional information of Mr Rajesh Ahuja, a proprietor, prepare trading and profit and loss account for the year ended 31st March, 2020 and balance sheet as at that date.

Trial Balance
as on ......

Particulars	Debit Balance (₹)	Credit Balance (₹)
Building	3,20,000	—
Wages	52,000	—
Machinery	32,000	—
Salaries and Wages	83,200	—
Debtors	67,400	—
Capital	—	4,46,200
Purchases and Sales	1,13,000	2,01,400
Creditors	—	25,000
Income Tax	4,000	—
Drawings	1,000	—
Total	6,72,600	6,72,600

Closing stock at cost ₹ 2,00,000 but at market price ₹ 1,77,000

12. What adjusting entries would you record for the following?
   (i) Depreciation   (ii) Discount on debtors
   (iii) Interest on capital   (iv) Manager's commission
   (v) Closing stock

Or From the following trial balance, prepare the trading and profit and loss account for the year ended 31st March, 2020 and the balance sheet as at that date.

Name of Accounts	Amt (₹)	Name of Accounts	Amt (₹)
Salaries	81,784	Sales	5,31,360
Bills Receivable	51,016	Capital	4,00,000
Investments	3,20,000	Provision for Doubtful Debts	20,000
Furniture	96,000	10% Loan (1st October, 2017)	80,000
Opening Stock	36,000	Discount Received	3,200
Purchases	2,32,000	Sundry Creditors	74,400
Sundry Debtors	1,60,000	Bills Payable	40,000
Interest on Loan	3,200	Outstanding Salaries	4,000
Insurance Premium	7,200	Bad Debts Recovered	1,600
Wages	36,800	Interest on Investments	16,000
Rent	12,160	Trading Commission	56,000
Bad Debts	9,600		
Carriage Outwards	4,800		
Cash at Bank	80,000		
Depreciation on Furniture	20,000		
Accrued Commission	8,000		
Advertisement	68,000		
	12,26,560		12,26,560

Additional Information
(i) Closing stock ₹ 40,000.
(ii) Goods costing ₹ 4,000 were taken by the proprietor for personal use.
(iii) A credit sale of ₹ 16,000 was not recorded in the sales book.
(iv) Maintain provision for doubtful debts @ 5%.

13. Balance sheet is not prepared under single entry system. Is it true? If not, identify the statement of financial position produced from incomplete accounting record.
Enumerate few points about it and show its format?

Or

M/s Shyama Sports Equipment does not keep proper records. From the following information, find out profit or loss for the year ended 31st December, 2020.

Particulars	31st December, 2019 (₹)	31st December, 2020 (₹)
Cash in Hand	6,000	24,000
Bank Overdraft	30,000	—
Stock	50,000	80,000
Creditors	26,000	40,000
Debtors	60,000	1,40,000
Bills Payable	6,000	12,000
Furniture	40,000	60,000
Bills Receivable	8,000	28,000
Machinery	50,000	1,00,000
Investment	30,000	80,000

Drawings ₹ 10,000 per month for personal use and fresh capital introduced during the year ₹ 2,00,000. A bad debts of ₹ 2,000 and a provision of 5% to be made on debtors. Outstanding salary ₹ 2,400, prepaid insurance ₹ 700 and depreciation on furniture and machinery @ 10% p.a.

14. "Accounting software is an integral part of the computerised accounting system", explain. Briefly list the generic considerations before sourcing accounting software.

Answers

1. The features of a trial balance are as follows (any three)
(i) Trial balance contains a list of all ledger accounts including cash account.
(ii) It is a statement, not an account.
(iii) It can be prepared at any time during the accounting period i.e., at the end of any chosen period which may be monthly, quarterly, half yearly or annually depending upon the requirements.
(iv) It is not an absolute proof of the accuracy of accounting records.
(v) It is prepared to check the arithmetical accuracy of the ledger accounts.

Or

In the Books of Shri Manmohan
Trial Balance
as on 31st March, 2021

Name of Accounts	LF	Debit Balance (₹)	Credit Balance (₹)
Capital		—	1,12,000
Purchases		28,800	—
Discount Allowed		960	—
Carriage Inwards		6,960	—
Carriage Outwards		1,840	—
Sales		—	48,000
Return Inwards		240	—
Return Outwards		—	560

Name of Accounts	LF	Debit Balance (₹)	Credit Balance (₹)
Rent and Taxes		960	—
Plant and Machinery		64,560	—
Stock on 1st April, 2020		12,400	—
Sundry Debtors		16,160	—
Sundry Creditors		—	9,600
Investments		2,880	—
Commission Received		—	1,440
Cash in Hand		80	—
Cash at Bank		8,080	—
Motor Cycle		27,680	—
Total		1,71,600	1,71,600

Note *Closing stock will not be taken in the trial balance because it represents a part of the goods purchased but not yet sold. As the total purchases have been included in the trial balance, there is no need of including closing stock again. If closing stock is adjusted against purchases, then only closing stock is shown in the trial balance.*

2. Notary public is an officer appointed by the central government or state government to exercise the power and functions relating to noting and protesting negotiable instrument for dishonour.

The following facts are generally noted by the notary public

(i) Date, facts and reasons of dishonour.

(ii) If the bill is not expressly dishonoured, the reasons why it is being treated as dishonoured.

(iii) The amount of noting charges.

Or

In the Books of Rao
JOURNAL

Date	Particulars	LF	Amt (Dr)	Amt (Cr)
2020				
Jan 1	Reddy Dr		20,000	
	To Sales A/c			20,000
	(Being the goods sold to Reddy on credit)			
Jan 1	Cash A/c Dr		10,000	
	Bills Receivable A/c Dr		10,000	
	To Reddy			20,000
	(Being the half of the amount received and acceptance for remaining half amount received)			
Feb 2	Cash A/c Dr		10,000	
	To Bills Receivable A/c			10,000
	(Being the cash received on due date)			

In the Books of Reddy
Rao's Account

Dr   Cr

Date	Particulars	JF	Amt (₹)	Date	Particulars	JF	Amt (₹)
2020				2020			
Jan 1	To Cash A/c		10,000	Jan 1	By Purchases A/c		20,000
Jan 1	To Bills Payable A/c		10,000				
			20,000				20,000

3. Errors which affect the trial balance are one sided errors and are disclosed by trial balance. Thus, trial balance does not tally if these errors are made.

Following are the errors which affect the agreement of trial balance

　(i) Error of casting

　(ii) Error in carrying forward

　(iii) Error of posting to the wrong side but in correct account

　(iv) Posting twice in an account

　(v) Error in posting with wrong amount

　(vi) Error of partial omission

　(vii) Error in totalling or balancing of an account

4.

JOURNAL

Date	Particulars	LF	Amt (Dr)	Amt (Cr)
(i)	Furniture A/c　　　　　　　　　　　　　　　　Dr		65,000	
	To Purchases A/c			65,000
	(Being the furniture purchased debited to purchases account, now rectified)			
(ii)	Salary A/c　　　　　　　　　　　　　　　　　Dr		10,000	
	To Golu			10,000
	(Being the salary debited to Golu's personal account, now rectified)			
(iii)	Repairs and Maintenance A/c　　　　　　　　Dr		64,000	
	To Building A/c			64,000
	(Being the white wash debited to building account, now rectified)			

5. (b) Adjusted Purchases = Net Purchases + Opening Stock − Closing Stock

6. (b) Contingent liabilities are not shown in the balance sheet. They are shown as a footnote just below the balance sheet so that their existence may be revealed.

7. (d) Direct expenses like royalty, consumable stores are shown to debit side of trading account.

8. (a)　　　　　$\text{Gross Profit} = 2,85,000 \times \dfrac{25}{100} = ₹\,71,250$

　　　Cost of Goods Sold = Sales − Gross Profit = 2,85,000 − 71,250 = ₹ 2,13,750

9. (c) Cash in Hand, Bills Receivable, Plant and Machinery, Land and Building.

10. Main components of computer are as follows

　(i) Input Unit　　　　　　　　　　　　　　(ii) Output Unit

　(iii) Central Processing Unit (CPU)

　　　It has two main unit

　　　(a) Arithmetic and Logic Unit (ALU)　　　(b) Control Unit

　(iv) Memory Unit

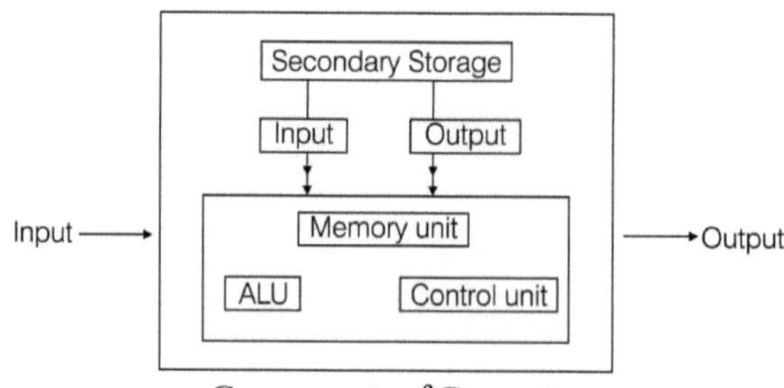

Components of Computer

Or

Types of software are as follows

(i) **Language Processors** It translate or interpret the program written in a programming language into machine language.

(ii) **System Software** It controls internal functions such as reading data from input devices and checking the system to ensure that its components are functioning properly.

(iii) **Application Software** It is designed and developed for performing certain specified tasks such as payroll accounting, inventory accounting , etc.

11. (i) Payment of rent ₹ 50,000 is revenue expenditure because it is incurred for day to day conduct of the business.

(ii) Custom duty ₹ 10,000 paid on import of a machinery is capital expenditure because it is incurred for the acquisition of a new asset.

(iii) It is a capital expenditure because the benefit of this expenditure will be available for number of years.

(iv) It is a revenue expenditure because it will not increase the value of the car and its benefit will be exhausted within the year.

(v) It is a revenue expenditure because it is a part of operating cost.

Or

Trading Account

Dr   for the year ended 31st March, 2020   Cr

Particulars	Amt (₹)	Particulars	Amt (₹)
To Purchases	1,13,000	By Closing Stock	1,77,000
To Wages	52,000	By Sales	2,01,400
To Gross Profit Transferred to Profit and Loss A/c	2,13,400		
	3,78,400		3,78,400

Profit and Loss Account

Dr   for the year ended 31st March, 2020   Cr

Particulars	Amt (₹)	Particulars	Amt (₹)
To Salaries and Wages	83,200	By Gross Profit	2,13,400
To Net Profit	1,30,200		
	2,13,400		2,13,400

Balance Sheet

Dr   as on 31st March, 2020   Cr

Liabilities		Amt (₹)	Assets	Amt (₹)
Capital	4,46,200		Building	3,20,000
(+) Net Profit	1,30,200		Machinery	32,000
(−) Drawings	(1,000)		Debtors	67,400
(−) Income Tax	(4,000)	5,71,400	Closing stock	1,77,000
Creditors		25,000		
		5,96,400		5,96,400

12.

JOURNAL

Date	Particulars		LF	Amt (Dr)	Amt (Cr)
(i)	Depreciation A/c	Dr		—	
	To Concerned Asset A/c				—
	(Being the depreciation charged)				
(ii)	Profit and Loss A/c	Dr		—	
	To Provision for Discount on Debtors A/c				—
	(Being the adjustment of discount on debtors recorded)				

Date	Particulars		LF	Amt (Dr)	Amt (Cr)
(iii)	Interest on Capital A/c	Dr		—	
	To Capital A/c				—
	(Being the interest on Capital adjusted)				
(iv)	Manager's Commission A/c	Dr		—	
	To Commission Outstanding A/c				—
	(Being the Manager's Commission adjusted)				
(v)	Closing Stock A/c	Dr		—	—
	To Trading A/c				
	(Being the closing stock adjusted)				

Or

Trading and Profit and Loss Account

Dr   for the year ending 31st March, 2020   Cr

Particulars		Amt (₹)	Particulars		Amt (₹)
To Opening Stock		36,000	By Sales	5,31,360	
To Purchases	2,32,000		(+) Sales not Recorded	16,000	5,47,360
(−) Goods Taken by Proprietor	(4,000)	2,28,000	By Closing Stock		40,000
To Wages		36,800			
To Gross Profit (Transferred to profit and loss account)		2,86,560			
		5,87,360			5,87,360
To Bad Debts	9,600		By Gross Profit b/d		2,86,560
(+) New Provision on Debtors	8,800	18,400	By Old Provision on Debtors		20,000
To Salaries		81,784	By Discount Received		3,200
To Interest on Loan	3,200		By Bad Debts Recovered		1,600
(+) Outstanding	800	4,000	By Interest on Investment		16,000
To Insurance Premium		7,200	By Trading Commission		56,000
To Rent		12,160			
To Carriage Outward		4,800			
To Depreciation on Furniture		20,000			
To Advertisement		68,000			
To Net Profit (Transferred to capital account)		1,67,016			
		3,83,360			3,83,360

Balance Sheet

as at 31st March, 2020

Liabilities		Amt (₹)	Assets		Amt (₹)
Capital	4,00,000		Debtors	1,60,000	
(+) Net Profit	1,67,016		(+) Sales not Recorded	16,000	
(−) Drawings	(4,000)	5,63,016	(−) New Provision on Debtors	(8,800)	1,67,200
			Bills Receivable		51,016
10% Loan		80,000	Investment		3,20,000
Outstanding Interest on 10% Loan		800	Cash at Bank		80,000
Sundry Creditors		74,400	Accrued Commission		8,000
Bills Payable		40,000	Closing Stock		40,000
Outstanding Salaries		4,000	Furniture		96,000
		7,62,216			7,62,216

13. Yes, Balance sheet is not prepared under single entry system.

Statement of affairs is prepared at the beginning of year and at the end of the accounting period. It is a statement of all assets and liabilities. Assets are shown on one side and the liabilities on the other, just as in case of a Balance sheet. It is also based on accounting equation, viz.

$$\text{Capital} = \text{Assets} - \text{Liabilities.}$$

Format of statement of affairs is given below

Statement of Affairs
as at...

Liabilities	Amt (₹)	Assets	Amt (₹)
Bank Overdraft	—	Cash in Hand	—
Bills Payable	—	Cash at Bank	—
Sundry Creditors	—	Bills Receivable	—
Outstanding Expenses	—	Sundry Debtors	—
Income Received in Advance	—	Stock	—
Capital (Balancing figure)	—	Prepaid Expenses	—
		Accrued Income	—
		Furniture	—
		Plant and Machinery	—
	—		—

Or

Statement of Affairs
as at 31st December, 2019

Liabilities	Amt (₹)	Assets	Amt (₹)
Bank Overdraft	30,000	Cash in Hand	6,000
Creditors	26,000	Stock	50,000
Bills Payable	6,000	Debtors	60,000
Capital (Balancing figure)	1,82,000	Furniture	40,000
		Bills Receivable	8,000
		Machinery	50,000
		Investment	30,000
	2,44,000		2,44,000

Statement of Affairs
as at 31st December, 2020 (before adjustment)

Liabilities	Amt (₹)	Assets	Amt (₹)
Creditors	40,000	Cash in Hand	24,000
Bills Payable	12,000	Stock	80,000
Capital (Balancing figure)	4,60,000	Debtors	1,40,000
		Furniture	60,000
		Bills Receivable	28,000
		Machinery	1,00,000
		Investment	80,000
	5,12,000		5,12,000

Statement Showing Profit and Loss
for the year ending 31st December, 2020

Particulars	Amt (₹)
Capital at the End of Year	4,60,000
$(+)$ Drawings $(10,000 \times 12)$	1,20,000
$(-)$ Additional Capital	(2,00,000)
Adjusted Capital	3,80,000
$(-)$ Capital in the Beginning of Year	(1,82,000)

Particulars		Amt (₹)
Profit Before Adjustments		1,98,000
(−) Bad Debts	(2,000)	
(−) Provision on Debtors	(6,900)	
(−) Depreciation on Furniture	(6,000)	
(−) Depreciation on Machinery	(10,000)	
(−) Outstanding Salary	(2,400)	
(+) Prepaid Insurance	700	(26,600)
		1,71,400

Statement of Affairs
as at 31st December, 2020 (after adjustment)

Liabilities	Amt (₹)	Amt (₹)	Assets	Amt (₹)	Amt (₹)
Creditors		40,000	Cash in Hand		24,000
Bills Payable		12,000	Stock		80,000
Outstanding Salary		2,400	Debtors	1,40,000	
Opening Capital	1,82,000		(−) Bad Debts	(2,000)	
(+) Additional Capital	2,00,000			1,38,000	
(+) Net Profit	1,71,400		(−) Provision on Debtors	(6,900)	1,31,100
(−) Drawings	(1,20,000)	4,33,400	Furniture	60,000	
			(−) Depreciation	(6,000)	54,000
			Bills Receivable		28,000
			Machinery	1,00,000	
			(−) Depreciation	(10,000)	90,000
			Investment		80,000
			Prepaid Insurance		700
		4,87,800			4,87,800

14. The following factors are usually taken into consideration before sourcing an accounting software

(i) **Flexibility** The choice of accounting software depends on the degree of flexibility it offers, in respect of data entry and the availability and design of various reports expected from it. The user should be able to run the software on variety of computer environments and machines.

(ii) **Cost of Installation and Maintenance** The cost of installation and maintenance are important considerations in the choice of software. Sometimes, certain software which are cheap involve heavy maintenance and alteration costs, e.g., cost of addition of modules, training of staff, etc. Conversely, the accounting software which are expensive may require least maintenance and free upgrading and negligible alteration costs.

(iii) **Size of Organisation** The choice of software also depends on the size of organisation and volume of business. The single user operated software may be useful for small organisations having less number of transactions. Whereas sophisticated software may be best suited for large organisations, to meet the multi-user requirements.

(iv) **Ease of Adaptation and Training Needs** The software must be capable of attracting users and be able to motivate its potential users. Some accounting softwares are user friendly and require simple training. However, some other complex softwares packages require intensive training on a continuous basis.

(v) **Utilities/MIS Reports** The choice of software also depends on the MIS report and the degree to which they are used in the organisation.

(vi) **Expected Level of Secrecy** The choice of accounting software also depends on the level of security features offered by it. Software should be able to prevent unauthorised access and manipulation of data.

(vii) **Exporting/Importing Data Facility** The accounting software should allow easy data transfer to other systems or software for flexible reporting such as organisations may transfer information directly from the ledger into spreadsheet software such as lotus or excel.

(viii) **Vendors Reputation and Capability** Another important consideration in the choice of accounting software is the capability and reputation of the vendor. This depends upon how long the vendor has been in the business of software development, whether there are other users of the software and extent of support available from people other than the vendor.

Practice Paper 2*
(Unsolved)

Instructions

- Time : 2 Hours
- Max. Marks : 40

1. There are 14 questions in the question paper. All questions are compulsory.
2. Question no. 1-4 and 10 are Short Answer Type Questions. Each question carries 3 marks.
3. Question no. 5-9 are Case Based MCQs. Each question carries 1 mark.
4. Question no. 11-14 are Long Answer Type Questions. Each question carries 5 marks.
5. There is no overall choice. However, internal choices have been provided in some questions. Students have to attempt only one of the alternatives in such question.

** As exact Blue-print and Pattern for CBSE Term II exams is not released yet. So the pattern of this paper is designed by the author on the basis of trend of past CBSE Papers. Students are advised not to consider the pattern of this paper as official, it is just for practice purpose.*

Part A
Financial Accounting–I

Short Answer (SA) Type Questions (3 Marks)

1. State whether the balances of the following accounts should be placed in the debit or credit columns of the trial balance.

   (i) Patents
   (ii) Sales return
   (iii) Provision for depreciation
   (iv) Salaries
   (v) Commission received
   (vi) Drawings made by proprietor

2. From the following list of balances extracted from the books of Kumar prepare a trial balance as on 31st March, 2021. The amount required to balance should be entered as capital.

Name of Accounts	Amt (₹)	Name of Accounts	Amt (₹)
Purchases	3,64,000	Proprietor's Withdrawals	12,000
Stock on 1st April, 2020	70,000	Sundry Debtors	72,000
Sales	8,00,000	Sundry Creditors	24,000
Sundry Expenses	3,000	Bad Debts	2,000
Leasehold Premises	1,00,000	Investment @ 10%	40,000
Freehold Premises	3,60,000	Interest on Investment	4,000
Return Inwards	5,000	Long-term Borrowings	1,20,000
Furniture and Fixtures	58,000	Loan from SBI	1,60,000
Equipment	1,60,000	Interest on Loan	13,000
Repairs to Equipment	1,000	Petty Cash Account	800
Depreciation	16,000	Balance at Bank	6,920
		Stock on 31st March, 2021 (not adjusted)	92,000

3. From the following information, complete the following journal entries.

JOURNAL

Date	Particulars	LF	Amt (Dr)	Amt (Cr)
(i)	.... Dr		1,750	
	....			1,750
	(Being bad debts written-off ₹ 1,750 on debtors were not recorded, now rectified)			
(ii)	.... Dr		63	
	....			63
	(Being discount allowed to debtor ₹ 63, on receiving cash was not recorded, now rectified)			
(iii)	.... Dr		7,500	
	....			7,500
	(Being bills receivable ₹ 7,500 received from debtor not recorded, now rectified)			

Or Briefly explain the following terms used in accounting of bills of exchange.

    (i) Drawer   (ii) Days of grace   (iii) Payee

4. Give journal entries to rectify following errors.

    (i) A motor car had been purchased for ₹ 68,000. Cash had been correctly credited but the motor car account had been debited with ₹ 62,800 only.

    (ii) Interest on deposits received ₹ 1,200 had been debited in the cash account but had not been credited to the interest account.

    (iii) The purchase of an office table costing ₹ 50,000 had been passed through purchase day book.

Or Following errors were detected in the books of Anuj Jindal, Delhi

    (i) Sale of old machinery for ₹ 80,000 was treated as sale of goods.

    (ii) Cash balance of ₹ 5,000 carried forward as ₹ 50,000.

    (iii) Wages paid to a worker for constructing building ₹ 5,000 were debited to wages account.

    State the nature of each of these errors.

Part B
Financial Accounting–II

Case Based MCQs (1 × 5 = 5 Marks)

Pooja, B.Com(h) graduate from Zakir Hussain College works as an accountant at Rajan's clothing in Karol Bagh. On 31st December, 2020, she prepared a trial balance after preparation of all accounts and subsidiary books. Her trial balance total also agreed. But when his senior accountant Anurag checked all books of accounts, he discovered some of the information which were not taken into consideration.

Following trial balance was prepared by Pooja and additional adjustments discovered by Anurag.

Name of Accounts	Amt (₹)	Name of Accounts	Amt (₹)
Capital	1,60,000	Insurance	1,200
Purchases	1,64,000	Salaries	25,000
Sales	2,20,000	Bad Debts	400
Return Outwards	2,000	Carriage on Purchases	400
Building	90,000	Commission (credit)	3,000
Opening Stock	30,000	Cash in Hand	10,000
Debtors	40,200	Cash at Bank	50,000
Creditors	56,000	Sales Tax Paid	10,000
Furniture	14,000	Sales Tax Collected	7,000
Wages	3,600	Interest on Investment	1,000
Rent	10,200		

Additional Information

(i) Closing stock was valued at ₹ 40,000. (ii) Outstanding salaries ₹ 2,000.

(iii) Unexpired insurance ₹ 100. (iv) Accrued commission ₹ 600.

(v) Provide depreciation on building @ 5% and on furniture @ 10%.

(vi) Provide for manager's commission at 5% on net profit after charging such commission.

5. Which of the following is amount of gross profit?

(a) ₹ 64,000　　　　(b) ₹ 66,000　　　　(c) ₹ 64,400　　　　(d) ₹ 68,000

6. Which of the undermentioned amount of salaries will be shown in profit and loss account?

(a) ₹ 27,000　　　　(b) ₹ 23,000　　　　(c) ₹ 25,000　　　　(d) ₹ 28,000

7. Value of furniture shown on assets side of balance sheet will be

(a) ₹ 14,000　　　　(b) ₹ 14,400　　　　(c) ₹ 12,600　　　　(d) ₹ 13,300

8. Closing stock is valued at ....

(a) cost price

(b) market price

(c) cost price or market price whichever is lower

(d) cost price or market price whichever is higher

9. Manager's commission is

(a) an outstanding expense　　(b) a prepaid expense　　(c) an unearned expense　　(d) an accrued expense

Short Answer (SA) Type Question (3 Marks)

10. Write a short note on CPU.

Or Write a short note on accounting information system.*Long Answer (LA) Type Questions (5 Marks)*

Long Answer (LA) Type Questions (5 Marks)

11. Shan started a firm on 1st April, 2020 with a capital of ₹ 60,000. On 1st July, 2020, he borrowed from his wife, a sum of ₹ 24,000 @ 9 % per annum (interest not yet paid) for business and introduces a further capital of his, amounted to ₹ 9,000.

On 31st March, 2021 his position was, cash ₹ 3,600, stock ₹ 56,400, debtors ₹ 42,000 and creditors ₹ 36,000. Ascertain his profit and loss taking into account ₹ 12,000 for his drawings during the year.

Or Andy keeps incomplete records. His capital at the beginning of year was ₹ 4,00,000 capital at the end of year ₹ 3,10,000. ₹ 1,25,000 was withdrawn by him for his personal use, as Andy needed money for expansion of his business, he asked his wife to help. His wife allowed him to sell her ornaments and invest that amount into the business which comes to ₹ 30,000. You are required to calculate profit or loss.

Also, mention any two uses of single entry system.

12. Show the treatment of outstanding expenses, provision for discount on debtors and goods distributed as free samples

(i) when given inside the trial balance　　(ii) when given outside the trial balance

Or The following balances have been extracted from the trial balance of M/s Haryana Chemical Ltd. You are required to prepare a trading and profit and loss account and balance sheet as on 31st December, 2020 from the given information.

Name of Accounts	Amt (₹)	Name of Accounts	Amt (₹)
Opening Stock	50,000	Sales	3,50,000
Purchases	1,25,500	Purchase Return	2,500
Sales Return	2,000	Creditors	25,000
Cash in Hand	21,200	Rent	5,000
Cash at Bank	12,000	Interest	2,000
Carriage	100	Bills Payable	1,71,700
Freehold Land	3,20,000	Capital	3,00,000
Patents	1,20,000		

Name of Accounts	Amt (₹)	Name of Accounts	Amt (₹)
General Expenses	2,000		
Sundry Debtors	32,500		
Building	86,000		
Machinery	34,500		
Insurance	12,400		
Drawings	10,000		
Motor Vehicle	10,500		
Bad Debts	2,000		
Light and Water	1,200		
Trade Expenses	2,000		
Power	3,900		
Salary and Wages	5,400		
Loan 15% (1st September, 2019)	3,000		
	8,56,200		8,56,200

Adjustments

(i) Closing stock was valued at the end of the year ₹ 40,000.

(ii) Salary amounting ₹ 500 and trade expenses ₹ 300 are due.

(iii) Depreciation charged on building and machinery are @ 4% and @ 5% respectively.

(iv) Make a provision of 5% on sundry debtors.

13. From the following balances extracted from the books of Shri Raman Tyagi on 31st March, 2020, prepare final accounts as at 31st March, 2020.

Name of Accounts	Amt (₹)	Name of Accounts	Amt (₹)
Opening Stock	30,620	Capital	5,00,000
Purchases	1,64,800	Drawings	96,000
Sales	5,12,000	Sundry Debtors	1,14,000
Sales Return	8,000	Sundry Creditors	28,000
Purchase Return	4,800	Depreciation	8,400
Factory Rent	36,000	Charity	1,000
Coal, Gas and Power	35,000	Cash Balance	8,920
Wages and Salary	73,200	Bank Balance	8,000
Discount Allowed	15,000	Bank Charges	360
Commission Received	2,400	Establishment Expenses	7,200
Bad Debts	11,700	Plant	84,000
Bad Debts Recovered	4,000	Leasehold Building	3,00,000
Rent Received	9,600	Goodwill	40,000
Productive Expenses	5,200	Patents	20,000
Unproductive Expenses	10,000	Trademarks	10,000
Carriage	17,400	Loan Taken	50,000
		Interest on Loan	6,000

The value of closing stock on 31st March, 2020 was ₹ 50,800.

Or Define expenditure and receipts. Also, explain various types of expenditure and receipts with examples.

14. List the distinctive advantages of a computer system over manual system.

Answers

2. Amount of Capital = ₹ 1,75,000; Total of Trial Balance = ₹ 12,83,000

5. (a)   **6.** (a)   **7.** (c)   **8.** (c)   **9.** (a)

11. Net Loss for the Year = ₹ 16,620 Or Profit for the Year = ₹ 5,000

12. *Or* Gross Profit = ₹ 2,11,000; Net Profit = ₹ 1,85,560; Balance Sheet Total = ₹ 6,73,060

13. Gross Profit = ₹ 1,97,380; Net Profit = ₹ 1,53,720; Balance Sheet Total = ₹ 6,35,720

Practice Paper 3*
(Unsolved)

Instructions

- Time : 2 Hours
- Max. Marks : 40

1. There are 14 questions in the question paper. All questions are compulsory.
2. Question no. 1-4 and 10 are Short Answer Type Questions. Each question carries 3 marks.
3. Question no. 5-9 are Case Based MCQs. Each question carries 1 mark.
4. Question no. 11-14 are Long Answer Type Questions. Each question carries 5 marks.
5. There is no overall choice. However, internal choices have been provided in some questions. Students
   have to attempt only one of the alternatives in such question.

* **As exact Blue-print and Pattern for CBSE Term II exams is not released yet. So the pattern of this
paper is designed by the author on the basis of trend of past CBSE Papers. Students are advised
not to consider the pattern of this paper as official, it is just for practice purpose.**

Part A
Financial Accounting–I

Short Answer (SA) **Type Questions** (3 Marks)

1. The following trial balance has been prepared by an inexperienced accountant. You are required to prepare
the trial balance in a correct form.

Trial Balance

as on ...

Name of Accounts	LF	Debit Balance (₹)	Credit Balance (₹)
Cash in Hand		20,000	—
Fixed Assets		—	25,000
Capital		—	77,200
Purchases		45,000	—
Sales		20,500	—
Discount Allowed		—	500
Return Inward		—	1,000
Return Outward		1,400	—
Wages and Salary		10,000	—
Debtors		2,680	—
Creditors		—	9,400
Drawings		—	2,000
Discount Received		—	700
Bills Receivable		2,340	—
Bills Payable		—	4,320
Rent		3,000	—
Interest Paid		—	2,000
Total		1,04,920	1,22,120

Or

Define trial balance and state any one importance of trial balance. Also, mention when closing stock is shown in the trial balance.

2. From the following information, complete the following journal entries.

In the Books of Nonu
JOURNAL

Date	Particulars		LF	Amt (Dr)	Amt (Cr)
2019 Feb 1	....	Dr		72,000	
	To .... A/c				72,000
	(Being goods worth ₹ 72,000 sold to Monu on credit)				
Feb 1	....	Dr		30,000	
	Bills Receivable (No. 2) A/c	Dr		24,000	
	....	Dr		...	
	To Monu				...
	(Being the acceptances received from Monu for 3 bills for 1 month, 2 months and 3 months respectively)				
Feb 1	Sonu	Dr		...	
	To Bills Receivable (No. 1) A/c				...
	(Being the 1st bill endorsed in favour of creditor Sonu)				
Feb 4	....	Dr		...	
	....	Dr		...	
	To Bills Receivable (No. 2) A/c				24,000
	(Being the 2nd bill discounted with the bank @ 12% p.a. on 4th February)				
Apr 30	....	Dr		18,000	
	To Bills Receivable (No. 3) A/c				18,000
	(Being the 3rd bill sent to the bank for collection on 30th April)				
May 4	....	Dr		...	
	....	Dr		...	
	To Bills Sent for Collection A/c				18,000
	(Being the bill collected by the bank and ₹ 150 collection charges deducted)				

3. Define bills of exchange and briefly explain parties to a bills of exchange.

4. Trial balance of Anita did not agree and she put the difference to suspense account. She discovered the following errors

(i) Purchases return to Arpit ₹ 3,125 was not posted to his account.

(ii) Installation charges on new machinery purchased ₹ 1,750 were debited to sundry expenses account as ₹ 175.

(iii) Rent paid for residential accommodation of Anita (the proprietor) ₹ 5,200 was debited to rent account as ₹ 5,000.

Rectify the errors and prepare suspense account to ascertain the difference in trial balance.

Or

What do you understand by suspense account? When and why is it opened?

Part B
Financial Accounting–II

Case Based MCQs (1 × 5 = 5 Marks)

Abhipriya after completing her B.Com (h) from Hans Raj College, has decided to pursue her passion of baking by starting her own venture "Oven's Batter half".

To cut her expenditure, she is maintaining books of accounts herself under single entry system.

Following is the information available

Name of Accounts	1st April, 2020 (₹)	31st March, 2021 (₹)
Machinery	2,80,000	3,70,000
Cash at Bank	81,600	4,63,000
Stock	1,31,600	3,41,200
Furniture	1,50,000	1,80,000
Building	3,20,000	3,60,000
Creditors	74,000	33,600
Debtors	49,200	1,72,400
10% Investment	4,00,000	4,00,000

During the year, he sold his personal investment of ₹ 10,00,000 and $\frac{4}{5}$ th part of it invested into his business. He withdrew ₹ 60,000 in each half year. Profit to be ascertained after making following adjustments

(i) Provide depreciation on building and furniture at 10% and 20% respectively.

(ii) Create provision on debtors at 5%.

(iii) Rent paid in advance ₹ 11,600.

(iv) Accrued interest on investment for 6 months.

(v) Salary due but not paid ₹ 4,400.

5. Which of the undermentioned is correct amount of opening capital?
(a) ₹ 22,53,000   (b) ₹ 13,38,400   (c) ₹ 14,12,400   (d) ₹ 17,38,400

6. Which of the following is correct amount of closing capital (before adjustments)?
(a) ₹ 22,53,000   (b) ₹ 13,38,400   (c) ₹ 22,86,600   (d) ₹ 23,20,200

7. Net profit after adjustment is
(a) ₹ 1,81,180   (b) ₹ 2,34,600   (c) ₹ 1,37,980   (d) ₹ 3,08,020

8. Closing Capital = Opening Capital + Profit + Additional Capital – ....
(a) Net Sales   (b) Interest on Capital   (c) Interest on Drawings   (d) Drawings

9. Which among the following can maintain its accounts under single entry system?
(i) Small firms   (ii) Cooperative society   (iii) Company

Alternatives
(a) Only (i)   (b) Only (ii)
(c) Both (i) and (ii)   (d) Both (ii) and (iii)

Short Answer (SA) **Type Question** (3 Marks)

10. What do you mean by procedures as an element of computer system? Also, discuss its types.

Or

Computerised accounting system is best form of accounting system. Do you agree? Comment.

Long Answer (LA) **Type Questions** (5 Marks)

11. Mention the steps required to be followed while calculating profit and loss by statement of affairs method. Also, prepare format of statement. Showing profit or loss under this method.

12. What is a balance sheet? What are its characteristics?

Or

From the following balances, prepare trading and profit and loss account and balance sheet.

Debit Balances	Amt (₹)	Credit Balances	Amt (₹)
Machinery	7,000	Capital Account	20,000
Debtors	5,400	Creditors	2,800
Drawings	1,800	Sales	29,000
Purchases	19,000		
Wages	10,000		
Bank	3,000		
Opening Stock	4,,000		
Rent	900		
Sunday Expenses	400		
Carriage	300		

Closing stock was ₹ 600

13. From the following balances, prepare trading and profit and loss account and a balance sheet as on 31st March, 2021.

Particulars	Amt (₹)	Particulars	Amt (₹)
Capital	16,40,000	Sundry Creditors	1,80,000
Life Insurance Premium	56,000	Sales	24,80,000
Plant and Machinery	1,00,000	Return Outwards	20,000
Stock in the Beginning	3,00,000	Special Rebates (Debit)	16,000
Purchases	17,44,000	Special Rebates (Credit)	24,000
Return Inwards	1,20,000	Rent for Premises Sublet	20,000
Sundry Debtors	4,20,000	Lighting	8,000
Furniture	1,82,000	Motor Car Expenses	1,26,000
Motor Car	8,00,000	Bank Balance	3,04,000
Freight and Duty	40,000	Loan from Vishal @ 12% p.a.	2,00,000
Carriage Inward	16,000	Interest on Loan from Vishal (Debit)	18,000
Carriage Outward	6,000		
Trade Expenses	3,08,000		

Additional Information

(i) Stock on 31st March, 2021 was valued at ₹ 5,00,000 (realisable value ₹ 6,40,000).

(ii) Stock of ₹ 1,20,000 was burnt by fire on 25th March. It was fully insured and the insurance company admitted the claim in full.

(iii) Goods worth ₹ 36,000 were distributed as free samples. Goods worth ₹ 30,000 were used for personal purposes by the proprietor and goods worth ₹ 10,000 were given away as charity.

(iv) Depreciate motor car by 15%.

(v) Included in trade expenses is insurance premium of ₹ 48,000 paid for the year ending 30th June, 2021.

Or

Prepare the trading and profit and loss account and a balance sheet of M/s Shine Ltd. from the following information.

Name of Accounts	Amt (₹)	Name of Accounts	Amt (₹)
Sundry Debtors	1,00,000	Bills Payable	85,550
Bad Debts	3,000	Sundry Creditors	25,000
Trade Expenses	2,500	Provision for Bad Debts	1,500
Printing and Stationery	5,000	Return Outwards	4,500
Rent, Rates and Taxes	3,450	Capital	2,50,000
Freight	2,250	Discount Received	3,500
Sales Return	6,000	Interest Received	11,260
Motor Car	25,000	Sales	1,00,000
Opening Stock	75,550		
Furniture and Fixtures	15,500		
Purchases	75,000		
Drawings	13,560		
Investments	65,500		
Cash in Hand	36,000		
Cash at Bank	53,000		
	4,81,310		4,81,310

Additional Information
 (i) Book value of closing stock is ₹ 35,000 and market value ₹ 40,000.
 (ii) Depreciation charged on furniture and fixtures @ 5%.
 (iii) Further bad debts ₹ 1,000. Make a provision for bad debts @ 5% on sundry debtors.
 (iv) Depreciation charged on motor car @ 10%.
 (v) Interest on drawings @ 6%.
 (vi) Rent, rates and taxes was outstanding ₹ 200.
 (vii) Create provision on discount on debtors @ 2%.

14. Define computer. Explain in detail about elements of a computer.

Or

"Cash withdrawal at an ATM" is example of which information system? Also write about it and explain in brief about various steps involved in it.

Answers

1. Trial Balance Total = ₹ 1,13,520   **4.** Difference in Trial Balance = ₹ 4,900

5. (b)   **6.** (a)   **7.** (a)   **8.** (d)   **9.** (a)

12. *Or* Gross Loss = ₹ 3,700; Balance Sheet Total = ₹ 16,000; Net Loss = ₹ 5,000

13.   Gross Profit = ₹ 9,76,000

           Net Profit = ₹ 3,78,000

    Balance Sheet Total = ₹ 23,18,000

Or   Gross Loss = ₹ 19,300

           Net Loss = ₹ 27,482

Total of Balance Sheet = ₹ 3,18,894

Printed by Libri Plureos GmbH in Hamburg,
Germany